Halo
and Philosophy

Popular Culture and Philosophy®
Series Editor: George A. Reisch

VOLUME 1
Seinfeld and Philosophy: A Book about Everything and Nothing (2000)

VOLUME 2
The Simpsons and Philosophy: The D'oh! of Homer (2001)

VOLUME 3
The Matrix and Philosophy: Welcome to the Desert of the Real (2002)

VOLUME 4
Buffy the Vampire Slayer and Philosophy: Fear and Trembling in Sunnydale (2003)

VOLUME 5
The Lord of the Rings and Philosophy: One Book to Rule Them All (2003)

VOLUME 9
Harry Potter and Philosophy: If Aristotle Ran Hogwarts (2004)

VOLUME 12
Star Wars and Philosophy: More Powerful than You Can Possibly Imagine (2005)

VOLUME 13
Superheroes and Philosophy: Truth, Justice, and the Socratic Way (2005)

VOLUME 17
Bob Dylan and Philosophy: It's Alright Ma (I'm Only Thinking) (2006)

VOLUME 18
Harley-Davidson and Philosophy: Full-Throttle Aristotle (2006)

VOLUME 19
Monty Python and Philosophy: Nudge Nudge, Think Think! (2006)

VOLUME 24
Bullshit and Philosophy: Guaranteed to Get Perfect Results Every Time (2006)

VOLUME 25
The Beatles and Philosophy: Nothing You Can Think that Can't Be Thunk (2006)

VOLUME 26
South Park and Philosophy: Bigger, Longer, and More Penetrating (2007) Edited by Richard Hanley

VOLUME 28
The Grateful Dead and Philosophy: Getting High Minded about Love and Haight (2007) Edited by Steven Gimbel

VOLUME 29
Quentin Tarantino and Philosophy: How to Philosophize with a Pair of Pliers and a Blowtorch (2007) Edited by Richard Greene and K. Silem Mohammad

VOLUME 30
Pink Floyd and Philosophy: Careful with that Axiom, Eugene! (2007) Edited by George A. Reisch

VOLUME 31
Johnny Cash and Philosophy: The Burning Ring of Truth (2008) Edited by John Huss and David Werther

VOLUME 32
Bruce Springsteen and Philosophy: Darkness on the Edge of Truth (2008) Edited by Randall E. Auxier and Doug Anderson

VOLUME 33
Battlestar Galactica and Philosophy: Mission Accomplished or Mission Frakked Up? (2008) Edited by Josef Steiff and Tristan D. Tamplin

VOLUME 34
iPod and Philosophy: iCon of an ePoch (2008) Edited by D.E. Wittkower

VOLUME 35
Star Trek and Philosophy: The Wrath of Kant (2008) Edited by Jason T. Eberl and Kevin S. Decker

VOLUME 36
The Legend of Zelda and Philosophy: I Link Therefore I Am (2008) Edited by Luke Cuddy

VOLUME 37
The Wizard of Oz and Philosophy: Wicked Wisdom of the West (2008) Edited by Randall E. Auxier and Phillip S. Seng

VOLUME 38
Radiohead and Philosophy: Fitter Happier More Deductive (2009) Edited by Brandon W. Forbes and George A. Reisch

VOLUME 39
Jimmy Buffett and Philosophy: The Porpoise Driven Life (2009) Edited by Erin McKenna and Scott L. Pratt

VOLUME 40
Transformers and Philosophy (2009) Edited by John Shook and Liz Stillwaggon Swan

VOLUME 41
Stephen Colbert and Philosophy: I Am Philosophy (And So Can You!) (2009) Edited by Aaron Allen Schiller

VOLUME 42
Supervillains and Philosophy: Sometimes, Evil Is Its Own Reward (2009) Edited by Ben Dyer

VOLUME 43
The Golden Compass and Philosophy: God Bites the Dust (2009) Edited by Richard Greene and Rachel Robison

VOLUME 44
Led Zeppelin and Philosophy: All Will Be Revealed (2009) Edited by Scott Calef

VOLUME 45
World of Warcraft and Philosophy: Wrath of the Philosopher King (2009) Edited by Luke Cuddy and John Nordlinger

Volume 46
Mr. Monk and Philosophy: The Curious Case of the Defective Detective (2010) Edited by D.E. Wittkower

Volume 47
Anime and Philosophy: Wide Eyed Wonder (2010) Edited by Josef Steiff and Tristan D. Tamplin

VOLUME 48
The Red Sox and Philosophy: Green Monster Meditations (2010) Edited by Michael Macomber

VOLUME 49
Zombies, Vampires, and Philosophy: New Life for the Undead (2010) Edited by Richard Greene and K. Silem Mohammad

VOLUME 50
Facebook and Philosophy: What's on Your Mind? (2010) Edited by D.E. Wittkower

VOLUME 51
Soccer and Philosophy: Beautiful Thoughts on the Beautiful Game (2010) Edited by Ted Richards

VOLUME 52
Manga and Philosophy: Fullmetal Metaphysician (2010) Edited by Josef Steiff and Adam Barkman

VOLUME 53
Martial Arts and Philosophy: Beating and Nothingness (2010) Edited by Graham Priest and Damon Young

VOLUME 54
The Onion and Philosophy: Fake News Story True, Alleges Indignant Area Professor (2010) Edited by Sharon M. Kaye

VOLUME 55
Doctor Who and Philosophy: Bigger on the Inside (2010) Edited by Courtland Lewis and Paula Smithka

VOLUME 56
Dune and Philosophy: Weirding Way of the Mentat (2011) Edited by Jeffery Nicholas

VOLUME 57
Rush and Philosophy: Heart and Mind United (2011) Edited by Jim Berti and Durrell Bowman

VOLUME 58
Dexter and Philosophy: Mind over Spatter (2011) Edited by Richard Greene, George A. Reisch, and Rachel Robison-Greene

VOLUME 58
Halo and Philosophy: Intellect Evolved (2011) Edited by Luke Cuddy

IN PREPARATION:

SpongeBob SquarePants and Philosophy (2011) Edited by Joseph Foy

Sherlock Holmes and Philosophy (2011) Edited by Josef Steiff

Philip K. Dick and Philosophy (2011) Edited by D.E. Wittkower

Inception and Philosophy (2011) Edited by Thorsten Botz-Bornstein

Breaking Bad and Philosophy (2012) Edited by David R. Koepsell

Curb Your Enthusiasm and Philosophy (2012) Edited by Mark Ralkowski

The Rolling Stones and Philosophy (2012) Edited by Luke Dick and George A. Reisch

For full details of all Popular Culture and Philosophy® books, visit www.opencourtbooks.com.

Popular Culture and Philosophy®

Halo and Philosophy

Intellect Evolved

Edited by
LUKE CUDDY

OPEN COURT
Chicago and La Salle, Illinois

Volume 59 in the series, Popular Culture and Philosophy®, edited by George A. Reisch

To order books from Open Court, call toll-free 1-800-815-2280, or visit our website at www.opencourtbooks.com.

Open Court Publishing Company is a division of Carus Publishing Company.

First printing 2011

Printed and bound in the United States of America.

Library of Congress Cataloging-in-Publication Data

Halo and philosophy : intellect evolved / edited by Luke Cuddy..
p. cm.—(Popular culture and philosophy ; v. 59)
Includes bibliographical references and index.
ISBN 978-0-8126-9718-6 (trade paper : alk. paper)
1. Halo (Game)—Design. 2. Video games—Philosophy. I. Cuddy, Luke, 1980-
GV1469.25.H36H35 2011
794.8—dc22

2011012571

To Bungie,
for putting out one of the greatest
First Person Shooter series
of all time

Contents

UNSC Briefing

FRED VAN LENTE

Rereading Thoreau's *Walden* at the same time as the chapters in this collection, I was struck by Backwoods Hank's assertion that "To be a philosopher is not merely to have subtle thoughts, nor even to found a school, but so to love wisdom as to live according to its dictates, a life of simplicity, independence, magnanimity, and trust."

When it comes to simple living, the most beggarly ascetic has nothing on Master Chief, the armored hero of Microsoft's *Halo* video game series. "See the Covenant, shoot the Covenant" (or, from time to time, The Flood) pretty well sums up both his *raison d'être* and the only *a priori* knowledge before a gamer picks up an Xbox controller to propel him towards his enemies.

In many ways game developer Bungie's genius in its creation of *Halo* can be summed up in the conception of this character, the quintessential player's cat's paw. While most narrative shooters have some square-jawed heroic type for the user to both identify with and embody, John-117 (Nerd Alert! Master Chief's given name) is both unique and generic in equal measure. His faceless visage is recognized the world over, yet still only the broadest outline of a human being inside his bulky MJOLNIR exo-skeleton which the player can fill with his or her own expectations and desires. At some point during the series a sex-specific pronoun or his name is evoked, thus saddling him with a gender; but entombed in that green shell he has no noticeable sexual characteristics. Since we never see him outside the carapace he has no demonstrable race or age. Most of the dialogue in the game is borne by Chief's glowing cybernetic AI Tinkerbell, Cortana; but when he does speak, it's in the unforgettable tones of Chicago DJ Steve Downes.

Everything else that is Master Chief is provided by the gamer, whether choosing to use the magnum or the AR to blow away Grunts, and any other thoughts or opinions that may manifest during the course of the ensuing fragfest. Indeed, he and the gamer come to life at literally the same time in *Halo: Combat Evolved,* the first game, as Chief is awakened from cryogenic sleep and taught how his MJOLNIR works, which cleverly teaches the gamer the configuration of his controller at the same time. Master Chief's life is not lived until the guiding force of the user is grafted onto his otherwise empty shell—not just an unexamined life, but an unconscious one.

As the gamer animates Master Chief in *Halo: Combat Evolved,* so *Halo and Philosophy* illuminates this video game series with a spark from history's great thinkers. As with many of the topics covered in the Popular Culture and Philosophy series, I imagine there will be some perfunctory hand-wringing over whether or not a First Person Shooter is an appropriate subject for serious critical study, blah, blah, blah. But if the unexamined life isn't worth living, then the unexamined game isn't worth playing; or, to turn that configuration on its head, a game worth playing is also worthy of being examined. And with worldwide sales of *Halo* merchandise reaching nearly two billion dollars as of this writing, Master Chief and friends (and enemies, particularly his enemies) are worth quite a bit to the Microsoft corporation and their legions of fans.

To speak in Aristotelian terms, if *Halo* the game takes Master Chief from a potential kicker of alien ass to an actual one, the authors of *Halo and Philosophy* take the actual game series and examine its social, political, and philosophical potential. It is a worthy goal, and I hope you enjoy reading these thought-provoking essays as much as I did.

Acknowledgments

Thanks to the folks at Open Court for their judgment, and to the authors for their fine contributions and superb *Halo* gaming experiences. Thanks also to Jason Vandusen of Vandusen design <vandusendesign.com>.

Eliminate Hostile Anti-Intellectual Units

LUKE CUDDY

When I play *Halo: Combat Evolved* and walk through the halls and passageways of the *Pillar of Autumn* it reminds me of *DukeNukem 3D* in its cold, futuristic splendor. But when I think of *Halo*, I also think of *Doom*. While I realize there are other obvious precursors to *Halo* (like *Half Life*, *Quake*, or Bungie's own *Marathon*) it's *Doom* that drew me into the First Person Shooter (FPS) genre as a teenager. Playing *Halo* sometimes takes me back to those days when a bad day at school would lead to hours of incinerating monsters with a Rocket Launcher or tearing through them with a Double Barrel Shotgun.

But is *Halo* just another mindless FPS, inclining its players towards aggression and desensitization (and stoking popular worries about what FPS games do to teenagers)? While *Halo* is violent, it sometimes gets a worse rap than it deserves. The *Halo* series has a more complex story than many others, taking elements of that story from science fiction, as we will see. Within gaming, *Halo* has paved the way for some newer games—*Borderlands*, for example, draws from *Halo*'s gun limitation. There is more to *Halo* than meets the eye philosophically as well. Watching a group of drunken males play a round of multiplayer doesn't do justice to the deeper philosophical issues that surround and inhabit *Halo* and *Halo* culture, from personal identity, to the Western notion of salvation, to elements of Buddhism.

***Halo*'s Roots in Science Fiction Literature**

In the first level of the first game of the series, *Halo: Combat Evolved*, you are introduced to one of the Halo structures from which the game gets its name. In fact, it's the first thing you see when you start playing the game: a backdrop of a planet in space with the ring-like formation in front of it. Such a ring-like formation was most famously fictionalized by Larry Niven in his Hugo-winning book *Ringworld*, which was succeeded by two other books to make a trilogy. Here Niven helps the reader conceptualize what he calls a "ringworld" (taking his inspiration from the concept of a partial Dyson sphere): "Take Christmas ribbon, pale blue and an inch wide, the kind you use to wrap presents. Set a lighted candle on a bare floor. Take fifty feet of ribbon, and string it in a circle with the candle at the center, balancing the ribbon on the edge so that the inner side catches the candle light."[1] You might think that a structure like this would be too thin, or too small, to sustain an atmosphere or for many people to live on. But scale is important and, as one of the characters in the book points out: "That's what it's all about. Six hundred trillion square miles of surface area is three million times the surface of the Earth. It'd be like having three million worlds all mapped flat and joined edge to edge" (p. 71).

Niven paints a vivid picture of how incredible one of these ringworlds would be. Since humans have yet to perfect interstellar space travel, it won't be anytime soon that such a ringworld will actually be discovered (let alone created) outside of a videogame. This makes it all the more cool that the *Halo* creators borrowed this logically possible construct from a science fiction novel because it gives gamers a chance to see it and explore it via, mostly, Master Chief.

The candle in Niven's description is supposed to be a metaphor for a sun, around which the ringworld was constructed. The Halo structures, on the other hand, are not this large. Another precursor to the *Halo* series in science fiction literature (also influenced by Niven) comes from the British author Ian M. Banks. Banks put out the *Culture* series of books, which envisions a slightly smaller structure called an "orbital"—probably closer to the Halo structures from the game.

---

[1] Larry Niven, *Ringworld* (Orion Books, 1970), p. 68.

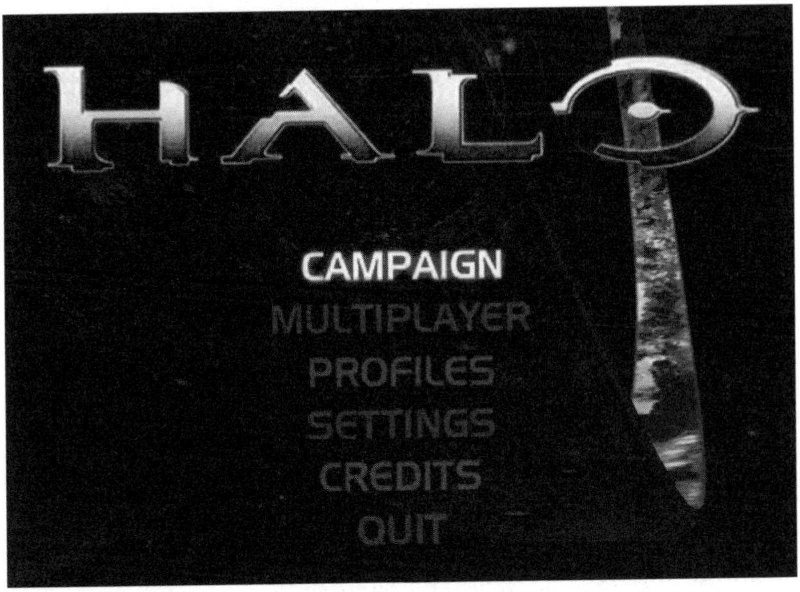

The opening screen of the first FPS Halo game depicts one of the Halo structures, as originally dreamt up by early sci-fi writers like Larry Niven and Ian M. Banks (Halo: Combat Evolved, 2001).

For anyone who has read these books, playing *Halo* for the first time can be pretty darned exciting. Not only do you get to see one possible vision of ringworlds or orbitals, but you get to explore them. After you kill all the Covenant soldiers and escape the *Pillar of Autumn* via the escape pod, you crash land on the ring in the escape pod. Before the *Pillar of Autumn* crash lands as well, you see the descent into the atmosphere of the Halo. This is Niven's and Banks' vision brought to life.

While the *Halo* storyline is certainly not pilfered from *Ringworld*, there are borrowed elements like a lost ancient super-race who created the rings (The Forerunners) or religiously devout aliens (The Covenant). In fact, someone who believes that the *Halo* universe is less complex than it is should take a look at the *Halo Encyclopedia* by DK publishing, which details *Halo*'s story, back-story, characters, races and much much more.

There's a sort of synthesis here between literature and videogames that is often overlooked, or simply not recognized. The concerned parent watching her son splatter aliens all over the wall while he maneuvers through a spacecraft probably doesn't realize that there are deeper science fiction concepts that underlie the game and the storyline. Understandably, perhaps *Halo* has an overemphasis on violence that is cause for concern, particularly in the multiplayer element. Nevertheless, the violence issue needs to be put in context before entirely condemning the *Halo* series on those grounds. After all, we are much more willing to accept violence in other media when it is coupled with something generally viewed as a greater cause (as in *Braveheart*) or with something that is artistically unique for its time (like *Pulp Fiction*).

Another way games and literature interact is through fiction based on a game. *Halo* the games have spawned *Halo* fiction. In addition to a trilogy and other books, there is a book of short stories called *Halo: Evolutions*. The stories in this collection consider perspectives that the game itself does not (or cannot because it would diminish gameplay). One of the authors, Fred Van Lente, shows the reader what it might be like if a team of Spartan's captured a particular sort of Drone. Karen Traviss speculates on what might go through Cortana's head when she's being "invaded" by the Gravemind while waiting for Master Chief to return. And B.K. Evenson imagines the life of a Spartan soldier that does *not* make it to frontline duty.

This all shows us the way media interact with other media. *Halo* borrowed some concepts from science-fiction literature to create their own universe. Then that universe was enhanced by other authors to give players more. And I haven't even mentioned parts of *Halo* culture like *Red vs. Blue* (Peter Ludlow's chapter in this volume discusses it in detail).

Why Think about Games?

When you play games with other people, in many cases, deeper elements of a player's personality can be revealed—whether it's your teammate on the wrestling mat or you during a friendly family game of *Hearts*. It is tempting to see the popular games in any given society as being a good measure of its general values and beliefs. The Romans had large arenas where people competed in games of life and death. Medieval Europeans strategized against each other in chess. At our current place in history, our society values sports and videogames, perhaps, more than any other types of games.

What underlies questions of whether or not *Halo* is worthy of philosophical analysis are questions of whether games in general are worthy of such analysis. Are they? Part of understanding videogames is understanding the way they differ from previous media. Roger Ebert, movie critic extraordinaire, recently took a side on the videogames-as-art question, for which he caught a great deal of flak from the gaming community.[2] Ebert suggested that, no, videogames are not art, nor will they be art for a very long time (if ever). Without actually disagreeing or agreeing with Ebert (though I have disagreed with him elsewhere), let me make you aware of the way Ebert went about coming to his conclusion. By playing them, you say? Maybe by watching gamers themselves play them? No, he reached his conclusion by watching online clips of some videogames, as noted by journalist Chris Suellentrop.[3] If you're reading this book, I'm assuming you see the problem here—or you at least recognize that there is a problem. As Suellentrop put it, judging games without playing them is something like judging a movie by only listening to the soundtrack.

When I teach logic, I will customarily spend at least a portion of class going over a logical fallacy called a "straw man." A straw man happens when someone misinterprets and distorts an idea, concept, argument, or phenomenon and then proceeds to come to a conclusion based on that weak interpretation. For instance, when someone who has never played *Halo* suggests that the game is nothing but blowing up aliens, it could be considered a straw man. Why? Because the game involves blowing up aliens, but much more—like the storyline or skill. It's a straw man because the person unfamiliar with *Halo* focused only on one aspect of the game, and one that is considered negative by many standards, then came to a conclusion ("that's all *Halo* is") prematurely. A straw man is dangerous because there is no reason for us to accept that conclusion (if it's based on a weak interpretation). You see straw men with extremists all the time: the videogame critic thinks that the bad aspects of games make all videogames bad; the videogame supporter thinks that the good aspects of games make them all good. In order to really understand what's going on, in order to really appreciate the negative and the positive of some phenomenon, we should be able to give a full and honest interpretation of it. Unfortunately, this doesn't always happen.

---

2 Roger Ebert, "Videogames Can Never Be Art," *Chicago Sun-Times* (April 2010).

3 Chris Suellentrop, "Inside the Box," *New York Times* (June 2010).

Surely Ebert's actions in not actually playing any videogames while coming to conclusions about them represents a generational divide (let's attribute it to this rather than to an inability to think critically, which Ebert *does* seem to possess in many of his movie reviews). It probably never occurred to Ebert that he was committing a straw man. The idea of directly interacting with something to experience it rightly (such as while playing a videogame) just never occurred to him because the media that were big in his generation (such as movies and music) do not require that sort of direct interaction. Critics of videogames have their place. I just have one request: do your research. It's best to understand something before you critique it. Otherwise, you might commit obvious fallacies. Lest we think that games themselves are simplistic or somehow inferior to other media, let's consider a quote from a book by Ian M. Banks (author of the *Culture* book series mentioned above). The main character in Banks's *The Player of Games* says:

> "All reality is a game. Physics at the most fundamental level, the very fabric of our universe, results directly from the interaction of fairly simple rules, and chance; the same description may be applied to the best, most elegant and both intellectually and aesthetically satisfying games. By being unknowable, by resulting from events which, at the subatomic level cannot be fully predicted, the future remains malleable, and retains the possibility of change, the hope of coming to prevail; victory, to use an unfashionable word. In this, the future is a game; time is one of the rules." (p. 48)

In the book, Banks envisions a highly advanced society called the "Culture" where game players (not just athletes) are well respected and held in awe. This is because, as the quote implies, this society sees games as more than mere entertainment. Games are something "elegant" and "aesthetically satisfying." Our society doesn't see them that way now, but maybe someday it will.

All of this is to say that *Halo* is worthy of philosophical investigation. It's taken some of its best elements from award-winning science fiction; it's created a storyline that raises questions about religious devotion, war, morality, and more; it's a videogame which are, more and more, becoming staples of our society; and it engenders deeper questions that are explored by contemporary science fiction authors via *Halo* fiction.

This Book and Its Chapters

This book is set up according to levels of difficulty, as the *Halo* games are. Don't assume, however, that the *Easy(er)* section will be a breeze. One of the reasons I've added the "er" is to suppress this assumption. The chapters in this section deal with some subject matter that is a bit easier to understand than the subsequent sections, but this doesn't mean it's easy in itself. For many people, philosophy is difficult in general. There, you've been warned. The subsequent sections grow in difficulty as you might expect. Still, if you are interested in a particular chapter, we can't stop you from turning straight to it.

In terms of the *Halo* universe, this book focuses on the three primary *Halo* games—*Halo: Combat Evolved*, *Halo 2*, and *Halo 3*—as well as the expansion *Halo 3: ODST* and the prequel *Halo: Reach* (but some of the chapters were written before the release of *Halo: Reach*, so it therefore wasn't possible to discuss it). Consequently, Master Chief is the main protagonist under discussion. This book also touches on the *Halo* backstory, fiction, and other *Halo* culture.

The authors consider the following questions:

- **Are campers really doing anything wrong?**
- **Does *Halo*'s music match the experience of the gamer?**
- **Would Plato have used *Halo* to train citizens to live an ethical life?**
- **What sort of Artificial Intelligence exists in *Halo* and how is it used?**
- **Can the player's experience of war tell us anything about actual war?**
- **Is there meaning to Master Chief's rough existence?**
- **How does it affect the player's ego if she identifies too strongly with an aggressive character like Master Chief?**
- **Is *Halo* really science fiction?**
- **Can *Halo* be used for enlightenment oriented thinking in the Buddhist sense?**
- **Does *Halo*'s weapon limitation actually contribute to the depth of the gameplay?**
- **When we willingly play *Halo* only to die again and again, are we engaging in some sort of self-injurious behavior?**

- **What is expansive gameplay and how can it be informed by the philosophy of Michel Foucault?**
- **In what way does *Halo*'s post apocalyptic paradigm force gamers to see themselves as agents of divine deliverance?**
- **Who is Master Chief really, and what can *Red vs. Blue* teach us about personal identity?**

Don't expect a conclusive answer to every question! If you do, you will drastically misunderstand philosophy. Philosophy does sometimes answer questions, but often philosophy is about simply pondering and exploring ideas, advancing general knowledge when possible, and enjoying the ride. As the subtitle of this book implies, evolve your intellect with this book the way you evolve your combat in *Halo*.

Easy . . . er

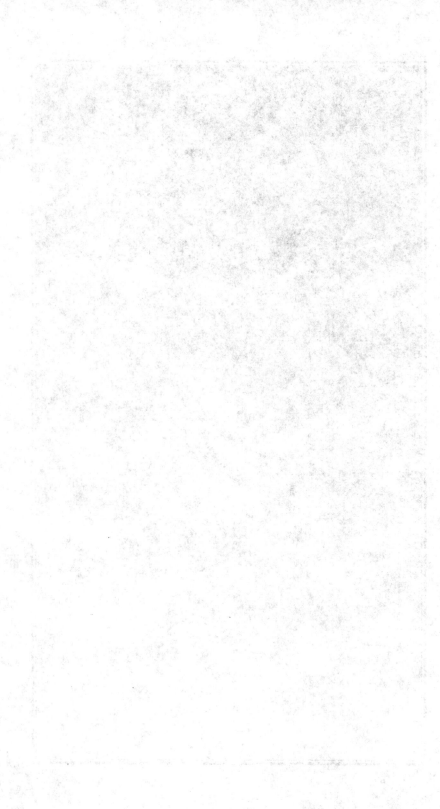

1

Who Is Master Chief?

JOYCE C. HAVSTAD

When you play *Halo*, you get to be Master Chief. But so does everyone else who plays *Halo*. Think about how many people are playing the game at this very moment—how many Master Chiefs are there *right now*? Now think about how many people have played any version of the game, all around the world, and ever since *Halo: Combat Evolved* first came out—how many Master Chiefs have there been, *ever*?

The *Halo* nation is incredibly vast; the number of Master Chiefs must be huge as well. Approximately six and a half million units of *Halo: Combat Evolved* were sold in the last decade. Add to that eight and a half million units of *Halo 2* and another nine and a half million units of *Halo 3*, and there have been almost twenty-five million units of the original trio of *Halo* games sold.[1] Even if only one person played the campaign of each unit of the game just once, there would still have been at least twenty-five million Master Chiefs.

So, who is Master Chief, really? Out of the millions of Master Chiefs that there have been, which one is the *real* one? Or, are *all* of them him? And what does the *actual* Master Chief look like? He is almost always wearing his helmet, so no one ever really gets to see his face, although the *Halo* novels do occasionally provide scant physical descriptions. For example, in *Halo: The Flood*, Master Chief is described as quite tall and muscular even without his armor, having serious eyes and strong features.[2] The most detailed

---

[1] These statistics are from a gamrFeed article by Jacob Mazel entitled "The 50 Best Selling Console Games of this Decade (So Far)," <http://gamrfeed.vgchartz.com/story/3364/the-50-best-selling-console-games-of-this-decade-so-far/>

[2] William Dietz, *Halo: The Flood* (Ballantine, 2003).

facial description of the character occurs in *Halo: The Fall of Reach*. But this novel begins when Master Chief is just a young boy, named John, with brown hair and freckles.[3]

When he's six years old, John is one of seventy-five children snatched from their homes by the United Nations Space Command (UNSC) and replaced with clones. The originals begin the training and enhancement that turns them into Spartans, cybernetically enhanced supersoldiers. And John, the young boy with brown hair and freckles, gradually becomes Master Chief Petty Officer John-117. The clones take the place of the originals, living in their homes and with their parents. So now, there are not just millions of Master Chiefs, but also at least two Johns. Which John is the real one? The clone, living in John's house with John's parents and being raised as John by people who believe he is John? Or the original, who is stolen from his home, numbered John-117, molded into a supersoldier, given growth hormone, physically augmented, linked with an AI, and who never returns to his parents or the place he was born?

Philosophers have puzzled for centuries over what makes and keeps a thing the particular thing that it is, and what makes someone stay the same person despite the many changes they experience in their life. This is despite the fact that identity seems like a straightforward, simple concept. And most people, not being fictional characters, having distinct faces, and not having been cloned, are not particularly complicated cases. Most people are nonfictional, have recognizable faces, and only one body. But Master Chief is different for all three of these reasons. In the real world, he is incarnated in many minds and on many screens. And his MJOLNIR armor is more recognizable than his actual physical features. Finally, even within the *Halo* universe, he is something of a copy of himself. He has been cloned at least once and frozen several times. For players of *Halo*, Master Chief is constantly resurrected. And for all of these reasons, understanding what generates and sustains Master Chief's identity is an especially tricky question.

The Same but Different

Identity is the relation that a thing has with itself. To say that something is identical is to say that it's the same. But things can also

[3] Eric Nylund, *Halo: The Fall of Reach* (Ballantine, 2001).

retain their identity over time, despite going through changes. For example, Master Chief is still Master Chief when he departs from the Covenant city-ship *High Charity*, despite leaving Cortana behind and going on without his AI. Master Chief goes through this and many other changes throughout his experiences in the series of *Halo* games, but he is still Master Chief. How does this work?

The possibility of identity over time is confusing, since the idea of identity seems like one of sameness, but it can also encompass difference. As a result of this complexity, questions about identity over time go back at least two thousand years. In philosophy, paradoxes are often used to demonstrate the puzzles inherent in seemingly obvious notions like identity.

One of the most famous paradoxes of the philosophical world is recounted by Plutarch, a Greek historian who lived in the first century. Plutarch is most remembered for his work *Parallel Lives*, a series of brief but insightful biographies of important figures in Greek and Roman history. The earliest "life" is that of Theseus, the hero who fought the Minotaur of King Minos on the island of Crete and who was the mythical founder of the unified Athens. In his description of the life of Theseus, Plutarch writes that:

> The ship wherein Theseus and the youth of Athens returned had thirty oars, and was preserved by the Athenians down even to the time of Demetrius Phalereus, for they took away the old planks as they decayed, putting in new and stronger timber in their place, insomuch that this ship became a standing example among the philosophers, for the logical question of things that grow; one side holding that the ship remained the same, and the other contending that it was not the same.[4]

In other words, the philosophers considered the case of Theseus's ship, and the fact that perhaps all of it had been replaced over time, and wondered whether it was really still Theseus's ship. They asked: was the ship's identity the same, despite the many changes that it had undergone? This paradox is known as The Ship of Theseus or Theseus's Ship.

Many centuries later, the British philosopher Thomas Hobbes complicated the matter even further. Hobbes is mostly remembered

---

[4] Translated by John Dryden in the late seventeenth century, <http://classics.mit.edu/Plutarch/theseus.html>.

for *Leviathan*, his 1651 work of political philosophy. But in a later work, *Elementorum philosophiae sectio prima De corpore* (more commonly known simply as *De Corpore* or *On the Body*), Hobbes discusses the original paradox of Theseus's Ship and then adds to it:

> Take the well-known example of Theseus's ship, which the sophists of Athens argued about long ago. The argument was about the difference between the original ship, and the one which was gradually remade through the continuous replacement of old planks by new ones. After all the planks had been replaced, was it numerically identical with the original ship? But if someone had preserved the old planks as soon as they were removed, and had later made a new ship by putting the preserved planks back again in the same arrangement, there is no doubt that this would be numerically identical with the original ship. We would then have two numerically identical ships, which is absolutely absurd. (Section 7, Chapter 11, Part 2)[5]

In this thought experiment Hobbes wonders which ship would be Theseus's ship, if not only were all the planks replaced, but if someone also collected all the old planks and put them back together into a ship. Then there would be two ships: one that has been called Theseus's ship throughout its history and despite many repairs, and another which has been reconstructed from all of the discarded pieces of the original ship. So, which ship is Theseus's ship, and why? If neither one is Theseus's ship, what happened to it? If both are Theseus's ship, how could there be two of them?

The paradox of Theseus's Ship can be recreated in many forms. Consider, for example, Master Chief's remarkable and iconic MJOLNIR armor. Imagine that a skirmish results in slight damage to a shoulder piece of Master Chief's suit. After the battle, he gets the damaged piece replaced. One day while sprinting, some of the lift and speed of the suit lessens. More parts must be replaced. Eventually the helmet has taken so many blows that the faceplate cracks and the entire piece must be swapped out. Finally a processor inside the advanced exoskeleton suit has to be taken out and a new one installed. But it gets fixed and Master Chief dons his suit of armor once again.

---

[5] Recently translated by George MacDonald Ross, <www.philosophy.leeds.ac.uk/GMR/hmp/texts/modern/hobbes/decorpore/decorp2.html>.

Imagine that, gradually, every single bit of the suit gets worn out and replaced. Master Chief doesn't even notice, but one day his MJOLNIR armor doesn't actually contain a single piece of the same material that it started with. Is it the same suit of armor? Or is it a different one? If it is a different suit, when did it stop being Master Chief's original suit of MJOLNIR armor and become a different one?

Now imagine that there is a technician responsible for making all of the repairs to Master Chief's armor. When Master Chief returns from battle with some damage to the armor, he goes to see the technician, so that she can remove the damaged piece and install a replacement. But instead of junking the discarded piece of armor, the technician saves it and restores it in her spare time. At first, the technician just has a dented shoulder piece. Then she gets some conduits and crystal. One day Master Chief brings a cracked and battered helmet to her. Eventually, the technician is able to entirely recreate Master Chief's suit of armor. Now there are two suits: which is Master Chief's MJOLNIR armor? The one Master Chief is wearing, but which doesn't have any of the original parts? Or the one in the technician's possession, which was broken into fragments and then restored and reassembled? Is it neither? Is it both?

At heart this puzzle is about what makes something stay the same, and what makes it different. Another way the puzzle can be described is as presenting two conflicting criteria for identity: historical versus material continuity. Material continuity is pretty simple—it's established via preservation of an object's physical matter. So, an object has material continuity just as long as it is made of the same stuff. Historical continuity is a bit more complicated—it is established via an unbroken temporal trajectory. In other words, an object possesses historical continuity when it is possible, despite the various changes it may have experienced, to trace the object's timeline in continuous stages from start to finish. Caterpillars and butterflies look like totally different creatures, but each butterfly was once a caterpillar, and it is possible to identify a particular butterfly as the same creature that was once a caterpillar by pointing to the unbroken timeline that leads from the caterpillar to the butterfly through a stage of metamorphosis. So, an object has historical continuity when it has an unbroken temporal trajectory, or a continuous history from one stage to the next.

In the case of the gradually repaired ship or suit of armor, there is clearly established historical continuity. Just as there's an unbroken timeline during which the Athenians continue to refer to the ship as Theseus's ship, despite many planks being taken out and replaced, so too there's an unbroken timeline during which Master Chief continues to use his armor and think of it as his suit of armor, despite the many pieces taken out and replaced. But there is also the case of the reconstructed ship or suit of armor, which has material continuity. Hobbes's imaginary second ship of Theseus is rebuilt from all the original planks, and thus is made of the same wood as Theseus's original ship, just as the technicians second suit of armor is rebuilt from all the original pieces, and thus is made of exactly the same physical stuff as Master Chief's original MJOLNIR armor.

Deciding which, if any, of the ships or suits of armor are the original ones depends on what seems more important to the determination of identity: historical or material continuity. If having an unbroken temporal trajectory as a certain object matters more than being made of the same stuff, then historical continuity determines sameness or identity. But if being made of the same physical material matters more, then material continuity dictates sameness or identity. Perhaps the best response to the puzzle is to consider both historical and material continuity when judging whether something is the same thing or different. But it is very difficult to construct a plausible and consistent solution to the general paradox that explains how to combine considerations of both historical and material continuity.

Making It Personal

The paradox of Theseus's Ship as well as the corresponding example of Master Chief's MJOLNIR armor are each about the identity of objects over time. These cases show that it is already a difficult matter to determine what makes a thing stay the same despite changes over time. Going beyond objects and talking about persons gets even more complicated, for several reasons. First, all persons are a kind of object, but not all objects are persons. To establish and maintain personhood must thus require something additional. Figuring out what that additional thing is and how to preserve its identity over time, despite changes, adds a new complication.

Second, neither historical nor material continuity seem like good criteria for the identity of persons over time. Persons lack strong material continuity. This is because most of the cells in our bodies are constantly replaced—so often, in fact, that less than ten years from now most of the cells in your body will not be the same as the ones there today.[6] But you'll still be you in ten years. This shows that material continuity must not be a very important criterion of personal identity: you won't be made of the same stuff, but you'll still be you.

Persons do often maintain a sort of historical continuity, but it's not clear that this is required for the maintenance of personal identity. Imagine that there was a time traveler who jumped one hundred years into the future. She would no longer have a temporally continuous personal history, but her personal identity would still be the same. This simple thought experiment reveals that possession of an unbroken temporal trajectory is not required for a person to stay the same person. And consider Master Chief, cryogenically frozen at the end of *Halo 3*, drifting in space with Cortana, awaiting rescue. He has entered a sort of suspended animation, waiting for his life to start again when he is needed. But despite this break in his personal history, he'll still be Master Chief when he wakes up. This shows that historical continuity must not be a very important criterion of personal identity: you can still be you even if there is a break in your personal timeline.

So, the identity of persons over time is complicated in a way beyond that of other objects, and requires criteria beyond that of material and historical continuity. The most obvious alternative candidate is known as psychological continuity. Psychological continuity refers to the continuity of various mental features deemed important to the preservation of personal identity. Relevant mental features might include memories, personality traits, emotional tendencies, and beliefs. When considering what makes persons unique and how they relate to themselves and other persons, it seems intuitively plausible that these sorts of mental features would be critical to the establishment and perseverance of a person's identity.

This importance of mental features is famously expressed by the English physician and philosopher John Locke, who lived during the seventeenth century. In his *Essay Concerning Human Understanding*, a treatise on the human mind and self, Locke considered the hypothetical case of a transfer of consciousness from one person to another. Locke wrote:

---

[6] For a popular discussion of this biological phenomenon, see Nicholas Wade's piece "Your Body Is Younger than You Think," *New York Times* (August 2005).

> For should the soul of a prince, carrying with it the consciousness of the prince's past life, enter and inform the body of a cobbler, as soon as deserted by his own soul, every one sees he would be the same person with the prince, accountable only for the prince's actions. (Section 15, Chapter 27)

This quote shows that, when imagining a person with the soul and consciousness of a prince in the body of a cobbler, Locke thinks that the identity of the person is determined by the intangible rather than the corporeal. In other words, consciousness determines the person, not the body their consciousness happens to be housed in. On this view, the prince-cobbler hybrid is really the prince trapped in the cobbler's body, not the cobbler inconvenienced by the prince's soul and consciousness. Additionally, Locke thinks that the idea being expressed here is not just his opinion, but a generally shared sentiment; that is what he implies when he claims that "every one sees" the case in the way he has presented it.

The ubiquity of Locke's own viewpoint can be tested by posing other, related thought experiments. Consider the Flood, and the way in which this parasitic life form infects sentient beings. Once the Flood has infected a host organism, it begins a process of evolution through various stages. The host is gradually transformed from itself into some form of the Flood, such as a Carrier or Combat form. At some point the host organism has lost its original identity and become a member of the Flood instead.

Although the Flood exists within the body of the original organism, and there is an unbroken timeline from the organism through infection to the Flood form, once the original sentience is gone it seems incorrect to say that identity is preserved. Often Combat forms of the Flood inhabit the bodies of Covenant soldiers, but it would be strange to blame the original soldiers for the actions of their bodies once the Flood form has taken over. The identity of the organism has changed: although there was once a Covenant soldier there, that being is gone and now there is something else in its place, a different creature. Agreement with this assessment of the situation demonstrates agreement with Locke's position: once psychological continuity has been lost, so too has personal identity.

A Psyche Connection

So, Locke's thought experiment with the prince and the cobbler is simply an early statement of the common feeling that psychological continuity determines personal identity. Locke himself focused on memory as the mental feature responsible for generating psychological continuity. But there are problems with this way of looking at identity.

Less than one hundred years after Locke's death, another philosopher named Thomas Reid offered a very powerful objection to Locke's account. Locke's view was that personal identity consists in consciousness alone, and that "whatever has the consciousness of present and past actions is the same person to whom they both belong" (Section 16, Chapter 27). This sounds relatively straightforward, but in his essay *On Memory*, the third of his *Essays on the Intellectual Powers of Man*, Reid posed the following scenario:

> Suppose a brave officer to have been flogged when a boy at school for robbing an orchard, to have taken a standard from the enemy in his first campaign, and to have been made a general in advanced life; suppose, also, which must be admitted to be possible, that, when he took the standard, he was conscious of his having been flogged at school, and that, when made a general, he was conscious of his taking the standard, but had absolutely lost the consciousness of his flogging. (Section 3, Chapter 3)

According to Locke, since the general remembers being the officer, the general is the same person as the officer, and since the officer remembers being the boy, the officer is also the same person as the boy. This logically implies that the general is the same person as the boy as well. But the fact that the general cannot remember being the boy means that, according to Locke, the general is not the same person as the boy. The general both is and is not the same person as the boy. Reid's example shows how Locke's view leads to contradiction, and is therefore illogical.

It is possible to reconstruct Reid's example with Master Chief's own history. Imagine John, a young boy just six years old, soon after his abduction from home and at the very beginning of UNSC's SPARTAN-II program. The newly renamed John-117 probably remembers being John, the boy from Elysium City. But by the time he's turned fourteen, he has undergone a rigorous training program, endured many physical and mental modifications, and is ready for his first mission. He might not remember being a normal boy as well as he did when the transformation had just begun. And after years of fighting as Master Chief, the supersoldier? He might not remember his life before becoming a Spartan at all. Imagine that Master Chief can remember training as John-117, and John-117 can remember being just John, but Master Chief can't remember just being John. Memories can connect each of the stages of his life to the one before it, but they don't reach all the way from the last to the first. This implies that Master Chief, the experienced super-soldier, both is and is not the young pre-abduction John. That's a contradiction, and views that contain contradictions are usually considered to be fatally flawed.

Reid's kind of case shows that relying on memory to establish psychological continuity is insufficient. But by taking various other mental features into account, perhaps it is possible to create a more robust account of psychological continuity. Recall that other potential candidates included personality traits, emotional tendencies, and beliefs. Combining these might be enough to generate an account of psychological continuity. But again, figuring out how to do that is tricky.

When defining things, philosophers often talk about necessary and sufficient conditions. Necessary conditions are the features that something must have in order to fit the definition of that thing. For example, a square is defined as a four-sided, two-dimensional, closed figure. Having four sides is a necessary condition of being a square. If a figure does not have four sides, it cannot be a square. But just having four sides does not make something a square. A pyramid with a triangular base has four sides, for example, but it is not a square. This is because having four sides is a necessary, but not a sufficient, condition for being a square. A sufficient condition is a feature that makes something qualify as the thing it is defined as. For example, being a square is sufficient for being a closed figure. If a figure is a square, then it must be a closed figure. But something does not have to be a square to be a closed figure. It could be a triangle instead. This is because being a square is a sufficient, but not a necessary, condition for being a closed figure.

This conception of necessary and sufficient conditions can be used to help evaluate the preceding discussion of personal identity. The constant replacement of bodily cells shows that, even under normal conditions, material continuity is not necessary for the preservation of personal identity. Locke's case of the prince and the cobbler shows that material continuity is not sufficient. The possibility of time travel shows that historical continuity, although usually a component of personal identity, is not necessary for the preservation of personal identity. And the transformation of sentient beings into Flood forms shows that historical continuity is not sufficient. But psychological continuity does seem necessary for the preservation of personal identity. Perhaps among the various mental features which make up psychological continuity, such as memory, personality, emotion, and belief, no single one by itself is necessary, but together they are sufficient.

Mastering the Chief

Establishing the identity of objects and persons over time is surprisingly difficult, as this discussion has shown, using a mix of cases from both the real world and from the fictional world of *Halo*. Notable examples from the history of philosophy, as well as the traditional philosophical method of constructing thought experiments, have been applied too. But there are some additional aspects of the particular identity of Master Chief that are worth further consideration. These are his status as a fictional character, his lack of a discernable face, and the fact that he has been cloned.

This has two important implications here: first, there's generally only one version of each real person, but there can be infinitely many versions of a fictional character. Philosophers like to make a distinction between types and tokens. Types describe a kind of thing, whereas tokens are instantiations of type. AIs are a type of thing, and each AI, such as Cortana, is a token of the type AI. Real persons are also a type of thing, and each of us are tokens of that type. Actually, each of us is also our own particular type of thing—but there's just one token of that type. The type that describes me, Joyce C. Havstad, only has one token of the type—there's just one version, a single instantiation, of me. This is not the case for fictional characters like Master Chief. The type that describes Master Chief has many tokens in it: in code, on disc, in novels, on screens, and in minds. There is a plasticity about fictional characters that allows for mass instantiation and creatively different versions—for many tokens to exist within the type. Real persons like you and me do not have this kind of plasticity, but fictional characters like Master Chief do.

Second, real persons are physical objects located in space and time, whereas fictional characters are mental constructs produced by imagination and narrative. Instead of being constructed and influenced by an assortment of material, biological, psychological, social, and historical factors, Master Chief's personal identity is determined by a group of story and game creators at Bungie. It is also, to some extent, determined by each player of *Halo*. This is an ingenious consequence of generating a character without a face. By never revealing, and perhaps never even creating, the face of Master Chief, the designers of the game allow each player to imagine Master Chief's face however they choose. Part of his personal identity is unfixed, and can thus be envisioned in a multitude of ways. Players can make up and relate to the character that they choose, enhancing the bond between player and character.

Lastly, what of the cloned boy left behind on Eridanus-II, replacing the original John who was abducted and taken to Reach? The clone was created by taking a tissue sample from the original John, replicating the DNA, and growing a copy in an accelerated process known as flash-cloning. It is true that clones share DNA with those they were cloned from. But this does not mean that they share personal identity.

For one thing, having the same DNA does not imply being the same person, even in the real world—identical twins share DNA but each have their own personal identities. For another, the clone and the original diverge in a host of different ways—they have different bodies, timelines, and psyches. Finally, the underdeveloped technology of flash cloning generates only poor copies of natural persons—flash clones do not share the memories of the original, have to be trained to walk and talk, and suffer from a host of genetic maladies. They never acquire full mental capacity and degenerate after only a few months.

And so, although there may have been two Johns for a short while sometime around 2517 C.E., in the world of *Halo*, there's really only one Master Chief. Luckily, in our world, there can be infinitely many.

2
Master Chief and the Meaning of Life

JEFF SHARPLESS

Large explosions from a volley of Brute fuel rod guns struck the advancing company of marines from the ridgeline some meters above. The precision ambush by Covenant forces effectively decimated the marines. Each plasma round rocked and obliterated the helpless men below, leaving only a few survivors. The debris clouds temporarily hid the surviving marines from the sights of Covenant snipers trained on them. Damaged and disoriented, the men of UNSC Bravo Company scrambled for cover behind a thin rock wall. It was only moments ago, the sergeant was screaming on the COM for support; now, only an assortment of body parts spread across the marble landscape. As the dust began to settle, Private Wilkes tilted his helmet back in the futile attempt to clear his vision of the blood from his fellow soldiers who had been destroyed by the explosions. Looking frantically for a weapon, he pressed his back to the wall anticipating the next barrage. What he felt was the force of a severe impact different from the energy blasts before. The impact shot dust, rock, and debris into the air, again blinding and disorienting. Emerging from the dust, with a sudden blinding speed, two Spartan warriors launched out of the cloud with weapons ready. The sight of Spartans immediately opening fire, one with an M6 Spartan Laser and the other an M19 SSM Rocket launcher, brought adulation and confidence to Wilkes and the other marines. The simultaneous fire hit the rock face above with precision and caused the precipice to fold. Dozens of Grunts fell to their deaths. The Spartans split and continued their assault with incredible ferocity. Within ten minutes the battle ended, over 200 hundred Covenants, 90 marines, and a Spartan lay dead on the battlefield. The remaining Spartan and marines were

> ***evac'd off the planet by a Pelican dropship to the UNSC battlecruiser in orbit. The battle on the ground was over, another battle would rage for the surviving Spartan.***

This battle scene reflects the environment of the *Halo* universe. For humanity, it's a future marked by the colonization of outer space and by terrible conflict. The same problems that have plagued humanity since the dawn of civilization, conflict and violence, continue in outer space. However, humans are not alone in the universe.

The Covenant, a technologically advanced alliance of different species led by the Prophets, deems humans inferior beings and begins massive assaults on the colonies. Earth unifies in a bitter struggle for survival. As the human colonies fall, there is a beaming ray of hope that strikes admiration and awe among the common soldier and citizen alike, the legendary elite Spartan warrior—genetically enhanced both physically and cognitively, and trained to be the ultimate soldier.

These heroic super-soldiers are deployed to achieve the unachievable. The famed Spartan Master Chief John-117 fights without question, thirsts for battle, and makes only one request, "I need a weapon," while going on to destroy the enemy with inhuman efficiency. The battle scene above illuminates why the Spartans garner such admiration and awe as heroes fighting to defend humanity from a malevolent enemy. However, Spartans have a dark history that raises questions of meaning for the warrior. Master Chief and his brothers and sisters face a challenge, as all humans do, to find a meaning to their existence. Yet for the Spartans, this search for meaning is far more desperate, partly because of their origins and partly because of their role. The Spartans are born from a hard-line military thinking which accepts that the ends justify the means.

The Spartan Warrior

At the close of the twenty-third century, humanity is in dire conflict with itself and the use of genetically enhanced soldiers is developed by the United Nations Space Command (UNSC) to control outbreaks of violence. The Spartan II Project, an offshoot of the previous Orion Project deactivated some years before, is a reaction to a tactical change from larger forces to small, highly skilled elite tactical units to put down insurrections on outer colonies and prevent civil wars. The brainchild of Dr. Catherine E. Halsey, the Spartan II Project is a new level of development attempting to integrate genetic enhancements with a new battle armor called MJOLNIR.

In 2517, seventy-five children approximately six years of age are selected based on their genetic profiles, to be used as candidates for the new project. The children are replaced with genetically defective clones to cover the conscription, records of the children's identities are erased, and the children are given a three-number code as their designation. In the years that follow, the children are subjected to rigorous physical and comprehensive academic training. In 2525, the fourteen-year-old candidates undergo a series of radical operations to enhance their skeletal, muscular, optical, and nervous system. According to reports, of the seventy-five original children only thirty-three survive the operations, thirty are lost, and twelve severely crippled by the process. After the final union of the candidates and the MJOLNIR armor, the Spartans are operational within the year, their first operation against rebels in an outer colony a great success. Since their deployment in 2525, the Spartans are embraced as heroes in the fight to save humanity against the invading Covenant Alliance.[1]

What Did They Die For?

Spartans fight and die as heroes, but for them the admiration is tainted by the facts of their origins. It will be in the moments of reflection that these warriors think about the meaning of their lives and call it into question.

> *As the Spartan stepped off the Pelican dropship, the voices on deck went silent, with only the hum of the ship breaking the silence. The light struck the green tint of the battle damaged MJOLNIR armor. Many of the workers on deck stopped what they were doing and watched the Spartan as he began walking toward the bridge to debrief with the Captain. They all wanted to catch a glimpse of the rarely seen elite Spartan II. Looking out through his visor at the faces of the men and women of the UNSC battlecruiser, he could see some people nodding their heads in acknowledgment, others brimming with*

---

[1] <http://halostory.bungie.org/spartan.html>.

admiration, others showing uneasiness and fear. The Spartan could hear the whispers and chatter from the personnel and wondered if they knew what he had lived through and sacrificed for them, and what his brothers and sisters had sacrificed.

Exhausted after the battle and debrief, the Spartan retired to his room. Resting alone, his thoughts turned to the battle and the loss of his brother, Spartan Kurt-051.[2] *His emotions surged as the overwhelming pain of loss hit him. Kurt was not merely a fellow warrior; he was a survivor of countless battles and a friend that stood fast before Covenant onslaughts. Kurt cared for humanity and his family of Spartans. Yet, for Fredric-104 he could not help feeling the pain of losing his people. He often chalked these feelings up to the need for good Spartans to win battles, but this was a guise. After each battle, the questions would grow in his mind. He could not help but ask, "What did they die for? Why are we here? Why was I taken from a normal life, experimented on, enhanced, and trained to be the most efficient ruthless warrior humanity has ever known?" He thought about his life and what was taken from him. He thought of the faces of the troops on the deck and felt the distance between what were to be his people, the human beings he was fighting for, the people his brothers and sisters died for, and the people that created him as an instrument of war. If war is a force that gives us meaning, then why does each battle and each loss only show its unending emptiness and cruelty?*

The Anti-Hero

The above is how I imagine a Spartan reflecting on the meaning of his or her life. A life of war will take its toll on any human beings, enhanced or not. To live with such violence as the core of our existence would lead many of us to question the psychological wherewithal of the Spartan. What the reflections of the Spartan show is only a fragment of what they have to understand as super-soldiers. What's missing in the Spartan's inner monologue is perhaps the most glaring and important, namely the fact that at the age of six these children were taken by their government and experimented on for the purposes of violence. To be taken and exploited does not seem to weigh heavy on his mind, but it is a crucial factor in a Spartan questioning his life. It's the combination of their history and

[2] *Halopedia* <http://halo.wikia.com/wiki/SPARTAN-II_Program.

their role as super-soldiers that render their lives, as philosopher Albert Camus suggested, absurd.

According to Camus, living brings with it a dense strangeness, an incomprehensibility as to the reasons why we are alive, and the certainty of death. There is anxiety, discomfort, and a palpable nausea that life has a genuine possibility of being meaningless. Through the history of the Spartans, we learn there is a reason for these soldiers, super-soldiers for a futuristic death squad against other human beings. It was only a war with the alien Covenant that made these Spartan warriors the "saviors" many see them as; they could have easily been seen as monsters bred to suppress the voices of dissent. The Spartans fight and die for a humanity that denied them their basic rights to dignity and self-determination; this is absurd. Yet, it is the reason for their creation, to fight for the governing oppressors as robot-like monstrosities. Their deaths are meaningless and all the killing they do is thoughtless. They are slaves of an uncaring master. The Spartan warrior must face Camus's claim in an acute way since their exploitation and abuse for the betterment of humanity is a possible interpretation of the meaning of their lives.

This rather disparaging narrative does capture the reality for Spartans in many ways—they are condemned to a life of war and murder, programmed to follow without question. Master Chief's famous statement, "I need a weapon," is a hollow, empty action of an absurd robot with a corrupted will. Nevertheless, human beings are experiential creatures who seek to make sense and meaning of their lives. The Spartan will want to make sense of his existence no matter what programming he or she has been fed. If a Spartan were to examine the meaning of his existence, I think it would be rather bleak, as I have described above, and the conclusion that life is absurd for the Spartan would ring true even more so than for the ordinary human being. If the Spartan were to see his life as absurd and his life and death meaningless, why not commit suicide? What keeps the Spartan going? We'll come back to this, but first we have to look at a myth.

The Myth of Sisyphus

Camus describes an ancient story that, for him, captures the nature of life and brings home the starkness of living to human beings and Spartans alike: the Myth of Sisyphus. It is the story of Sisyphus, a king's son condemned by the God Zeus for his crimes to push a rock up a hill and watch it fall back down for all eternity. This chronicle, for Camus, is the plight of humanity—each of us is born, we grow up, we live the variety of possible lives one can live, and then we die. All that goes on between birth and death is but an empty platitude and each person is condemned by fate, the Gods, or God, to a life of pushing a rock up the hill and watching it fall down.

Camus says, "At the end of the awakening comes, in time, the consequence: suicide or recovery."[3] The story of Sisyphus becomes tragic when he becomes aware that this is his fate for eternity; just as the worker realizes she too is locked into a life of possible toil; or the Spartan, who becomes aware of the absurdity of his existence, each battle, each loss, and the imminent threat of pain, suffering, and death. The Spartan will see his own rock being pushed up the hill. Suicide is a tempting option for escape, but Camus believes that even in the face of such a desolate understanding of life, there is a response that defies the conclusion of suicide. He points to the moment in the story of Sisyphus where he has pushed the rock up the hill and it begins to roll back down. Sisyphus turns to walk down the hill; he is exhausted and tormented, yet in that moment of turning and beginning his descent, there is a sense that revolts against the toil, pain, and torment. Camus illuminates this point:

> At that subtle moment when man glances backward over his life, Sisyphus returning toward his rock, in that slight pivoting he contemplates that series of unrelated actions which becomes his fate, created by him, combined under his memory's eye and soon sealed by his death. Thus, convinced of the wholly human origin of all that is human, a blind man eager to see who knows that the night has no end, he is still on the go, the rock is still rolling. (Camus, p. 123)

For Master Chief and the other Spartans, the meaning to their existence is challenged by their creation and their lives are filled with violence and pain. But as Camus shows, their absurd life has meaning in the fleeting moments where they are aware that they are still fighting and still standing. They are not heroes but anti-heroes,

---

[3] Albert Camus, *The Myth of Sisyphus* (Vintage, 1991), p. 13.

standing fast in an absurd and hostile environment of their lives. They go on fighting and sacrificing to defend the undeserving humans who created them. They push their rock uphill and stand defiantly as it falls down; in that moment for human beings and Spartans, there is something we might call happiness. The answer to the question "Is life worth living?" is a defiant yes!

This seems a fair philosophical interpretation of life at times and perhaps more so for the Spartans. Nevertheless, we can question the conclusion that Camus draws about life being absurd, since the term absurd can be ambiguous and it is a rather extreme way to interpret living. Could we not argue that we merely do not understand the so-called strangeness of being alive? What in life leads us to think it is absurd? In addition, it is unclear that life is similar to the Myth of Sisyphus. Life can certainly appear so and, in the Spartan's case, it does seem to hold up as a narrative. They are not heroes but anti-heroes. Yet, it is equally possible that the Spartan's life is more than a sorrowful tale of exploitation by militaristic government. Millennia before Camus talked about the absurdity of life, the Greeks showed that life for the Spartan can have meaning and happiness.

The Stoic Warrior

In the time of *Halo*, some three thousand years will have passed since the group of thinkers known as the Stoics suggested another path to meaning. As we saw in the previous section, the Spartan warrior faces incredible challenges that may lead him to think life is meaningless, but he stands fast defiantly as the anti-hero. The ancient philosopher Epictetus suggests that even with the difficulties that human beings face we can live with peace and tranquility; this can be true for the Spartans as well. Epictetus and his fellow stoic philosophers teach a "fundamental rule" where there are things within our control and things outside our control. It is only when one is clear and can distinguish between the two, that human beings can cultivate tranquility. It is the attitude of the mind that determines the meaning and worthiness of life, not the situation in which one finds oneself.

The fundamental premise of Epictetus's thought is that by understanding what is within our control we can better master our desires. Those things that are outside our control, we are to ignore. The highest good is virtue, living in accordance with one's nature as a rational being or right reason while evil is living contrary to virtue, right reason. Human suffering and the occurrence of severe events such as natural disasters, slavery, or being conscripted for a military experiment, for example, result in physical pain, but the problem lies in how we respond to pain and the psychological movements of thought that occur from our habits of experience.

Epictetus would say that events like the Spartan II program, where the children are kidnapped, genetically engineered, and trained to be super-soldiers, are all instances beyond the control of the individuals. What we experience or possess in life can come and go and people are genuinely helpless to do anything about what is outside their control. What we do have control over is how we manage our psychology. Stoic psychology breaks down impressions (the things we experience through the five senses) from sensations (more developed feelings from these impressions). Stoics argue that we can give "assent" to, or make a choice to accept, certain impressions and deny others; there are actions and instances that are "up to us" and "not up to us." This is where we can assert our control. Our goals and our attitudes are up to us, and in giving assent we allow those thoughts, experiences, and emotions to influence us. Epictetus says, "When we suffer setbacks, disturbances, or grief, let us never place blame on others, but on our own attitudes."[4] The Stoics believe we can select the positive thoughts, experiences, and emotions, and deny, or not give assent to, the negative thoughts, experiences, and emotions. To give into negative thoughts is considered an error in judgment, by placing importance on things that elude our control.

The proper recourse for the Spartan is to learn what is "up to him" and to master his desires by understanding negative emotions and focusing on what is important for a good life for him. The Stoic program argues that if we learn to control ourselves and cultivate our virtue, there will be much less suffering and little evil in the world. Suffering and painful experiences are genuine, but the emotions we accept are self-imposed even when someone is being harmed. For example, when the marines are attacked by the Covenant troops from an elevated position, the stoic Spartan is as fearful as the rest of the marines; the difference, however, is the way the stoic Spartan then frames this fear. To go from "there are

---

[4] Epictetus, *A Manual for Living* (HarperCollins, 1994), p. 17.

Covenant troops firing rockets from above" to "there are Covenant troops firing rockets from above and we are all going to die" gives assent (makes the choice) to negative emotions of distress. These movements to negative emotions are misjudgments and, according to the Stoics, emotions are not automatic since there is a choice to make in the movements.

If we understand the rational self, then we understands that movements of thought are part instinct and part choice. It may seem counter-intuitive in not moving to negative emotions when they are warranted; for example, if there are soldiers at your front door and you know they mean possible harm, you will naturally be *terrified* that they will harm you or your family. The Stoic advice is to know what is "up to you" and you will be fine.

It is not that Stoics are indifferent to loved ones, but it is "not up to you" if they are harmed or not, nor does it entail passivity to the situation; a Stoic may fight because living in accordance with nature may require one to sacrifice oneself. However, the Stoic must minimize the attachments to contingent things, like family, because we cannot control whether they live or die; failing to see this as true is to fail to understand the fundamental rule of becoming enslaved to negative emotions. Epictetus asks, "Do you wish to be invincible? Then don't enter into combat with what you have no real control over" (Epictetus, p. 31). The Spartan can be invincible if he understands that the meaning to his life is independent of the conditions that surround him.

Master Chief has to face his past, the exploitive feature of his creation, and the questionable reasons for why he fights. He has to accept his present nature as a warrior sworn to defend humanity. He can be faithful to the cause as an antidote to the bitterness that his past may foster. What we learn in the mostly silent character of Master Chief is the complete Stoic warrior that is strong in his own understanding of his past, present, and future. His statement, "I need a weapon," is a claim that understands who and what he is. Epictetus reminds us, "Nothing can be taken from us. There is nothing to lose. Inner peace begins when we stop saying 'I have lost it' and instead say, 'It has been returned to where it came from'" (Epictetus, p. 23). If this follows, Master Chief and the Spartans can live with harmony and tranquility even in the war-torn *Halo* universe.

The criticism often leveled against Epictetus and the Stoics is that they minimize the emotional connections and attachments that are very important to most human beings. The Spartans must minimize their attachments to their fellow soldiers and the people they are sworn to defend. They can only fight on. Epictetus's argument that it is out of their control and they must ignore it would minimize the terrible injustice suffered by the children of the Spartan program. The Stoic ideal seems rather troubling and hard to bear in this instance.

In the end, the contemplative Spartan will seek to make sense of his or her difficult life—be it the anti-hero or the Stoic warrior, only the Spartan will know. The two views offered, of Camus and Epictetus, are but two of the possibilities to be explored in the effort for greater understanding of life. Yet, both Camus and Epictetus capture something about what Master Chief has to concentrate on in finding meaning to a life less ordinary. Camus captures the strangeness and absurdity of living that can seem rather hopeless and meaningless. Master Chief and his kind could easily become disillusioned by the facts of their origin, the constant battles, and loss of life. These things are the rock being pushed up the hill and it falling down. If the Spartans embrace Camus, they can find meaning in the fleeting moments of defiance as they survive and fight on.

On the other hand, Epictetus captures an understanding that suggests that even if the world may appear absurd and rather mad, there's still a choice. The Spartan can respond to the facts of her past and present by being clear with what is up to her and ignoring what she cannot control. In that understanding, tranquility is possible. Each of these philosophical perspectives addresses the possible meaning for the Spartan warrior. Those who play the games and read the stories of the Spartan warriors observe a solemn being facing a life of war and carnage—a being who faces that life with a quiet reserve that ordinary humans will sympathize with, but struggle to grasp. Even in the darkness and turmoil of the *Halo* future, Master Chief can find meaning to his actions and his life.

3

Why Plato Wants You to Play *Halo*

ROGER TRAVIS

What would Plato have thought of *Halo*? Plato knew a lot more about videogames than we usually give him credit for, and he was as familiar as anyone could be with *Halo's* illustrious forebears, *The Iliad* and *The Odyssey*.

Despite his famous opposition to the ethics of what he called *mimesis*—that is, really, playing pretend the way we do when we play *Halo*—Plato would have welcomed *Halo* as a proper training for the citizens of a just nation.

Plato saw the theatrical epics he knew as a threat, but there's also an under-appreciated irony in Plato's position on *mimesis*—especially with regard to epic, a genre in which *Halo* is fully entitled to membership. That irony has everything to do with the status of works like *Halo* that help members of a society learn to behave as steadfast warriors in the face of threats to their communities. It's no coincidence that even as Plato, through his character Socrates, is condemning stories that people perform by playing pretend, he's performing such a story himself: *The Republic*.

Am I foolishly going to suggest that *Halo* is a deep philosophical treatise? Of course not—but according to the ancient understanding of philosophy, *Halo is philosophy*, because in its own way *Halo* trains us in the ethical life. Plato might well have welcomed it as a warlike supplement to *The Republic*.

Context of Platonic Ethics in *Halo*: Education

It certainly doesn't seem on the face of it as if *Halo* has anything to do with the questions with which Plato was most concerned—the questions of ethical philosophy that we might boil down to "What does it mean to do, and to be, good?" Even if we somehow dignify *Halo* with the title "epic," it's still just a space-epic videogame about a super soldier fighting aliens, right?

It's definitely that, but, strangely, Plato had a great deal to say about the ethical philosophy of (space-)epic, and about videogames; indeed, dealing with the philosophical influence of works very much like *Halo* was a key part of his reason for inventing what we know simply as "philosophy."[1] Those works were *The Iliad* and *The Odyssey*, and Plato felt he needed to deal with them for both a practical and a theoretical reason.

Practically, Plato saw that if his new way of doing life—that is, the practice of philosophy—was going to have the effect he wanted it to have on the world, he was going to have to reform education. In Plato's Athens, the Homeric epics constituted the bedrock of education—and also a great deal of the edifice built upon that bedrock. Young Athenians learned their Homer before they learned anything else, and Plato himself ironically demonstrates that learning over and over in his dialogues, as interlocutor after interlocutor spouts endless bits of Homer the way moderns with a religious education can spout sacred texts.

We can see epic's dominance reflected in the works for which classical Athens is justly famous. When Herodotus and Thucydides go to write history, they begin with the "author" they thought of as a man named "Homer." (They were wrong to think that way. There was no single author Homer, but a bunch of different people whom we call "the Homeric tradition." But that doesn't affect the use the Greeks made of what they thought of as Homer.) When Aeschylus, Sophocles, and Euripides go to write tragedy, it's Homer's *Iliad* and Homer's *Odyssey* that they count on their audience knowing, if their tragedies are going to make sense. *The Iliad* and *The Odyssey*, and, to a slightly lesser extent, a whole bunch of other, similar-but-inferior, epics that we've now lost, were the textbooks of the Athenian educational system.[2]

---

[1] Since this chapter takes a highly contextual view of Plato, it's probably worth saying that there are writers before Plato who are usually called "philosophers"—specifically, they're called "pre-Socratic philosophers" (their names include Heraclitus and Parmenides)—but 1. they didn't call themselves that, and 2. their work was very unlike what we know as philosophy.

[2] We know next to nothing for certain about the procedural—as opposed to

Plato on the Attack

When Plato wants to talk about reforming the way Athenians—and people in general—learn to be Athenians, and good people, it's Homer he attacks: in the *Ion* and especially in *The Republic*. In the *Ion*, Plato has Socrates take on Ion the rhapsode—that is a reciter of the epics of Homer—as a proxy both for Homer "himself" and for the entire educational system that Plato saw as founded upon "his" works. In fact, Ion's name is a tell here, because it indicates that he's standing in for the educational tradition that came from Ionia, which is where the Homeric epics originate.

It might help to imagine for a moment what it would be like if *Halo* were the key textbook that kids were learning from today. You might find them quoting Sergeant Johnson, the Master Chief, Captain Keyes, and Cortana in appropriate situations, and bragging to one another about their accomplishments in the game. . .

Oh, wait. Kids already do that, don't they?

In fact, we're already in an educational system not that far from the one Plato experienced, in which being a person involved much more playing epic pretend than you notice when you first turn your attention to it; it's just that the idea we have of "school" being the most important educational practice of childhood and early adolescence gets in the way of our seeing where and what our children are really learning.

The idea of "playing epic pretend" gets us into the theoretical part of the reason Plato's ethical philosophy can't be separated from Homeric epic—and thus can't be separated from *Halo* either. The theoretical side of all this is where *The Republic* comes in, and now we have to dive into the thorny problem of *mimesis*. We could do a lot worse than to simply define it from the start as "playing epic pretend," but let's start with the more familiar translation: "imitation."

Halo as Mimesis

Although *mimesis* is usually translated as "imitation," imitation is not what's going on when we play *Halo* or listen to a bard sing *The*

---

the substantive—side of Athenian education; in fact, most of what we do know comes from Plato, who's hardly an unbiased source. For the state of the art, such as it is, in research on ancient education, see W.A. Smith, *Ancient Education* (Philosophical Library, 1955).

Iliad, or watch a Greek tragedy, or watch a romantic comedy on TV. What's really going on is that we're pretending.

In fact, Plato's word *mimesis* (which was already a reasonably old word meaning "pretend performance" in ancient Greek) had the sense of both "performance" and of "copying." Plato makes it clear that he understood the word to mean "pretend performance." Our word "imitation" has the sense of "copying" but not of "performance."

The reason we see *mimesis* translated as "imitation" so often is that in the tenth book of *The Republic* Plato makes his famous argument about how a painting of a bed is (as we usually see it) a "copy of a copy," because a "real" bed is actually a "copy" of the idea of Bed—usually called "the form of the bed." But Plato is provocatively de-emphasizing the performance side of the word and heavily emphasizing the "copy" side not with the intention to *redefine* the term *mimesis* but with the intention of *critiquing* it.

More simply put, in *Republic* 10, Plato's emphasizing the part of performance that may be viewed as sheer copying, or mimicry as we usually define that word. He's saying "You think this *mimesis* thing is awesome, but, let me tell you, too much of it is mimicry, and you don't realize how dangerous that makes it."

In terms of *Halo*, when you pretend to be the Master Chief, you're doing *mimesis* in the Book 3 sense: that is, you're pretending to be somebody else. Plato's Book 10 Socrates—if he's even serious at that point—would like you to think about the harm you're doing yourself ethically in that you're also copying the actions the game gives you to copy: shooting aliens, just to choose *Halo*'s most prominent mechanic. If it seems insane to think that you could do yourself ethical harm that way, well, really it's no more insane than saying that a painting of a bed is twice-removed from the metaphysical realm of the forms, which contains some sort of divine Bed: that is, it's insanity with a philosophical reason, and an ironic philosophical reason at that (more about the irony in a moment).

There's something to be said for Plato's notion of ethical harm when we consider the kind of actions *Grand Theft Auto* gives you to copy: certainly the idea that people could become walking performances of criminal characters is one that's pretty familiar to any gamer who's tried to defend games like *Halo* as ethically okay, much less one who's tried to persuade even gamers that the game might be ethically valuable. Plato knew it well, too: *The*

Republic brings its critique of *mimesis* to a head with the following passage:

> Therefore, Glaucon, I said, whenever you meet with any of the eulogists of Homer declaring that he has been the educator of Hellas, and that he is profitable for education and for the ordering of human things, . . . we are ready to acknowledge that Homer is the greatest of poets and first of tragedy writers; but we must remain firm in our conviction that hymns to the gods and praises of famous men are the only poetry which ought to be admitted into our State. For if you go beyond this and allow the honeyed muse to enter, either in epic or lyric verse, not law and the reason of mankind, which by common consent have ever been deemed best, but pleasure and pain will be the rulers in our State.[3]

By playing epic pretend, people learn to let their appetites overcome their reason, Socrates says here. By playing *Halo*, you don't just learn to be like Master Chief, but because *Halo* appeals to your appetites—for blood, for sex—you also learn to let those appetites control you.

Note carefully also the way Homer and tragedy have come together; it will be very important in a moment. It's a shortcut, but not an inaccurate one, to say that the elements of tragedy we see in *Halo,* like the deaths of Commander Keyes and Sergeant Johnson, and the suffering of Cortana, demonstrate the same coming together: from a Platonic point of view *Halo* is both epic and tragedy, just as *The Iliad* is both epic and tragedy.

Plato's student Aristotle also chooses to group Homeric epic and Greek tragedy together in his famous *Poetics.* Aristotle's view, though, is directly opposed to Plato's: for Aristotle, playing pretend is just what humans do, and when we do it in an epic or a tragic form we learn to be *better* at philosophy (that's where his famous idea of *catharsis* comes in), not worse. At the end of this chapter, I'll suggest that if we're willing to let a little Aristotle in to leaven our Plato, the ethical picture for *Halo* gets even better. But even if we go with Aristotle on the basic ethical nature of *mimesis*, Plato's analysis of its relation to education and culture keeps its power—the power I'm exploring here in connection to *Halo.*

---

[3] Here and throughout this chapter, I use heavily adapted versions of Benjamin Jowett's translation of the works of Plato.

All bad? No

Plato's Socrates's pronouncement, though, if we wanted to take it at face value, deciding that Socrates speaks Plato's mind, would spell doom for our attempt to make Plato the rabid Bungie fanboy we want him to be. But it's not the sum total of what Plato has to say about videogames, because in his final work, *The Laws*, he returns to the matter of *mimesis* in the course of designing another ideal city, this one substantially different from the one designed by Socrates and the people he talks to in *The Republic*. In *The Laws* Socrates is—almost uniquely in all of Plato's dialogues—absent. His role is taken by a character called only "Athenian." This Athenian takes a different view of what kind of playing pretend belongs in the city, but one that brightly illuminates what we just saw in *The Republic* Book 10.

First, *mimesis* is now explicitly the vehicle of education in the form of choral poetry (thus, a different kind of *mimesis* from the harmful kind outlined in *The Republic* Book 10). Second, in a memorable and unfortunately rarely-analyzed passage, the Athenian says that if tragic poets should come to the lawgivers and ask to put on tragedy in their new city, the lawgivers should respond that—wait for it—*they* are tragedians themselves, and there can only be one.

> **Athenian:** And, if any of the serious poets, as they are termed, who write tragedy, come to us . . . I think that our answer should be as follows: Best of strangers . . . we also according to our ability are tragic poets, and our tragedy is the best and noblest; for our whole constitution [*politeia*] is a performance [*mimesis* (or what did you think?)] of the best and noblest life, which we affirm to be indeed the truest tragedy. You are poets and we are poets, both makers of the same strains, rivals and antagonists in the noblest of dramas, which true law can alone perfect, as our hope is. . . . First of all show your songs to the magistrates, and let them compare them with our own, and if they are the same or better we will give you a chorus; but if not, then, my friends, we cannot.

Okay, here's the most amazing thing, and this is the reason I gave you the Greek for "constitution." *Politeia* is the word that, when given as the title of a dialogue of Plato, is translated "Republic." Here at the end of his life, in his last and summative work, Plato admits that *The Republic* was *mimesis*. Yes, the same thing he had

Socrates say would have to be chucked out. More, the Athenian is saying via this play on words that mimetic performances of *The Republic* would be admissible in the ideal city.

Ironic Killtacular

What are we to make of this? Well, here's where *Halo* itself comes in. *The Republic*—and we can use this one mega-dialogue as an emblem of the entire Platonic corpus—as *mimesis* seeks to train its audience, readers and listeners, to be like the characters performed in the dialogue. Indeed, *The Republic* is a training simulation course in dialogue itself. Its values are the values of the fantasy of the philosophical city, and those values are pushed into the audience through the power of playing philosophic pretend, the same way the Socrates of *The Republic* tells his listeners that Homeric epic pushes all sorts of potentially-questionable values into the audience of epic.

If we can prove that *Halo* is somehow a training in philosophy, we might be able to bring our 360's to Magnesia (the name of the city the lawgivers of *The Laws* are founding).

The most important objection Plato made to the Homeric epics was that their main characters—Achilles, Agamemnon, Hector, Odysseus—are not worthy of emulation. Achilles deserts in a fit of pique; Agamemnon is an incompetent commander; Hector runs away from Achilles before turning around only because he has no choice; Odysseus lies like a rug.

Such is not the case of the characters of *Halo*. Captain and Commander Keyes, Sergeant Johnson, Cortana, the noble and infinite marines and ODST troopers: all of these NPC's do their duty, uttering only the occasional wry remark, and help you save the universe in the process.

Most importantly, of course, there's *you*, Master Chief. You have no choice but to do your duty; to do otherwise is to fail to play the game (from a practical standpoint, to fail to finish the level you're on and move to the next). And when you see yourself in the cut scenes, the basic nobility of your character is absolutely manifest. Your care for Cortana, your relationship with Johnson, the way the marines look up to you: all of it declares the Master Chief to be our last, best hope of saving the universe.

And the mechanics, direct as they are, vehemently reinforce this *mimesis* of nobility: the things that you *do* to play the Master Chief are the things that you *should do* to save our species. Whether it's hitting the sweet spot on a Hunter with a pistol or jacking a Wraith to take out a plasma-gun emplacement, you're doing it for the UNSC and for the planets it protects.

The same is true of the Arbiter. Even in *Halo 2,* before the Arbiter and the Master Chief join forces, the Arbiter is fighting the Flood—the very same enemy, of course, that UNSC and the Master Chief are fighting. When the Covenant splits, the Arbiter is of course on the "save the universe, including the humans" side.

What about the Violence?

The violence of *Halo,* like the violence of many other popular videogames, is of course what critics of the medium always seem to concentrate their fire on. From Plato's perspective this factor would have posed not the slightest problem. Ancient Greece was a place where war was a fact of life. To make a young man unwarlike would have seemed to Plato just as bad as to make him a quitter or a liar.

Shooters of armed conflict, so to speak, tend to take less criticism on this score than ethically-ambivalent games like *Grand Theft Auto.* Mainstream culture tends, for largely the same reasons as Plato, to pay less attention to violence done in the name of a notionally—and nationally—good cause.

On the other hand, the concerns of parents and educators about kids spending many hours immersed in this violence, however universe-saving it might be, also have a Platonic side: this is where the criticism of *mimesis* that bequeathed to us the translation "imitation" comes in. Is there something about this kind of playing epic pretend that, as Plato's Socrates says, makes pleasure and pain be "the rulers of our state"?

The very existence of *The Republic* and the rest of Plato's dialogues says no. To grasp this truth we have to make a final stop, in the famous cave of *Republic* Book 6.

This is a story about education and culture, and the lack of those things. That's what Socrates says, but very few readers even notice him saying that. Imagine a bunch of people forced to sit and play *Super Mario Bros.* all day every day. *Super Mario Bros.* is all they know of the entire universe. Their arms and legs are tied down to the couches they sit on. They're playing co-op, and the levels are never-ending. Now imagine that one of them is released, and dragged out of the house; somebody shows him the sky (of which of course the nearly ever-present sky of *Super Mario Bros.* is a representation—that is, a *mimesis,* a play-performance), and he grows to like it. He goes back to help the others see what he's seen, but even if he can untie them, they won't get up.

He tries to play *Super Mario Bros.* again to get their attention, but they pwn him because his reflexes are shot from having spent so much time outdoors, and so when he tries to tell them that they should get up, they kill him. So who's educated and cultured, in this scenario? That's the trick—both the *Mario*-playing prisoners and the guy who went outside are educated; they're just educated differently.

Plato's shadow-puppet play—the one the prisoners of the original cave watch projected on the wall—is *mimesis,* just as the Homeric epics are, just as *Mario* is, and *Halo* is. To be released and to go outside *seems* to mean being free of that closed world of *mimesis* in which you do the things you play because that's what you know of the world.

But when we consider that *The Republic* is itself *mimesis*—a dialogue—things start to look different. Imagine that you're playing a game in which you play as the person released from the couch, and when you get back inside after seeing the sky, Covenant forces are trying to kill the rest of humanity, still tied to the couches.

Mario may be ineffectual, ethically, but *Halo* is about waking up (literally, in *Combat Evolved* and *Halo* 3, in which you as the Master Chief wake up from cryogenic sleep and paralysis respectively) to a reality in which you must save the universe.

The Republic is about becoming a hero, philosophically-speaking. Plato is seeking to replace the tales of heroism of *The Iliad* and *The Odyssey* with a new tale, the tale of Socrates, because, of course, Socrates is the hero who tried to release the other prisoners, and died for it. In the *Crito* he is explicitly compared to Achilles.

Is *Halo* philosophy, then? Yes, in the ancient sense—the Greek sense devised by Plato himself. Like *The Republic, Halo* is a way of thinking about how to live an ethical life: how to live up to our obligations, how to help others, above all, how to protect others from forces poised to destroy them. Achilles was the protector of the Greeks, Hector of the Trojans, Odysseus of his household on Ithaca, as the Master Chief is the protector of humanity.

Guardian Training

In Books 2 and 3 of *The Republic* we hear about the stories Plato's Socrates thinks are fit for the Guardians to hear in the course of their education. We hear that almost all of the myths with which Plato himself was raised are unsuited for the task, because they depict ethically bad acts by supposedly heroic characters, like Achilles grieving over Patroclus. That discussion transitions into the first discussion of *mimesis,* and comes to a head in the following passage:

> If [the Guardians] play pretend at all, they should play pretend from youth upward only those characters which are suitable to their profession—the courageous, temperate, holy, free, and the like; but they should not depict or be skillful at playing any kind of illiberality or baseness, lest from playing pretend they should come to be what they play. Did you never observe how playing pretend, beginning in early youth and continuing far into life, at length grows into habits and become a second nature, affecting body, voice, and mind?

The word I translate "playing pretend" here is of course *mimesis.* When we think of the Master Chief in light of this passage, we see that even if we need Aristotle's ideas about *mimesis* to acquit *Super Mario Bros.* from the charge of making its players go through life trying to jump on mushrooms, *Halo* ends up looking like remarkably good training for guardians.

This Platonic analysis of the ethics of *Halo* leaves us with some big questions about playing space-epic. Can we imagine a world where this kind of violent Guardian training is no longer necessary? If we can imagine that world, should we try to get there, given that testosterone seems like a biological fact of life?

Neither Plato nor the *Halo* series can help us answer those questions, but both can help us ask them more compellingly.

4
Does Cortana Dream of Electric Sheep?

MONICA EVANS

There's a moment near the beginning of *Halo: Combat Evolved* in which Cortana is ordered to evacuate the boarded *Pillar of Autumn*. Between gunfights in the ship's hallways and heavy fire from a dozen Covenant ships, Cortana takes a few seconds to glance around the bridge, as if she's going to miss the place, before hanging her head and letting the Master Chief yank her from the system. It's a surprisingly human moment, not only for an AI character, but for a game that is primarily concerned with run-and-gun shooting, combat tactics, and competitive multiplayer.

In science fiction, we tend to focus on the spaceships, the robots, and the aliens, but it's the emphasis on small human moments that often define the best work in the field. As a genre, science fiction is valuable for exploring the nature and purpose of humanity, especially as it is one of the few genres in which we can step outside humanity and look back at ourselves from alien eyes, extreme futures, and the vantage point of our very best and worst potential as a species. Science fiction has never been about the future, but about the present: about us as we are now, contrasted with what we hope or fear to become.

But science fiction gets its point across through stories, and computer games, while they have great potential for storytelling, are an interactive, immersive medium, one that must present players with an engaging experience but not necessarily a traditional story. There are a wide variety of games that include science-fiction imagery, rhetoric, and themes. Some of the best-loved and most critically acclaimed game series fall into this category, including but not limited to *Doom, Fallout, Half-Life, Metroid, Starcraft, Space*

Quest, Resident Evil, Final Fantasy, Unreal Tournament, and *Metal Gear Solid*, as well as games that take place in the *Star Wars*, *Star Trek*, *Matrix*, and *Chronicles of Riddick* worlds. The Game Developers Choice Awards, arguably the most prestigious awards in the commercial games industry, have named a "Game of the Year" eleven times; seven times, the award has gone to a science fiction-themed game, and at least one has been nominated every year.[1]

More than this, computer games *are* science fiction. They are the feelies of *Brave New World* and the interactive wall screens of *Fahrenheit 451*, the dangerous cyber-playgrounds of *Neuromancer* and the metaverse of *Snow Crash*, and they are quickly becoming the not-quite-human intelligence systems of *Blade Runner* and the works of Asimov and Ellison. Yet more often than not the science-fiction content of games is limited to the superficial, present only in the visual atmosphere of alien worlds and the names of weapons. Too often, computer games fail to include the social commentary, fundamental questions, or examinations of humanity at the extremes that define the best science fiction in other media.

Looking at the *Halo* series, we can't deny that it has been hugely successful, both critically and financially, and that it has had a significant impact on the medium of games. We also can't deny that *Halo* is science-fiction-themed. Alien races, slipstream capable battleships, and cybernetically enhanced soldiers aside, the core of the game's single-player campaign—not to mention the series' title—is the exploration and eventual control of a ring-shaped structure inspired by a partial Dyson sphere that immediately brings Larry Niven's *Ringworld* to mind. The question is not whether *Halo* looks like science fiction, but whether the series addresses the same fundamental questions as its references and inspirations, and what it has to say about the nature of humanity when faced with its greatest and most insidious threats.

I Was Gonna Shoot My Way Out. Mix Things Up a Little

Science-fiction writer Theodore Sturgeon once said, when he was fed up with defending the genre, "Ninety-percent of science fiction

[1] The seven winning science-fiction games are *Metroid Prime, Star Wars: Knights of the Old Republic, Half-Life 2, Gears of War, Portal, Fallout 3*, and *Uncharted 2*. "Archives: Best Game" (2010), <www.gamechoiceawards.com/archive/bestgame.htm>.

is crud, but then, ninety percent of everything is crud." His point, that a genre shouldn't be dismissed for including some less than brilliant works, was a response to science fiction's most vocal critics who habitually used "the worst examples of the field for ammunition."[2] (Game developers and players faced with a similar argument would do well to take note.)

In the twenty-first century, science fiction has at long last become mainstream. Author Thomas Disch notes that science fiction is currently so pervasive in our culture that "its basic repertoire of images . . . are standard items in the fantasy life of any preschooler."[3] Science fiction is nothing if not relevant today, in our technological, interconnected culture that values personalization, individuality, and breadth of knowledge over depth, a future seen by at least some of the writers of the last decades.

Despite its current popularity, defining science fiction is apparently an impossible task. John Clute and Peter Nicholls in their *Encyclopedia of Science Fiction* come right out and say that there "really is no reason to expect that a workable definition of science fiction will ever be established. None has, so far." Author Damon Knight's flippant definition is amusingly one of the most widely used: "Science fiction is what we point to when we say it."[4] Nevertheless, there are some common elements among the different definitions. To many, science fiction is primarily concerned with the nature of humanity, and with humanity's relationship with science and technology. A great deal of science fiction falls into what Neil Gaiman calls the "what if" or "if this goes on" kind of story, one that explores an extrapolated future to look more closely at an aspect of present society, culture, or technology.[5]

In computer games, the definition most commonly used seems to apply to iconography: if there's a spaceship, a robot, or an alien race, it's a science fiction game. Sidestepping the contentious issue of story and games, we can at least say that defining

[2] "Sturgeon's Law" (2010), at <http://en.wikipedia.org/wiki/Sturgeon%27s_law>.

[3] *The Dreams Our Stuff Is Made Of: How Science Fiction Conquered the World* (Touchstone, 1998), p. 1.

[4] John Clute and Peter Nicholls, *The Encyclopedia of Science Fiction* (Orbit, 1999), p. 314.

[5] Noted in his introduction, "Of Time and Gully Foyle," in the new edition of Alfred Bester's *The Stars My Destination* (Vintage, 1996).

a subset of interactive games by way of a narrative genre presents difficulties. If the substance of science fiction is primarily expressed through narrative, computer games as a medium have a two-fold problem: game designers are not authors, although their creative processes may be similar, and players are not necessarily paying attention to the designer's planned experience as much as their own personal narrative, which may be as simple as "I killed those three guys really effectively," or "I beat level six in nine minutes."

Computer games are based on deterministic systems, and many of the major issues explored in science fiction, including social and political commentary, morality, ethics, love, otherness, and reality, are extraordinarily difficult to reproduce or express in black-and-white terms. On the other hand, there are a number of standard mechanical conventions that may seem to address science-fiction themes, but are taken for granted by players. The fact that a given computer game includes multiple lives and save states does not mean that it has anything profound or meaningful to say about the ethics of cloning or the potential for radically extending human life expectancy. Games that do "hang a lantern" in this way run the risk of overemphasizing mechanics that are often seen as fundamental to games.

Computer games also progress along a learning curve: as players become more skilled, the game world becomes more challenging, and more tools and options for overcoming those challenges are presented. For realistic games, particularly those that take place in present day, introducing future tech as the game progresses is a common way to increase both difficulty and the player's options. Once the shotgun, double-barreled shotgun, and combat shotgun have been exhausted, introducing the *plasma* shotgun may be the easiest way to increase a player's arsenal, and suddenly the game has become science fiction, at least superficially.

These and other issues may account for the sheer number of science-fiction-themed games, but they offer little help to designers who not only intend to create great science fiction in games, but to tell stories and ask questions that are best or perhaps only expressed through games. For examining humanity at its extremes, through the lens of an "other", or in relation to advances in science and technology, the interactive nature of computer games must be leveraged in service of the science fiction content to create meaningful, substantive experiences for the player.

The Right Man in the Wrong Place Can Make All the Difference

You can create an excellent game with a science-fiction setting that does not address larger philosophical concerns. The *Metroid Prime* series, for example, perfectly captures the feeling of being alone and isolated on a hostile alien planet, but goes no farther than that. Given that the series is focused solely on gameplay, primarily balancing exploration and platforming puzzles with first-person combat, no deeper exploration of human issues is required, and in fact might be detrimental to the game experience.

For a game that does intend to explore larger issues, the medium of computer games can be used to startling effect. One of the most successful examples is *Half-Life 2*, a game that makes a clear commentary on the nature of human survival and how easily we can convince ourselves of normality as things around us are spiraling out of control. In *Half-Life 2*, the science-fiction elements—such as the pervasive Breencasts, the concentration-camp-like City 17, or the character of Dog—are supported by a structure in which fundamental questions of humanity are first raised by the gamespace and then explored through the player's actions.

The human race is presented in the context of survival in three major groups: those working with the alien Combine that have enslaved the human race, believing they can save their own lives; those who have given in and keep their heads down, hoping to stay alive as long as possible; and those who are actively fighting against the Combine regime, believing that revolution is the only way to save the human species.

The player character, theoretical physicist Gordon Freeman, is in this last group, as *Half-Life 2* is an action-oriented First Person Shooter (FPS), but the active nature of the character allows the player to see as much of the devastated world as possible. Freeman's somewhat remarkable transformation from research physicist to hard-core soldier and messiah figure is never directly explained by the game, but the fact that Freeman's skills improve at the same rate as the player's makes it easier to accept. Here the game's learning curve works in service of the story, rather than as a separate mechanic.

Half-Life 2 avoids many of the pitfalls of science-fiction games by presenting a world and a problem rather than a traditional story. The player learns everything they need to know about the Combine in the first five minutes of the game, a quietly harrowing train ride to City 17 (motto: "It's safer here"), where humans are treated like cattle and the Combine soldiers look like nothing so much as concentration camp guards. The mission-based plot is more straightforward, often consisting of little more than "Here is a problem, go and fix it" or "Bad things are coming, escape them!" but the player's motivations and Freeman's are always in tandem. The player is part of the action, not separate from it, making the claustrophobic, defeated space at the game's beginning all the more compelling: you aren't simply told that things are bad, you live it for the space of the game's introduction.

It's also nicely ironic that Gordon Freeman fights against the Combine and Dr. Breen, the game's human antagonist, through the literal application of the human survival instinct, something Dr. Breen urges the rest of humanity to overcome in his pro-Combine propaganda (most notably in response to a "concerned citizen" who wants to know why the Combine have effectively sterilized all humans within reach).

One can of course play through *Half-Life 2* without paying any attention to the surrounding details, and a great deal of the game's success depends on the fact that it is, regardless of story, an excellent game. Nevertheless, the vision of the game is not undermined but supported by its interactive nature, and both the pure narrative moments and the complex interactive experiences in *Half-Life 2* are enough to make at least the philosophically-minded player consider what humanity might look like when survival is the only remaining option.

Our criteria for science-fiction games might be that they not only include the props of science fiction—the robots, spaceships, and aliens—but also challenge the player to consider humanity in a new light, particularly in terms of scientific and technological advances. Additionally, the science-fiction game creates experiences that are best explored or understood in an interactive medium, and that are enhanced by the mechanics of the individual game and the medium as a whole. The science-fiction game is one in which fundamental, philosophical questions are handled with as much care as core game mechanics, and in which the player is inspired not only to win, but to think.

This War Has Enough Dead Heroes

In *Halo: Combat Evolved*, we can see a clear pattern in the way humanity is represented: in the world of *Combat Evolved*, we are fighters, and no strangers to sacrifice. The nameless soldiers that accompany the Master Chief on many of the game's missions do not often survive, nor are they expected to unless the mission objectives call for it. Likewise, the eventual fate of Captain Keyes and the destruction of the *Pillar of Autumn*, both intended to prevent the Halo installation from eradicating all sentient life in the galaxy, emphasize that humans, or at least those of the United Nations Space Command, are willing to sacrifice themselves for the greater good of the species.

The one human seemingly exempt from this description is the Master Chief, who is constantly presented as hero and savior, the person other people make sacrifices for. It's no accident that the Chief is woken from cryosleep to the sounds of a hushed choir and the awe of the two technicians in attendance. While the Master Chief is presented as different from other humans, no comment is ever made about the specifics of that difference: that as the last survivor of the SPARTAN II-project, he is a fully-augmented, cybernetically-enhanced human. On the contrary, the Master Chief's augmented status simply makes him a better soldier, and in the narrative serves primarily to help the player feel more like the hero of the game.

In terms of the alien antagonists, both the Covenant and the Flood appear in the first *Halo* as faceless enemies, albeit with differing visuals and tactics. The brief story sequences present the Covenant as an advanced theocratic civilization and the Flood as a parasitic, nearly mindless organism, but in practice they amount to no more than two types of bad guys to kill. Given that the first half of the game is dedicated to fighting the somewhat traditional Covenant forces, the introduction of a second, radically different enemy faction was intended to create "surprise, drama, and impact"[6] in the vein of Ridley Scott's *Alien*; but while the Flood's appearance complicates the story and forces the player to adopt new combat tactics, no deeper exploration of their species is ever offered. Both Flood and Covenant serve the same purpose as the Master Chief's augmentation: to support the player's sense of heroism, and to provide a variety of challenges for the player to overcome.

Ironically, the two most fully-developed characters in *Halo* are the two A.I., Cortana and Guilty Spark 343. Cortana may be the most human individual in the game: she is often witty or sharp-tongued,

---

[6] "The Fauna of Halo" (2010), <http://web.archive.org/web/20060210224125/http://www.bungie.net/News/TopStory.aspx?story=prexboxhistory040904>.

occasionally smug about her intelligence, clearly cares for the Master Chief, and is the only character in the game to truly lose her temper. Her commentary during missions is usually limited to guiding the player through the latest set of objectives, but even then she feels more human than any of the marines following the Chief through a given mission.

Guilty Spark, on the other hand, is presented as an advanced, albeit eccentric machine intelligence, in that he sees the world primarily in terms of outcomes. The casual, cheerful way in which he informs the Master Chief that the Halo installations are intended to wipe out the Flood by destroying their food source—all sentient life in the galaxy—and the equally cheerful way in which he instructs the waiting Sentinels to "save his head" speak to an intelligence that thinks very differently than the other characters and factions. Guilty Spark's priorities regarding sentient life are also quite different. He is prepared to scour the galaxy of life without batting a digital eyelash, but is "shocked, almost too shocked for words" that the Master Chief and Cortana would think of destroying the *Pillar of Autumn* and its extensive records of human history. To Guilty Spark, the existing humans are less real, and certainly less worthy of study and categorization, than the digital artifacts they left behind.

Looking at the whole of the game, one can see that *Halo: Combat Evolved* presents an immersive science-fiction world but lacks substance in many ways. Apart from the bright spots of Cortana and Guilty Spark, the game includes the trappings of science fiction without the philosophy, and settles for creating a world that players can enjoy without questioning, with no hard choices and no expectations of those players other than mechanical skill. The core of the *Halo* series has never been the story-driven, single-player campaigns but the multiplayer capability, and the continued success of the series owes much to that community of players. Nevertheless, one can see the seeds of something greater in this first attempt, and the potential for more complex and insightful science fiction in future versions of the characters, factions, and gameworld.

Politics . . . How Tiresome

The opening sequence of *Halo 2* stands as one of the more surprising risks taken in the name of narrative by a development studio, particularly given the runaway success of the previous title.

Where the experience of *Halo: Combat Evolved* can be fairly described as "Master Chief blows up alien bad guys," *Halo 2* begins not only by humanizing the Covenant, but by turning one Elite soldier into a sympathetic, tragic hero and setting him up as a foil of equal skill and prowess to the Master Chief.

The opening sequence, in which the Master Chief's accolades for destroying the Halo ring are juxtaposed with the Elite's trial, torture, and effective excommunication for allowing him to do so, also explores a great deal of the Covenant's theology and political structure. Their subsequent attack on the Earth's defense platforms can be somewhat jarring for players who have just become invested in their side of the story, but must immediately go back to killing faceless hordes of Covenant forces.

Over the course of the game, the personality conflicts between the Prophets of Truth, Regret, and Mercy, the Brute Tartarus, and the Arbiter himself turn the Covenant into a complex, fractured culture, as well as a collection of allies and villains with individual desires and agendas. The religious schism among the Covenant leadership also places them in stark contrast with the united human front, making their eventual alliance an interesting comment on the desperate measures of two civilizations in peril.

As for the Arbiter himself, his character fits the *Halo* series's abiding interest in struggle, suffering, and sacrifice. When presented to the Prophet of Truth, he has fallen so far from grace that he considers himself already dead. Rather than have him hung by the entrails and his corpse paraded through the city—as the Council apparently voted—the Prophet makes him into a literal instrument of vengeance. As the Arbiter, he is expected to do everything in his power to secure the Covenant's future, but he is also expected, even encouraged, to die in the attempt. The Arbiter's crisis of faith, eventual betrayal by his masters, and alliance with his former enemies is a common story in both science fiction and fantasy tales, one with far more potential for explorations of the nature of humanity than the Master Chief's equivalent missions.

Other old enemies are also presented in a new light with the introduction of the Gravemind, the cryptic and manipulative entity that is both the voice and the collected intelligence of the Flood. Physically formed from the corpses of the infested fallen, the Gravemind seems more specifically inspired by body horror than by science fiction in general. In terms of its actions, however, the Gravemind is an exceptional politician, sending both the Arbiter and the Master Chief on distracting errands to allow itself to invade and infest the civil war-torn Covenant city of High Charity in *Halo 2*, and changing allegiances on a seemingly daily basis in *Halo 3*.

Critical reaction to the Gravemind as a character was poor, both for its confusing and seemingly inconsistent motivations and its often clichéd villainous dialogue.[7] That said, presenting the Flood not as a mindless parasite but as an intelligent character with ambitions and fears of its own suggests that the world of *Halo 2* and *Halo 3* is a place of more substance than the original game.

For the most part, the recurring human characters are presented as more fully-developed versions of their previous selves. In *Halo: Combat Evolved*, the nameless friendly marines complain about kill-stealing and say "My bad" during friendly-fire, making single-player missions feel like surrogates for an XBOX-Live experience. In the sequels, the chatter is humorous but more believable, and many soldiers are presented as at least names and faces, if not fully developed characters.

Johnson, Lord Hood, and Miranda Keyes are among the few individuals with major roles to play, and all three have character arcs closely tied to *Halo*'s themes of struggle and sacrifice. Both Johnson and Keyes sacrifice themselves for the greater good; Keyes to prevent herself and Johnson from being used as surrogates by the Prophet of Truth, and Johnson as the man in the wrong place at the wrong time when Guilty Spark realizes what the humans intend for the Ark. Lord Hood is left to give the fitting eulogy in the penultimate cinematic of *Halo 3*:

> Let us never forget those who journeyed into the howling dark and did not return, for their decision required courage beyond measure. Sacrifice, an unshakeable conviction that their fight, our fight, was elsewhere. . . . They ennobled all of us, and they shall not be forgotten.

In terms of sacrifice, the character that most stands out is the Master Chief, who is presented in even more heroic terms than in the first game. At the end of *Halo 2*'s first mission, the Chief discovers a Covenant bomb on the Cairo defense platform. Rather than defuse it, he drags it to an airlock, pushes itself and him out into space aimed at a Covenant ship, drops it off, and leaps into space again as it explodes behind him, to land safely on the surface of the *In*

[7] "Gravemind: Reception" (2010), <http://en.wikipedia.org/wiki/Gravemind>.

Amber Clad—a sequence that is so over-the-top in its heroics that it nearly comes across as parody. When controlled by the player, the Chief has to work for his victories, but the story sequences present him as an inhumanly powerful force—which, given his augmentations, is an arguable point.

The moments in which the Master Chief seems most human are those that he shares with Cortana, who evolves into something like a love interest in *Halo 3*. In fact, the third game begins with Cortana explaining how she was allowed to choose her Spartan, and that she chose the Master Chief because he had something special: he was lucky, a nice reference to the fact that the player, regardless of skill, has an infinite number of chances to win against the most difficult foes. Much of *Halo 3* involves the Master Chief's search for and rescue of Cortana from the Gravemind, and their reunion is another of the small human moments that raises the emotional impact of the narrative.

Arguably, the only moment of sacrifice associated with the Master Chief occurs at the very end of *Halo 3*, when the remaining Earth forces believe he has died destroying the Ark. In fact, he returns to cryosleep in the floating remnants of the *Forward Unto Dawn* with Cortana watching over him, ready to wake him in humanity's next hour of need—a moment that seems more appropriate to Arthurian legend than science fiction. The relationship between science fiction and fantasy is easily as contentious as that between gameplay and story, but the more heroic aspects of the Master Chief suggest that the *Halo* series might have as much in common with the works of Tolkien, Fritz Leiber, and Robert E. Howard as with Asimov, Clarke, and Bester. Despite the spaceships, aliens, and AI, the experience of *Halo* may be as easily if not better explored through the lens of fantasy than through the questions of science, technology, and humanity raised by science fiction.

Just Dust and Echoes

In April of 2006, the developers of *Halo* published the *The Bungie Guide to Sci Fi*, in which they continue to list the numerous inspirations for the series. The list begins with *Ringworld*, Iain Banks's *Culture* series, and *Starship Troopers*, and takes a moment to address fan concerns that they "ripped off" the idea for the ring-shaped structure of the Halo installations: "Ring-shaped artificial worlds have also been used by Iain M. Banks and others because they are cool. And that's why we used one. Because it's cool and therefore the type of thing a Forerunner civilization would build."[8]

Additional influences include Ridley Scott's *Aliens*, *Blade Runner*, *Snow Crash*, *Rendevous with Rama*, *Dune*, *Robocop*, and *Terminator*, and older games such as *Homeworld* and the original *Half Life*. The developers at Bungie may not be science-fiction scholars, but they are proudly self-admitted fans, and their guide reads not only as an introduction to science fiction for those new to it but as a list of the high standards to which they held themselves while creating the *Halo* universe.

The question is not whether Bungie attempted to create meaningful science fiction, but whether they succeeded. It's worth mentioning that the fan reaction to *Halo 2*, while overwhelmingly positive in general, was somewhat critical of the story elements, both for their focus and their execution. In particular, the Arbiter missions in *Halo 2* were criticized for distracting from the Master Chief's story and the defense of Earth,[9] suggesting that for many players the attempt at narrative substance was less interesting than the new vehicles and multiplayer maps.

The story that unfolds across the three core games makes for a compelling, often thought-provoking frame for the single-player gameplay experience, particularly for players who know their science fiction. For the average player, *Halo* may not necessarily inspire deeper explorations of humanity or critical insights as to our relationship with science and technology, and it may not always live up to the classics of science fiction that were its partial inspiration. But *Halo* does reach its narrative goals in terms of pure engagement: emotional impact, dramatic twists, and letting the player feel like they're the only one that can save the universe. And sometimes, even in science fiction, that's enough. Whether Theodore Sturgeon would qualify *Halo* as part of the ninety percent crud or the ten percent brilliance, or whether the game qualifies as meaningful science fiction, may not be as important as the fact that sometimes it's just really fun to be the Master Chief for a few hours.

After all, we're only human.

---

[8] "The Bungie Guide to SciFi" (2006), <http://www.bungie.net/News/content.aspx?cid=7994>.

[9] "Arbiter (Halo): Cultural Impact" (2010), <http://en.wikipedia.org/wiki/Arbiter_%28Halo%29#Cultural_impact>.

Normal

5

The Initiatory Journey to Legendary Play

SÉBASTIEN HOCK-KOON

I'll be the first to admit it: I'm not that good. I don't have incredible reflexes. I'm not particularly, or naturally, good at aiming or at dodging bullets. I play better than many people on Earth, sure, especially those who never or rarely play videogames. But among gamers, I am certainly not a star. Now, before you start thinking "Then what the hell are you doing writing a chapter in a book on a videogame?" just read on.

Despite my shortcomings, I finished *Halo* in legendary mode all by myself, without looking for help or tricks or cheats. And I achieved it because I was persistent and because I am a game designer. More precisely, I was studying game design at SupInfoGame when I first encountered *Halo: Combat Evolved* (*Halo* will refer to this first episode for the rest of the chapter). I did not play and replay it as homework but only because I enjoyed it. And yes, playing videogames is considered homework in a videogame school.

Thanks to this game, I have learned many things about game design. I would like to share this experience with you.

I Was Once Wrong about *Halo* . . .

The first time I played *Halo*, it was on a computer in October 2003. The Xbox version had been released for more than a year and a half. It was far more colorful than many First Person Shooters (FPSs). But the gameplay itself was just average. From the very beginning, I had been wondering what people found so amazing about *Halo*. So I borrowed an Xbox and the game from my school, for the holidays (it's the kind of thing you can do in a game design school). I first finished the game one time, in easy mode. It was good, but already far better on console than on computer.

The thing is, I have not been astonished or even surprised by the game. The once incredible graphics looked bad a year and a half later. The novelty of vehicles did not touch me because I had played *Battlefield 1942* a lot. The small number of weapons was ridiculous compared to the real gun fetishist's FPS (a.k.a. *Perfect Dark*). The game was entertaining; I had no major issues with it. At the time, I didn't realize the implications.

At the school I was attending, I was taking a game design and project management course. Half of my homework was about game design. I was taught to see a videogame's defaults and qualities. And I did not find any of the first in *Halo*. Not being able to find any flaw should have warned me but it did not. When I bought my own Xbox, I did not buy *Halo*. I waited until its release in the "Classics" collection (which, naturally, cost half the price of the original). Then, I finished the game in normal mode. It did not change my opinion much, but it was desperately enjoyable to play. So I tried to beat it in heroic mode. This was when I really started to see how great *Halo* is.

The Real *Halo* Begins in Heroic Mode

I didn't realize it while playing in heroic mode. It only became obvious, even unavoidable, on legendary mode. Roughly speaking, I saw a pattern. In order to finish easy mode, I had to master two things: shooting the right enemy and moving at the same time. In normal mode, I needed grenade throwing mastery. The heroic mode required weapon mastery—choosing my two weapons wisely and switching cleverly between them while fighting. Finally, in legendary, I had to add the melee attack.

It worked this way for me (it certainly was not the same for you, if you made it all the way to the legendary mode). Dajez notes the difference between the basic and the expert use of a videogame character's action repertoire.[1] Progressing in *Halo* cannot be considered linear (although the plotline might be regarded as such).

---

[1] Frédéric Dajez, "La figurine interfacée, à propos de l'Odyssée d'Abe," in *L'image actée: scénarisations numériques, parcours du séminaire L'action sur l'image* (Editions L'Harmattan, 2006).

There is not an overall "FPS skill" that you have to improve. There are many different skills. Your level in each skill is independent of the others. A player may aim perfectly, like an e-sport team member, while not having the ability to expertly throw a grenade in order to maximize the amount of Grunts that get blown to hell.

The key, for me, was that I had mastered all these features after the first level of the easy mode. It took me four times the length of the game to master and use them all. Let's stick to Dajez's metaphor. Consider each new skill as a new word. Your vocabulary gathers all the words you know. Your lexicon contains the words that you use in your everyday life, in other words, the ones that you master. For example, when the tutorial teaches you how to throw a grenade, you learn a new word/skill that widens your vocabulary. This word/skill will go to your lexicon, when you are able to throw a grenade wisely in combat. To progress, I did not improve the skills I already had. I acquired new ones and used all of them together. The order I followed came naturally. It was not imposed on me by the game. It was certainly possible to change it.

This means that every player may create his or her own way to reach the end of the game. The main features are given at the beginning of the game. The player decides which to master and when to do so. It coheres with James Paul Gee's "Multiple Route Principle." This principle allows players "to make choices, rely on their own strengths and styles of learning and problem solving."[2]

At the same time, it goes against another principle. According to Gee's "Explicit Information On-Demand and Just-in-Time Principle," good videogames should make the right information available at the right moment. In *Halo*, it can only be applied to tutorials and objectives. It works in easy mode. Against further difficulty levels, you're on your own. The game won't tell you the way to success; you must find it by yourself. Naturally, it is possible to cheat or to ask for help. But I, like many gamers, consider this route to be admitting defeat.

Learning and Unlearning

Let's move beyond learning in a game and consider more specific mechanics, particularly concerning weapons. There were many

[2] James Paul Gee, *What Video Games Have to Teach Us about Learning and Literacy* (Palgrave Macmillan, 2003).

points during my *Halo* tenure when I found myself realizing that I was wrong about something, and how dumb I had been previously. As my skills changed, my comprehension of the game changed.

My Dear Needler

The simplest example was the Needler. Before heroic mode, I thought it was the worst weapon of the game. Seriously, it is the only Covenant weapon that has to be reloaded. It launches shards that do not explode on impact. If you send enough on an enemy there is a big explosion, but only after a few seconds. This explosion is lethal, but because of the delay, you may waste ammunition and time shooting an already dead Elite. If you don't shoot enough shards, you will only injure and not kill the target.

I changed my mind in heroic mode as my understanding got sharper. The Needler is not usually a good weapon. Its qualities are circumstantial. Most of the time, it's less effective than other weapons. But against the right situation and with the right technique, it may just be awesome. The higher the game difficulty is, the more attention you must pay to this kind of detail.

Until normal mode, Covenants' shields are not a real problem. They are annoying; but it is not necessary to deal specifically with them. In heroic and legendary mode, you have to care about them, especially those of the Elites. You cannot allow yourself to waste ammunition and time in combat any more. The fact that Covenant weapons tend to be more effective against those shields eventually becomes significant. Thus, you tend to use them more and more, because their advantages become obvious and relevant.

But let's return to the Needler. It has many features that make it great against Elites. First, no matter the difficulty, the explosion is fatal. Other weapons generally become less and less effective, especially human ones as the difficulty increases. Secondly, with experience, I realized that the shards were slightly homing to the target. It allowed me to focus a little less on aiming and a little more on dodging and analyzing the situation, so that I could stay alive. Thirdly, the delay between the last shard necessary for explosion and the explosion itself may be counter-balanced.

When you are shooting at an enemy, you generally stop when the enemy is dead. The best is to stop right after the "killing" bullet is shot rather than when the enemy actually falls. While you are firing, you are exposed. It means that you can also be shot. Most bullets are too fast, it is impossible to profit by this delay. With the Needler, you have a few seconds between the shot of the "killing" shard and the explosion.

When you think that you have fired enough, you can hide and wait safely for the sound of the explosion. Thanks to the Needler's fire-rate and homing shards, you can reduce significantly the time during which you're exposed. More importantly, this weapon tells you without any doubt whether or not your enemy is dead. You can also fire shards in order to detect enemies. If the trajectory is curved, there is an enemy around. The Needler may provide you with something often neglected and yet vital in combat: information.

I think this kind of evolution is somehow typical in FPSs, at least in good ones. But it is often neglected by researchers. Linderoth, Lindström and Alexandersson made two girls play *Perfect Dark* in deathmatch mode. The girls found the Reaper good compared to other weapons.[3] When I read this, my first thought—well the polite version of my first thought—was "What the hell? The Reaper is the worst weapon of the game!" It was a gamer's reaction. In *Perfect Dark*, the Reaper is the Skeddar version of the minigun. It is heavy and absolutely not accurate. When you press the trigger, it takes a few seconds to warm up before firing. I would rather use the basic pistol than this useless fan-like weapon.

After this, I checked on the Internet to see whether my view was shared among players. And yes, according to many people, the Reaper is definitely one of the worst weapons in *Perfect Dark*. Anyway, I decided to consider that these girls had a good reason to appreciate it. I asked myself what its characteristics were and in which situation they could make it a better weapon.

The Reaper has a high dispersion rate, so it is difficult to aim precisely at someone. When it fires, its rotating blades turn it into a melee weapon at the same time. If you do know how to aim, the Reaper reduces your chances to touch your opponent. But if you don't know how to aim correctly, the Reaper actually increases your chances to touch with bullets or blades.

The efficiency of a weapon does not rely only on the weapon itself. The skills of the user and the situation can change everything. A beginner should use a Shotgun rather than a Railgun, on the contrary an expert would be far more dangerous with the second than

---

[3] Jonas Linderoth, Berney Lindström, and Mikael Alexandersson, "Learning with Computer Games," in *Toys, Games, and Media* (Erlbaum, 2004).

with the first. While I was progressing, my perception of the Needler changed. I could tell the same kind of story about each common weapon of *Halo*. Some revealed their real value in time, while some lost their interest to me. This evolution is about understanding the true power of a weapon and the best way to use (or not use) it. The very best way is generally learned where you need it, in heroic or legendary mode. You could have used it in easy mode. It would have worked as well, even if it was not necessary in order to win.

My Dear Grenades

There's a particular weapon whose use changes according to the difficulty: grenades. At the beginning, I just wanted to write about Plasma Grenades. I did not use Fragmentation ones much. I found their trajectory too random and they could not stick to an enemy. I certainly could have learned to use them properly but I did not. So I finished the legendary mode without using them. I thought I couldn't say much about them, but I was wrong—it will often happen in this chapter.

The fact that I could go through the game all the way without Fragmentation Grenades is definitely relevant. It means that it's not necessary to master every part of gameplay in order to beat the highest difficulty level. It sends us back to Gee's "Multiple Route Principle." In order to progress, the player can choose what to improve and what to ignore. So I created my own way of playing *Halo*, which is one among many. In my way, I almost only used Plasma Grenades.

In normal mode, I used them quite normally. You throw them to a group of enemies and they explode, killing or at least hurting them. As mentioned above, I did not need them in easy mode, so I did not use them. Sadly or happily, things changed in heroic mode. It became almost impossible to get several enemies with one grenade. They would dodge or jump away. The only way to be sure to kill one was to make the grenade stick. Because of this, I suddenly found them far less effective. I considered Plasma Grenades useless in heroic mode. But I did judge a bit too fast. Yes, it became very hard to kill with a grenade, but no, they were not useless. After a while I realized that when an Elite dodged the explosion, its trajectory was rather unsurprising and moreover it was absolutely not shooting at me.

Throwing a grenade to a group changes a potentially chaotic system into a predictable one—at least for a few seconds. A well placed grenade may help you shoot your enemies. Sure, Plasma Grenades are less effective in heroic or legendary mode. But they may be effective if you really know how to use them.

Halo as a Game Design Lesson

Playing *Halo* taught me many things about the game itself. But I also learned about game design. *Halo* is the game that really made me understand what "gameplay depth" means. Depth in gameplay is often related to complexity or variety. I do not understand it that way. I consider that depth is the ability of a game to allow a progression based on the mastery of mechanisms that were not told but discovered by practice. Depth is about acquired skills based on self-discovery of hidden knowledge. Naturally, you can search the Internet for tips, but you will miss the most important part of the game.

This definition may be applied to the Needler. However, in the next section I want to address two weapons I have not yet said anything about: the Plasma Rifle and the Plasma Gun.

My Only Two Weapons

At first sight, it seems awkward. Why on Earth should I be limited to two weapons? It's especially true when you have played, and loved, *Perfect Dark* and its plethora of weapons. It's often said that limited weapons forces the player to choose wisely which weapons to pick up. It is certainly true, but is that it?

Consider the following. You are just about to enter the *Truth and Reconciliation*. You have to choose among many available weapons. A casual gamer would choose his or her two favorites, but a hardcore gamer would want the weapons best suited to dealing with the level in question. There are many possibilities. You know that one is the best, but you don't know which one. If you were playing *Perfect Dark*, the best decision would be evident: take every weapon you find. In *Halo*, you have to evaluate each combination. Actually, the two weapons limitation does not reduce choices, it increases the number of possible choices as the best one is not obvious. I argue that it makes the player "stop, think, and (most importantly) *care*"[4] about his or her weapons. And making people think and care about a videogame is absolutely not a bad thing.

According to Salen and Zimmerman, a key element of good game design is "meaningful play."[5] This expression means that the actions of the player are taken into account by the videogame and that the player can see the outcomes of his or her actions. I would replace "actions" by "progression" and consider meaningful progression.

Meaningful progression means that the progression of the player is taken into account by the videogame and that the player can see the outcomes of his or her progression.

Inside the *Truth and Reconciliation*, you have to fight two Hunters. They are tough enemies unless you have the right weapon and the right technique. Three different weapons may kill them in one shot: the Pistol, the Sniper Rifle, and the Shotgun (at very close range and it may take two shots). Only the Sniper Rifle is available in this level. In order to kill the two Hunters easily, you should keep it. But, in order to do so, you have to know that you will face them onboard as well as the right way to kill them. Let us imagine two different players; Player A is doing the level for the first time, while Player B already knows that there are Hunters inside. They both know how to kill Hunters easily.

If it was possible to carry every weapon without counterpart, players A and B would both take them all. They would both have the right weapon to face the Hunters. There would be no differences between the results of their play. Player B's additional knowledge would be meaningless. As they could only take two weapons, Player A may have made a wrong choice. Then, there would be a difference in the result. Player B would have the advantage.

In the first case, the game would have given meaning to their progression because they were both able to kill the Hunters easily. In the second case, the game gave more meaning to the progression of Player B. As far as I'm concerned, better skills or knowledge, in the way one plays, should always lead to better results.

---

[4] Alexander Kerezman, "The Player and The Game" (2010), <www.gamasutra.com/blogs/AlexanderKerezman/20100414/4927/The_Player_and_The_Game.php.>.

[5] Katie Salen and Eric Zimmerman, *Rules of Play: Game Design Fundamentals* (MIT Press, 2004).

I could probably stop here, but I am not done yet with the limitation. Judging from the comparison I made between *Halo* and *Perfect Dark*, one could think that the first is better than the second. Fortunately, it is not so simple. As I mentioned before, *Perfect Dark* is a gun fetishist FPS. Its fun lies in firepower, playing it is about having too many far too powerful weapons. On the other hand, the fun of *Halo: Combat Evolved* lies in combat. It's about choosing the right two weapons and getting the most out of them by choosing the right tactic according to the situation.

In *Perfect Dark*, changing weapons is not a common fighting action. It takes too long to do in combat, as you generally have many of them. In *Halo*, switching between your weapons requires only the press of a button. As you only have two, you can reach the other one very fast. If you make a mistake or change your mind, just press the button once more. Switching between weapons is a fighting action in *Halo*. These two games are very good ones, they are both considered FPSs, but they are definitely not alike.

My Dearest Plasma Rifle and Plasma Gun

I loved the Plasma Rifle from day one. I found it far more useful than the Plasma Gun. Once more, I was wrong, but that's not the point right now. The Plasma Rifle made me understand how to use switching to increase my firepower. More precisely, it taught me how to fire longer without stopping. In order to do so, I combined the Plasma Rifle with the Assault Rifle.

First you start with the Plasma Rifle. When it overheats; you switch to the Assault Rifle. Once your magazine is empty, you switch back to the Plasma Rifle which has cooled down. And you can fire again. I used this combination as an example of depth during the final presentation of my first year at SupInfoGame.

Now, I know it was a mistake. Someone could have asked "Hey, Sébastien, why don't you take a Plasma Gun instead of the Assault Rifle? You could fire endlessly." No one did, but my answer would certainly have been "Well, perhaps because I am stupid." Combining the two Plasma weapons was actually obvious, even desperately obvious. Yet, at this moment I had not thought about it. The two rifles combination was enough at the beginning of heroic mode. It did not need more firepower, so I did not look for it. But I had to, later. I also had to understand the subtleties of these two Plasma weapons.

The Plasma Gun may seem simple and it is. You press and release the trigger, it shoots. You press and hold it, the gun charges. You release, a big Plasma ball is fired and the gun overheats. But this Plasma ball is not only more powerful, like the Needler's shards, it is also slightly homing. And it can annihilate an Elite's shield. The charged Plasma Gun is perfect to start a skirmish by destroying the leader's shield.

The Plasma Rifle is harder to master. At first sight, you may think that pressing to fire is all that you have to do. To be precise, this weapon has two fire rates: a fast one (compared to the Plasma Gun) and a faster one. The second rate is reached after holding the trigger for a few seconds. It is more powerful and less accurate but it also heats up much more.

As far as I know, the most efficient way to use the Plasma Rifle is to keep shooting at the first fire rate. To do so, you need to press and release the trigger at the right rhythm. It allows you to fire longer with a fast and accurate weapon. I came to know, and like, so much about it that the Plasma Rifle is one of the reasons why I stopped playing *Halo 2*. There are two Plasma Rifles in *Halo 2*: the Elite blue one and the Brute red one. The first was supposed to be *my* dearest Plasma Rifle, but it was not.

First, it did not look exactly the same (though this didn't bother me much). Secondly, its sounds were different, but I could have worked it. The really annoying thing was that its rhythm had changed; its feeling was completely different. Not mastering new weapons is quite normal, I could bear it. But I could not suffer being once again a beginner with the Plasma Rifle. This change made all things I had learned about this weapon, and all the time I spent to learn them, meaningless. I know it may sound extreme but it felt like a betrayal.

My Two Unforgettable Moments

After gameplay depth, let's consider another critical aspect of the game: emergence. *Halo,* in its very structure, has the ability to create unpredictable and yet logical experiences. This became clear to me after two remarkable episodes.

The first moment happened while I was sneaking around, looking for the right place to start my next attack on a Covenant unit. Just after rounding a corner, I came face to face with an Elite. Actually, I was facing its back. I used the Melee Attack for a stealth kill. Then I laughed and I certainly got killed right after because I was laughing. The difficulty was high (heroic or legendary); a surprise meeting with an Elite should have resulted in a tough situation.

I knew I had just lived a rare and unpredictable moment, so rare it only happened once. I knew that because of my many hours playing *Halo*. You almost never get a free stealth kill on an Elite. I mean a "real" free kill, not one decided by the game designer. It may happen though, because the game is scripted but not completely. Its small parts of randomness allow these kinds of moments to occur.

My second unforgettable experience took place in legendary mode. I was facing a Jackal in an open space, with nowhere to hide. It was at about ten meters. I saw a green light on its gun and made one step to the right, one to the left, and one more to the right. These steps made me dodge three bursts of three Plasma bullets. After the last one, I ran to the Jackal and threw it off balance with a Melee Attack. Then I could shoot its feet and make it fall before finishing it.

I did not plan to act like this, it just came naturally. It was not a matter of reflex but only knowledge and anticipation. I felt like a superhero dodging bullets by reading the enemy's mind. At that very moment, I became aware that I knew almost perfectly the Jackal's fire pattern. This knowledge was not enough to avoid all the bullets, but it was all that was necessary.

Once again, it happened because the game allowed it. The Jackal's pattern was both complex and predictable. Dodging it was very difficult, yet doable. It gave meaning to a higher progression. Killing a Jackal in legendary mode without grenade or charged fire is not easy. Doing so without being touched requires even more skill. It could have been impossible. Believe me, an unavoidable pattern is easy to create, it is also true for one that must be easy to avoid. A "hard but not impossible to avoid pattern" requires a lot of work and testing.

Uncertainty, the Dark Side of Learning

Learning in a videogame is uncertain. It's uncertain because you're not forced to play a specific game. If I did not play *Halo*, I would not have written what you are reading at the moment. It is uncertain because the game allows you to not understand. Tutorials aside, *Halo* never forces you to understand one particular thing. Information is available but you have to decide to look for it. So you may as well miss it. There is nobody behind you telling how you should play—well, there could be someone, but in my case there wasn't. You can finish the game in easy mode while ignoring most of what we have discussed here. I finished it in legendary mode and I know I did not master everything.

You only have to learn when you're facing difficult situations and when you want desperately to overcome them. But there are so many different skills that it's impossible to predict which one you will acquire or improve in order to do so. The game designer can only hope that the player will not give up the game. For example, it isn't possible to foresee what a player will have learned after finishing the game once. This is why learning in videogames, and particularly in *Halo*, is unpredictable and deeply uncertain.

But instead of fighting this uncertainty, as a teacher would, *Halo* embraced it. Each play is different and some playthroughs are more significant than others. Each skill or mechanism may be understood roughly or deeply according to the needs of the player. He or she may choose which new skill to acquire and which to leave undeveloped. Giving meaning to a deep understanding or knowledge rewards the attention paid to the game and makes the player aware of his or her own progression. Even if the game gives every reason to work in order to progress, the decision is always up to the player. This is the main difference between learning in videogames and learning in school.

6

Halo and Music

BEN ABRAHAM

In August of 2005, amateur film maker and die-hard *Halo* enthusiast Cody Miller recorded a video of his single life, legendary difficulty completion of the *Halo 2* campaign. Miller had practiced for weeks leading up to his three-hours-plus marathon gaming session. To do it he had to memorize the location of every single instant-kill jackal sniper, figure out the fastest and safest routes through every map, practice each shortcut until he could make every grenade jump, first time every time, and generally be an extremely good player.

Watching this feat of almost superhuman ability and endurance gives us the distinct impression that the game was never meant to be played like this. And yet Miller's subversive play style did not require the changing of a single line of code.

The hectic pace Miller keeps occasionally forces music to be cut short or begin playing one over the top of another, confounding the intended effect of the otherwise separate pieces. And yet he never breaks a game rule and never dies. And because of this, his now enshrined speedrun video is an entirely valid "telling" of the *Halo 2* story. This gives rise to an awfully important question: if this is a valid arrangement of the myriad possible strands of the *Halo 2* narrative then why does it seem as if the music is so unprepared for Miller? Why is it unable to keep up with the pace he set?

This question goes to the heart of fundamental issues with the nature of both music and videogames, and whether the two are even compatible.

> assured: in ten or so versions there will always be a few that create amazing points of synchronisations and moving or comical juxtapositions, which always come as a surprise.[1]

He called these happy accidents of synchronization "forced marriage" and the phenomenon demonstrates audiovisual synchronisation occurring even with music composed with no regard for the visual elements they will be thrust upon. While this effect has largely been acceptable in the history of videogames to the current point, no one has yet figured out what to do if they want to make the *Psycho* shower scene of videogames.

Our identified incompatibility between unpredictable, interactive videogames and pre-composed "linear" music is only an issue if a piece of music is composed, rather than performed or assembled live. In fact, the incompatibility is actually only an issue for a certain preconception of what music actually is, and more specifically, for the conception of music that arose from the Western musical tradition. If we were to expand our conception of music beyond what is heard in the concert hall or through the TV set, the perceived incompatibility between games and music might dissolve entirely.

Music According to Whom?

Using the term "song" rather than the broader term "music," Plato places the following assertion into the mouth of Socrates in Book II of *The Republic*: "song consists of three elements: words, musical mode, and rhythm." Acceptable notions of what constitutes a musical work have changed drastically throughout the ages. At the very least the necessity for music to contain words as found in Plato's time is nowhere to be seen today. Furthermore, the idea that a piece of music requires a tonal center, what Plato referred to as "musical mode," itself an early version of the key signature, has been questioned by various movements throughout the twentieth century.

Murray Schafer in his landmark book *The Tuning of the World* attempts a more catholic definition of music, partially in response to developments in recording technology and artistic practice. As Schafer says:

---

[1] Michel Chion, Walter Murch, and Claudia Gorbman, *Audio-Vision: Sound on Screen* (Columbia University Press, 1994), p. 188.

> To define music merely as *sounds* would have been unthinkable a few years ago, though today it is the more exclusive definitions that are proving unacceptable. Little by little throughout the twentieth century, all the conventional definitions of music have been exploded by the abundant activities of musicians themselves. (p. 5)

Schafer identifies the ancient roots of our modern conceptions of music by noting two competing Greek myths that explain the origins of music. In the first, the Apollonian, music is borne out of the emotional expression of the gods, and implies that music is itself emotion made manifest. In the latter, the Dionysian myth, music was conceived when a god discovered the resonant properties of a tortoise shell, and therefore music has its origin in the properties of the material world. They bear different implications for what can be called "music" and Schafer describes them as "the cornerstones on which all subsequent theories of music are founded."[2]

Schafer is still only addressing the history and conception of music in the West, however. John Miller Chernoff in his study of African music, *African Rhythm and African Sensibility,* tells his Western readers, "we must be prepared to open our minds . . . to the possibility that they may have an entirely different conception of what music itself is."[3] Chernoff goes so far as to say that

> When a Western friend for whom you might play some African music says in disgust, as he sits fidgeting in his chair, "That's not music," he is ironically both right and wrong. African music is not just different music but is something that is different from "music." (p. 33)

And yet leaving non-Western music-making to its fate as "not music" seems an unappealing prospect and carries overtones of cultural imperialism. Famed ethnomusicologist John Blacking in his pioneering study *How Musical Is Man?* advocated that music departments perform a recategorisation of their study of music: "more modestly, as a system of musical theory and practice that emerged and developed during a certain period of European history."[4]

For one thing, Western musicality has a preoccupation with the musical object (usually the "score") as the determining aspect of a

---

[2] *The Tuning of the World* (Knopf, 1977), p. 6.

[3] Chernoff, *African Rhythm and African Sensibility*, p. 31.

[4] John Blacking, *How Musical Is Man?* (Faber, 1976), p.3.

piece of music (replaced more recently perhaps by the recording artifact), a preoccupation not shared by many oral musical cultures. For example, indigenous Australian musicality lacked any form of notation at all, and songs were transmitted orally through the practise of performing the song. It's particularly hard for our Western minds to comprehend the inability to separate the practice of performing a piece of music from its very existence, but for these musicians, and indeed for many other oral traditions, there is nothing beyond the memory of the song and its performance to point to as the definitive form.

The idea of a musical "work" comes with some serious cultural baggage. As Marcia Citron notes in *Gender and the Musical Canon*, "important social variables such as power, class, and gender can be inscribed in a work" (p. 121). For Citron then,

> music, like its sister art forms, grows out of a specific social context. It expresses in various ways fundamental assumptions about the culture in which it originates. Aesthetically music entails communication, and this can take place at many levels and in varied combinations of work, composer, performer, and receptor. (p. 120)

On a rather different tack, The Javanese and Balinese gamelan orchestra sounds, to Western ears unaccustomed to their unique scale and tuning, like the mad crash and clatter of un-tuned gongs. But they are in fact just another product of a very different idea of what makes sound musical.

Music the *Halo* Way

So where does O'Donnell, and the *Halo* series, stand on the subject of music? We've seen that O'Donnell thinks of music as telling basically linear stories, which places him well and truly within the Western classical tradition. In defense of tradition O'Donnell notes that, despite interactivity, when a person is done playing the game they have inevitably had "a linear experience because that *is* all you have, when you play a game you are having a linear experience . . . you play for ten minutes, you have a ten-minute experience." For O'Donnell then, since duration is the uncontrollable factor, he places much importance upon being able to successfully manage this aspect of a piece, dealing with the problem of interactivity by fixing the beginning and end sections and making the middle malleable.

As part of his writing process O'Donnell composes whole pieces of music, and the majority of these, he told me, were written while keeping in mind what would be happening in each level. Working closely with the level designers he attempted to write music for "the emotional journey [they wanted] the player to have." It's not too much of a stretch to assume that what is being designed by the level designers is primarily meant to be seen, and therefore onscreen. So it would seem there is a desire for the music and visuals to synchronize or complement each other.

As *Halo* stands, while an explosion onscreen may not trigger a musical stab from the cello section, O'Donnell will still have the knowledge in advance of which sections explosions are likely to occur in, and this has the potential to influence the music he creates. But the point of music in *Halo*, O'Donnell notes, is not to convey this kind of semantic information. When asked whether he used or was interested in applying the techniques of the *Leitmotiv*,[5] he replied, "That's not the composer that I want to be. I'm not writing *Peter and the Wolf*, as much as I love *Peter and the Wolf*." O'Donnell doesn't seem to be composing, then, with explosions in mind. Instead, he says, "music creates emotional enhancements that work best when you have reasons for music to exist," which is, to use Murray Schafer's earlier term, an Apollonian view of music—music is emotion; connotation rather than denotation.

When pressed about the potential for a closer relationship between music and visuals in the *Halo* games, O'Donnell pointed to the success of the synaesthesia game *Rez* which places the emphasis on music being generated by the player's actions. The visual information is informed and constrained by the music, and O'Donnell agreed that attempts to find a similar approach that worked within a more traditional FPS game is "a great place to explore." Naturally, he had reservations, saying that while "it works great for electronica and that sort of genre," if the game needs to have a more orchestrally scored epic feel, "you struggle with that."

The experiential result of O'Donnell's musical philosophy and implementation is that music in *Halo 2* is linked on an emotive level with the game narrative, as determined by O'Donnell and the other game designers. It is linked, however, only on the most broad

---

[5] A *Leitmotiv* (German for 'leading-motive') is a musical theme used recurrently to denote an object, a person, an aspect of character, or some other element in a story.

strings of sounds become familiar to the player adding a rhythmic dimension to otherwise un-pitched sounds.

Sound, Music, and Vision

The in-game sound effects of *Halo 2* are infused with a musicality through pitch, timbre, and rhythmic elements which contribute to an overall soundscape that is highly musical. The musicality of sound effects works to bridge the gap between music and sound effects and helps overcome the incompatibilities between music and vision as identified earlier–because all of these sound effects are synchronised with their onscreen actions already.

To repurpose an earlier example: Martin O'Donnell may not be able to make the cello section perform a musical stab whenever a plasma grenade explodes, but he can place within the sound effect of a plasma grenade an aural connection to a cello stab that happens elsewhere. He could even choose to use the cello to form part of the plasma explosion sound effect. This achievement is centrally important for how it changes the relationship between music and visuals; it enables a new kind of audio-visual relationship that works exceptionally well in interactive videogames. *Halo 2*'s music-infused sound effects present a picture of a unique new way for music—and music meant in the broadest possible sense—to operate within videogames that is almost unlike anything else in the medium.

7
Personal Identity in Blood Gulch

PETER LUDLOW AND
CHIARA REPETTI-LUDLOW

One of the more remarkable fan-created spinoffs of the *Halo* videogame franchise has been the *Red vs Blue* (*RvB*) machinima series. Machinima, for those who don't know, is a form of movie made from video captures of videogame play. These video captures are edited and mixed with voice, music, and sound effects to create a (hopefully) coherent story line. Typically the action in a machinima video is staged and rehearsed, just as in a standard film production. The difference, of course, is that the "actors" are videogame player characters being operated by the producers of the show.

RvB is a machinima web series that is produced by Rooster Teeth Productions, based in Austin, Texas. The episodes appear weekly (premiering each Monday night at 9:00 P.M. Central). The show typically has nineteen episodes per season and is now in its eighth season. There are also two important mini-series that appeared between seasons and that fleshed out details of the narrative. In addition to the web broadcasts, the episodes are released on DVD.

There has been lots of critical acclaim for the series, including the remarks of Graham Leggat, former director of communications for Lincoln Center's film society, describing *RvB* as "truly as sophisticated as Samuel Beckett."[1] That may be over the top, but as we'll see, the *RvB* series is not only great entertainment, but it also engages philosophical questions in a very deep way.

---

[1] As reported in K. Delaney, "When Art Imitates Videogames, You Have '*Red vs Blue*': Mr. Burns Makes Little Movies Internet Fans Clamor For, Shades of Samuel Beckett," *Wall Street Journal* (April 9th, 2004), p. 1.

This is a scene from the machinima web series Red vs. Blue (RvB, *Rooster Teeth Productions, 2003*).

Some of these questions center around the nature of personal identity—what it means to be a person and under what conditions a person continues to survive. We think the series has a serious philosophical contribution to make on this topic. Surprisingly, the classic philosophical positions on personal identity are undermined by the thought experiments given in the *RvB* plot line.

Welcome to Blood Gulch. Meet the Red Team

RvB begins in a location called Blood Gulch, with what appears to be a standoff between two teams of combat troops—the Red Team and the Blue Team—but the story line rapidly evolves into much more, incorporating elements of videogame criticism, commentary on digital culture, artificial intelligence, personal identity, and the meaning of life. The dialogue is fresh, sometimes ridiculous, but also at times quite deep. When we're introduced to the *RvB* characters, it initially seems as if we're watching an existential conversation between two members of the Red Team. But then the conversation takes a turn and it becomes a discussion about the absurdity of online multiplayer mode (in which users are assigned to either a red or blue team and then take part in player vs player combat against the other team), and perhaps also about the absurdity of war.

SIMMONS: You ever wonder why we're here?

GRIF: That's one of life's great mysteries isn't it? Why are we here? I mean, are we the product of some cosmic coincidence, or, is there really a God, watching everything, you know, with a plan for us and stuff? I don't know, man, but it keeps me up at night.

SIMMONS: What! I mean why are we out here, in this canyon?

GRIF: Oh, uhhh. Yeah.

SIMMONS: What was all that stuff about God?

GRIF: Uhhhh, hm, nothing.

SIMMONS: You wanna talk about it?

GRIF: No.

SIMMONS: You sure?

GRIF: Yeah.

SIMMONS: Seriously though, why are we out here? Far as I can tell, it's just a box canyon in the middle of nowhere. No way in or out.

GRIF: Uh hmm.

SIMMONS: The only reason we set up a Red Base here, is because they have a Blue Base over there. And the only reason they have a Blue Base over there, is because we have a Red Base here.

GRIF: Yeah. That's 'cause we're fighting each other.

SIMMONS: No, no. But I mean, even if we were to pull out today, and if they would come take our base, they would have *two* bases in the middle of a box canyon. Whoopdee-fucking-doo.[2]

While the narrative drives an independent story line, it also makes an effort to connect with the broader *Halo* story. This is clear throughout the *RvB* narrative, and is introduced in the very first episode in the conversation between Grif and Simmons:

SIMMONS: What's up with that anyway? I mean, I signed on to fight some aliens. Next thing I know, Master Chief's blown

---

[2] From *RvB* Season 1, Episode 1, transcript at <http://roostertooths.com/transcripts.php?eid=1>.

up the entire Covenant armada and I'm stuck in the middle of nowhere, fighting a bunch of blue guys.

GRIF: Talk about a waste of resources. I mean, we should be out there finding newer and intelligent forms of life, you know, fight them.

SIMMONS: Yeah, no shit. That's why they should put us in charge.

With this clever comic move, the narrative for the series is embedded within the *Halo* universe, and is able to draw on elements of that universe. In this case, we have a reference to Master Chief, the player character hero of *Halo: Combat Evolved*, and we also have a reference to the initial goal of that iteration of *Halo*—stopping the Covenant.

Whether we think of *RvB* as fiction within the *Halo* universe or a completely independent fictional world, it raises interesting questions in the themes that come up in its narrative. As we suggested earlier, these themes can be thought of as philosophical thought experiments.

Thought Experiments in Philosophy

Throughout its history, philosophy has utilized thought experiments as part of its methodology. This dates at least to Plato, who used the analogy of the cave to illustrate the relation between forms and particulars. Other thought experiments have not merely illustrated ideas, but have played an important part in philosophical arguments.

Thought experiments involving personal identity were introduced by John Locke in the seventeenth century and then by Bernard Williams, Derek Parfit, and others in the mid-twentieth century. Locke's thought experiment was designed to show that a person should not be identified with his or her body. Would it be possible for the consciousness of a prince (all his memories, thoughts, and desires) to be placed in the body of a cobbler and vice versa? In other words, the prince would be walking around in the Cobbler's body and the Cobbler would be walking around in the prince's body, much like the plot of the movie *Freaky Friday*. Locke drew upon this scenario to show it was possible that a single person might occupy different physical bodies. So what's required for the persistence of personal identity between the bodies of prince and cobbler?

What makes it the case that the prince is the same person when his consciousness occupies the cobbler's body? Locke felt that memory was the key element.

More recently, several thought experiments have been designed to show that Locke's memory answer can't be right. Bernard Williams constructed the following thought experiment.[3] Consider a person who appeared having all the memories and personality traits of a long deceased person named "Guy Fawkes." Perhaps, following Locke, we are tempted to say "well, I guess then it must be Guy Fawkes." But Williams then asks us to suppose that *two* such characters appear. Can they *both* be Guy Fawkes? It seems not. The original Guy Fawkes cannot be identical with the resulting individuals (one thing cannot be identical to two, after all) even though the memories survive intact.

Williams took his argument to show that bodily identity is required for personal identity, but other thought experiments have called this into question. Consider the thought experiment of Sydney Shoemaker in which a person's brain is removed and placed in a new brainless body, resulting in a person with the same characteristics as the original. We're tempted to think it's the same person as the original.[4] But now consider a wrinkle added by David Wiggins:[5] Suppose that we split the brain of the original person (let's call him "Guy") and put each half in a brand new body (people have survived the loss of half a brain, so this seems reasonable). Suppose that each half has the same psychological characteristics and memories as Guy. Now the objection used against Locke has returned, since there are two individuals with the same psychological characteristics as Guy (even the same brain as him more or less), but two things can't be identical to one, so both can't be the same person.

Derek Parfit held that the real moral of cases like this is that *identity* is not the important thing, but rather psychological continuity is.[6] That is, while we might say that Guy is not identical with either of the split-brained individuals that come from him, it would be another matter to say that Guy therefore does not survive the

---

[3] "Personal Identity and Individuation," *Proceedings of the Aristotelian Society* 57 (1956-57), pp. 229–252.

[4] *Self-Knowledge and Self-Identity* (Cornell University Press, 1963).

[5] *Identity and Spatio-Temporal Continuity* (Oxford University Press, 1967).

[6] "Personal Identity," *Philosophical Review* 80 (1971), pp. 3–27.

brain splitting and re-embodiment. Survival and identity are two different things. In a case of splitting (what Parfit calls "fission") we may not have identity, but we have survival. Parfit also pointed out that psychological continuity was important to assessing personal plans and goals. So while the split-off individuals might not be identical with Guy, they would naturally maintain the plans and goals of Guy.

While thought experiments like this have been used in all manner of cases in philosophy, some philosophers have questioned the reliability of the method. Why should we rely upon our intuitions (or judgments) that something is possible, and why should our judgments of what is possible have anything to do with what is actually the case? The answer is that thought experiments are designed to probe the nature and character of individual concepts. Is it conceivable that we could have a mind without a body? Well then we at a minimum have established that there is no conceptual restriction on saying the mind and body are distinct.

Recently a lot of work in so-called experimental philosophy (known to its practitioners as "X-phi") has argued that the suppositions of Western philosophers about what is conceivable don't square with what is considered conceivable in other cultures.[7] One way to take these results (assuming they're correct) would be as a caution against appeals to notions of conceivability in philosophy altogether. But of course another way to take the results would be as a reminder that more may be conceivable than we might suppose upon first reflection.

If this is right, then what we should be looking for are ways to pump our intuitions about what is conceivable—to take our intuitions beyond what they might ordinarily be in our cultural or historical situation. Science fiction is especially good at this, and if science fiction is good at intuition pumping, videogames are even better, since they incorporate the same science-fiction narratives while at the same time providing an immersive experience that makes distant possibilities more salient and plausible. Fiction woven from familiar videogame experiences (like *RvB*) is in a position to prime our intuition pumps even more.

---

[7] See J. Knobe, and S. Nichols, eds., *Experimental Philosophy* (Oxford University Press, 2008).

AIs and Personal Identity in *RvB*

There are several points where the *RvB* narrative raises interesting questions about the nature of the person. In the *Halo* games there is an important role played by AIs—the artificial intelligence agents that guide figures like Master Chief (and, of course, guide the user through the gameplay). AIs in fiction are nothing new, but the intimate role that they play with their assigns in *Halo* adds a twist—the AIs are an ever-present inner voice that can offer suggestions, provide data, and counsel courses of action. In *RvB* the tightness of this bond is highlighted, and the potential downside of an ever-present voice is noted.

Among the characters in *RvB* are a group of special agents who are assigned their own personal AIs. As we will see, these AIs are problematic in several ways, and one of the special agents—Agent Washington—was temporarily driven crazy by his AI and had to have it removed. It seems Washington was at one point unable to distinguish his own thoughts from those of the AI.

The intimate link between these special agents and their AIs (and even between *Halo*'s Master Chief and his AI, Cortana, for that matter) suggest new and better ways of illustrating the extended mind hypothesis advocated by David Chalmers and Andy Clarke—the thesis that our minds include certain external tools that we use.[8] Chalmers has been known to wave his iPhone, declaring it to be part of his extended mind. But this is not as effective an intuition pump as playing a game in which your personal AI assistant is constantly guiding you or, for that matter, imagining a scenario in which a special agent has such an AI 24/7 and the AI is having destructive psychological effects.

The *RvB* narrative is also effective at illustrating new ways in which artificial intelligence agents might be realized. One of the Blue Team members, Church, turns out to be an AI. He and the team discover that he can jump into both human bodies and robots, basically reprogramming them. The scenario is not, as far as we can tell, a "ghost in the machine" scenario. Church is not a little person inside another person—a homunculus—but rather the host body is rewired (reprogrammed) for the duration of Church's occupation of it. There are also elements where the homunculus story seems to be in effect, as when Church and another AI enter

[8] "The Extended Mind," *Analysis* 58 (1998), pp. 7–19.

into the cavernous mind of the Blue Team member Caboose, but this doesn't appear to be a case of take-over and reprogramming so much as visitation.

Church also is able to appear as a ghost-like form when disembodied (in fact he even takes himself to be a ghost). How do we make sense of this? One possibility is that there's an additional medium that is programmable but which is causally inert until it can enter into a programmable physical system like a human body or a robot. We could think of it as being like the "soul stuff" discussed by Hilary Putnam[9] or as dynamic patterns of information that are (at least temporarily) self-sustaining without the usual physical or biological substrate.

Project Freelancer

For our new thought experiments the relevant story line revolves around Project Freelancer, a twenty-sixth-century military-industrial R&D project under the control of one Dr. Leonard Church, otherwise known as "The Director." The goal of Project Freelancer is to equip elite soldiers with enhanced armor and dedicated AIs to assist them in the operation of the armor and presumably in other matters.

The initial plan of Project Freelancer is to have forty-nine special agents (each one code named for one of the remaining states in the United States—Florida has gone rogue) and each is to be assigned an AI.

As we write this, the plot line is still unfolding, but as far as we can determine, the following is the case. At some point shortly after its inception, Project Freelancer is terminated with only two AIs having been created. One is an AI based upon the Director—this AI is sometimes known as "The Alpha" and sometimes as "Church," and the other is based upon memories of a woman in The Director's past—sometimes known as "Alison" and sometimes as "Tex."

It's unclear at this point whether Tex/Alison was made by The Director or by The Alpha. It's possible that the plot could evolve in such a way that The Alpha is identical to The Director. That mind-bending possibility doesn't undermine the thought experiment we are imagining here, which only requires that they *could* be distinct even if psychologically continuous.

---

[9] "Philosophy and Our Mental Life," *Mind, Language, and Reality: Philosophical Papers, Volume 2* (Cambridge University Press, 1975), pp. 291–303.

The Director is undeterred by the cancellation of the project (or cancellation of funding for the project) and finds a way to generate AIs on the cheap. This is not as trivial as it sounds because apparently these AIs are not replicable in the way that typical computer programs are. Exactly why is never explained, but we can speculate. Perhaps the complexity of the AIs is such that simple copying is not possible. Or, it may be that they employ elements of quantum computation in which a read/write copying mechanism would not work because the attempt to read the state of the The Alpha would have the effect of altering its state (the idea being that quantum states cannot be precisely observed without changing those states).

Whatever the reason for the copying problem, The Director finds that he can fracture off fragments of the original AI by torturing the AI until it undergoes a kind of psychological fission—for example separating the memory from various emotional components. Once the AI's personality has undergone this fission bits of each component can be fractured off. This isn't a copying process but a process in which new AIs are chipped away from the original. It seems that the psychological fission allows more AIs to be created, or perhaps the fission is necessary for the fracturing to be possible (we'll say more about this in a bit).

It may be hard to see how this could work from a scientific point of view, but we can imagine various scenarios. Suppose we thought of the AI as being like a hologram. The interesting thing about a hologram (the physical film, not what appears to us) is that every point in the hologram records light from the entirety of the original scene, so that in principle the whole scene can be reconstructed from any arbitrarily small piece of the hologram (although one loses resolution—that is, the image becomes fuzzier).

If psychological fission is required before fracturing off AIs, then we can speculate that The Director discovered that one could not get a holographic fragment of the whole, but only from the sub-components. This is certainly plausible on the assumption of the modularity of the mind as advocated by Jerry Fodor—there would be no uniform central processing but rather a number of sub-components of the mind that act in concert with each other.[10] One can only get fragments from these sub-components because

---

[10] *The Modularity of Mind* (MIT Press, 1983).

the sub-components are "encapsulated"—none of them carry information about the entire Alpha AI.

The individual AIs are thus produced via fracturing, each having the distinctive features of certain aspects of The Alpha's (Church's) psychology. For example, The Epsilon unit contains a number of relevant memories; The Omega unit has distinctive emotions such as anger. (Given that The Epsilon unit retains the memories of being tortured it is no surprise that things did not go well when it was assigned to agent Washington.)

A key element of the plot line involves one of the Freelancer agents, Agent Maine, who has gone about collecting the various AIs and incorporating them with his own. This agent is also called "The Meta." The Meta becomes quite powerful at one point by virtue of acquiring the AIs and the enhanced armor components that they deploy. Although it is not explicitly stated, one may also speculate that The Meta is driven by a desire to recombine the components that were fractured off of The Alpha.

Where Parfit Went Wrong

This is a very partial description of the plot line, but we can already see many elements of the philosophical thought experiments we discussed earlier. On the one hand, the fact that AIs can have different forms of embodiment argues against materialist theories of personal identity for such agents—theories that say identity is constituted by the body. At first glance, this seems to be consistent with Locke's argument. We might therefore think that Locke's theory of personal identity fits well within the story line, but it really doesn't; in *RvB* the memory component is important but it is not sufficient to secure the identity of the AI.

Is *RvB* then a thought experiment that lends support to Parfit's theory of personal identity? At first glance the answer seems to be "yes," however there are important ways in which the *RvB* scenarios cause trouble for Parfit's position. The first and most obvious problem is that for Parfit, psychological continuity is the key element in the survival of an agent, yet in the RvB story line when AIs are made by cracking off bits of The Alpha there is plenty of psychological continuity between the source and the "copy" (arguably more continuity than in the split-brain cases), but little intuitive pull to think this ensures the survival of the source. For example, the various AIs that are extracted from The Alpha could all be combined into something—let's say The Meta—with the psychology of The Alpha, but it doesn't follow that we would think The Alpha could survive the destruction of its "soul stuff" simply because The Meta is still around.

Why is this? Perhaps it's because there's no reason to think that the fractured off pieces of The Alpha are significant enough chunks to ensure The Alpha's survival. The split-brain cases discussed by Parfit are different because the continuing individuals retain substantial portions of the original brain. If smaller bits are fractured off—bits that carry the psychology of the whole (like a bit of a holographic film can carry the entire image)—we do not get the intuitions that the original object (hologram or AI or person) can survive its material destruction simply because psychologically continuous fragments of it are still around. The intuitions go against Parfit in such cases.

This is even more clear if the fragments must be recombined into something like The Meta before we get something that is psychologically continuous with the original object. Suppose that The Alpha is destroyed but that The Meta is assembled from fragments of The Alpha. We resist saying that The Alpha has survived in such a case. Once The Meta is assembled it may have the psychology of The Alpha, but something about its history—being fractured off of mental modules and *then* assembled—seems to undermine our intuition that The Alpha has survived.

Parfit addresses cases of simple fission where two halves are rejoined, but what are the intuitions for cases where there is a massive fission of the original, not into functional halves but into more or less dysfunctional components that are then recombined into a functional whole in the form of The Meta? Again, we think the intuitions break against Parfit.

If Parfit's story is weak here, is there an alternative? The *RvB* story line suggest an account of personal identity in which it is possible (at least for AIs) to have a kind of disembodied existence that is nonetheless organized computationally. This is actually a possibility—discussed by Putnam—that the computational theory of mind could apply just as well to "soul stuff" as to minds. In the *RvB* universe, it seems that the soul stuff (or whatever substance explains the visible manifestation of the AI when disembodied) may well be the key to survival for an AI. Carve off a little bit and you may get something psychologically continuous with the source, but you won't thereby get the survival of the source, and you won't get something with the goals and plans of the source.

The question here is not whether the story is an accurate picture of how things in fact stand, but whether such a scenario is conceivable and thus illuminating of our concept of personal identity. Perhaps we did not see this as a possible position before *RvB*. If so, then we can think of *RvB* as an exercise in philosophy, designed to get us to see possibilities that had previously escaped our attention.

In a famous passage from Shakespeare (*Hamlet* Act 1, Scene 5), Hamlet cautions Horatio about the limits of philosophy: "There are more things in heaven and earth, Horatio, Than are dreamt of in your philosophy."

The cautionary advice can be flipped on Hamlet, because if we extend the limits of our philosophical intuitions with *RvB*-like thought experiments, what we can dream of may well outrun the furnishings of our real world. Coming to Horatio's defense, we might put it this way: "There are more things in Blood Gulch (and our philosophy), Hamlet, than are found in your heaven and earth."

8

Enlightenment through *Halo*'s Possible Worlds

LUKE CUDDY

Consider the following scenarios from *Halo 3* right before you rescue Cortana at the end of *Floodgate*, both of which are true, sort of:

> **Scenario 1:** My checkpoint begins. There's a Flood running at me with a tentacle-like claw swinging menacingly in the air. He jumps, but I still have six rounds left on my Brute Shot, and one of them has this Flood's name on it. But when I shoot I miss, causing me to panic and miss again. He swipes me in the face twice with his claw, taking my power down almost half way. I fire again in a continued panic, but the Flood is right in front of me now, and the Brute Shot is too powerful: the shot kills us both.

> **Scenario 2:** My checkpoint begins. There's a Flood running at me with a tentacle-like claw swinging menacingly in the air. He jumps, but I still have six rounds left on my Brute Shot, and one of them has this Flood's name on it. A split second later his appendages and insides are splattered all over the rock wall to my right and the canyon to my left.

How is it that I can say these are both true, when they seem to be competing instances in time? Both cannot have actually happened, right? But both scenarios are possible worlds that exist in my playing of *Halo 3* (though I would prefer the second to be the actual world). Some philosophers and, in recent scientific history, scientists have suggested that the existence of possible worlds is a real possibility. In other words, these people suggest that possible worlds besides the one we live in *actually exist*, as we'll see.

Something else to consider is that the possible world of scenario 1 will never again occur. It's suspended in time (somewhere on my Xbox?) in that specific state. One could wonder what happens to that future and the creatures in it. For those of us who've used emulators (software that fully reproduces old videogame consoles like NES, Atari, or Genesis), possible worlds are very familiar because of save states. Save states allow you to override the constraints of the original game by saving your progress at any point. For example, in the original *The Legend of Zelda*, when you die, you either start at the beginning of the last dungeon you were in (minus most of your hearts), or at the beginning point in the overworld. But while running this game on an emulator, you can save it at any point, including right before a very difficult dungeon boss, or at a room in a dungeon where there are three doors. If you don't know where these doors lead, you can create a save state in that room, then try one door in one possible world, then the other, then the last. Of course, if you try one door and it's a dead end or too difficult, you can start that save state over and try another. It makes the game much easier, but it also illustrates possible worlds in videogames.

In games like *The Legend of Zelda* on emulators, we have more time to reflect on our choices in these possible worlds, whereas in the *Halo* series we don't. In *Halo*, we don't care about what happens in what future; we don't care about what puzzles of space and time are illuminated by the concept. We only care about achieving the future where we can actually move on to the next part of the level! In the context of *Halo*, as we will see, possible futures can potentially lead to a high emotional state, such as anger or frustration, via both single player and multiplayer—something that doesn't occur the same way in other videogames. *Halo*'s ability to produce this state in its players is what makes it a ripe candidate for leading those players to enlightenment oriented thinking in the Buddhist sense.

Possible Worlds

In philosophy one could argue that the notion of possible worlds goes back to Gottfried Liebniz's idea that the *actual* world we live in is the best of all *possible* worlds. According to Liebniz, there are other possible worlds out there that we *could* live in, but we don't because God instead created our world which is, apparently, better than any other possibilities. David Lewis, the twentieth-century American philosopher, wrote about possible worlds in relation to language. For instance, when you get pwned by a seven-year-old in *Halo 3*'s multiplayer, you might say, "Yeah, he pwned me but I could have pwned him." If you didn't pwn him, then how can it also be true that you could have pwned him? According to Lewis, statements like the latter can have a truth value because there actually is another world where they are true, existing in time simultaneously with our world.

In the realm of science, the idea of possible worlds came to the fore with the advent of quantum physics and, eventually, string theory. Today, string theory is hotly contested but remains a frontrunner for the theory of everything—a theory that unites our understanding of the physical world at the quantum (small stuff) and Newtonian (big stuff) levels. Among other things, string theory suggests that there are, in fact, parallel worlds existing alongside our own. Although string theory has yet to be backed up by hard observable evidence, its acceptance by many members of the scientific community has made the notion of possible worlds more appealing to our culture in general.[1]

Whether or not there really are other worlds, existing alongside our own, for the first time in human history we have games like those of the *Halo* series, which present an artificial turf, so to speak, where the idea of possible worlds can be explored. Although there are a number of fascinating metaphysical issues to be explored (concerning *Halo*, videogames, and possible worlds), as noted, I am interested in the use of this possibility for enlightenment oriented thinking and behavior in the Buddhist sense.

The fact that *Halo* games present the players with infinite lives gives them a lot of possible worlds to create. Most of the time, players are not aware that they are creating these worlds. They die, get angry, then reload their Shotgun and try again. But, as we've seen, each death represents another possible world, lost somewhere in virtual space and time once the player reverts to her previous checkpoint. The key element for Buddhism here is *anger*. The difficulty of some of the levels in *Halo* games, combined with the infinite lives/possible future scenario, makes players angry! Really

[1] As John Gribbin notes in *In Search of Schrödinger's Cat* (Bantam, 1984), science-fiction authors in the early 1980s would routinely "discover" the idea of possible worlds and then run with it for a story (p. 289).

angry! But what if this anger could be harnessed, or consciously mitigated? In that case, *Halo* might be seen as a tool for Buddhism, which advocates the mitigation of anger in general and, consequently, the growth of compassion.

Fuck This Game!

Consider the following scenario from *Halo 3* multiplayer online:

> **Scenario 3:** I just picked up a Needler—an underrated weapon in my book, and there's always the chance that you'll get a one shot kill. LITTLESHIT232[2] comes at me, but I unload a barrage of pink spikes into him, head level, killing him instantly. Sensing an imminent threat I wheel around to see HAPPY_SMILE001 aiming a Brute Shot in my direction, but my Needler is quicker, and I still have enough ammo to take him out before he can finish me. I go on to have a great game, coming out in first place.

Now consider this:

> **Scenario 4:** I haven't been playing multiplayer too long. Just long enough to get my UNSC Spartan Super Soldier patch. I'm feeling pretty confident. I just had a good game [described in scenario 3]. I know I'm not the best. But I'm getting better, improving. The new game starts, and immediately THEPDIDDY1200 melees me from the side. *It's okay*, I tell myself, *it's only one frag*. But then my next death comes from BIEBERBOT_41—he outsmarts me in a one-on-one with the Shotgun. The game continues on in this fashion—I almost get a kill, but then I die. Almost, then death. Finally, it looks like I'm going to get my *first* kill (everyone else has at least ten by now). I'm taking down The45YEAROLDVIRGIN and he's almost dead, but then in comes THEPDIDDY1200 to take care of both of us. Fuck this game!

Halo multiplayer creates possible worlds in a different way than single player. Each, for instance, Slayer match can be seen as a possible world, whereas deaths do not create possible worlds. This is because each time the player dies it does not reset the match; the match continues since other players are there to inhabit the level on which it's being played.

---

[2] Names have been changed to preserve identity.

Here possible worlds contribute to the player's generation of emotion in a different way. In single player, the possibilities are repeated over and over again as the player dies before the next checkpoint. But in multiplayer each death does not engender another possible world; it simply shows the player how bad he's doing relative to other players in the match. In Slayer, possible worlds come into play in the reiteration of the same level. That is, after one match ends, another one will begin with different players. Although the players are variable, we can still consider multiple iterations of the same level possible worlds. All the other variables are the same, from the physical setting to the possible weapons and items. (Of course, if you're playing Slayer with friends on split screen, then the players *are* the same.)

Scenario 4 above is likely familiar to any players of *Halo* multiplayer. While some of us might pride ourselves on skill, everyone has the occasional bad game, or games. Sometimes the possible worlds we create in multiplayer are all ones where THEPDIDDY1200 tramples us. This can make us as players very, very prone to emotion—particularly anger! Walk into a house where there's a *Halo* tournament going on and, if you stay long enough, you're bound to hear (repeatedly) the phrase scenario 4 ended with. *Halo* is intense, whether you're playing single player or multiplayer. But before getting further in our analysis of *Halo*'s ability to generate emotions, we need to talk a bit about Buddhism.

Upāya and the Parable of the Burning House

When your small child is watching his older sister play *Halo*, and he asks whether the violence on the screen happens in real life, what do you tell him? Well, on the one hand, the violence on the screen is clearly simulated, so you can tell the child that it's fake. But, on the other hand, the child did ask whether it happens in real life and, if history has taught us anything, violence *does* happen in real life. Humans kill other humans mercilessly. So what do you tell the child? Most parents would probably work out some compromise where they, in a nice way, tell the child something like this: "You see, son, violence does occur in real life, but it's not like the human vs. Covenant violence on the screen, and, in real life, violence only occurs because of bad people." Or, the parents would just lie.

The point is that sometimes it's necessary to withhold some or all of the truth from a child because the truth is often harsh, and telling it to a child at a young age might damage his perception of reality. This is why parents don't tell their child that Santa Claus doesn't exist until she's good and ready to hear it.

In Buddhism, there is something called "upāya." From Sanskrit, it roughly translates as "skillful means." One of the most common methods of getting this concept across is through the parable of the burning house from the Buddhist text *The Lotus Sutra*. This parable is the tale of a rich father who owns an old and decaying house filled with hundreds of people, including his sons. When a fire breaks out in the house the rich father thinks that he can escape to safety through the flaming gate, but his sons are inside playing games, completely unaware of the dire situation they are in. The father wonders how he's going to get his sons out. He first decides to yell to them to come out but the sons are absorbed in their games and won't listen. The father finally decides to employ some sort of skillful means to get his sons out of the house. He promises them goat-carts, deer-carts, and ox-carts if they leave. At this, the sons emerge from the house, demanding what was promised. But instead the rich man gives to each of his sons . . .

> a large carriage of uniform size and quality. The carriages were tall and spacious and adorned with numerous jewels. A railing ran all around them and bells hung from all four sides. A canopy was stretched over the top, which was also decorated with an assortment of precious jewels. . . . Each carriage was drawn by a white ox, pure and clean in hide, handsome in form and of great strength... At that time each of his sons mounted the large carriage, gaining something he had never had before, something he had originally never expected.[3]

The father employs skillful means in order to save his sons from burning to death. His sons are not coming out of that house, so the father engages in what some would call trickery. He promises his sons three kinds of carts to get their attention, then once they come outside to demand their carts, the father gives them an even greater gift: the large carriage. Plus, he has saved his sons from burning to death in the house. Trickery or not, the father's perceptive knowledge of the mental states of his sons, and his subsequent ability to get them out of the house, is itself a skill—skillful means, upāya.

---

[3] *The Lotus Sutra* (Columbia University Press, 1993), pp. 57–58.

This parable is a metaphor for the Buddha's relationship to all unenlightened beings. The Buddha is the father, trying to employ skillful means to bring his children (unenlightened beings) to enlightenment, to Buddhahood. But what is enlightenment? A difficult concept to get across, enlightenment is usually described as an eternal bliss or a state of mind brought on by a full understanding of illusions of the world around you.[4] The burning house can be seen as the Saha-world, or the world of illusion created by the human mind. We're hemmed in by this world of illusion we ourselves create, and the Buddha's path can lead us out of this illusion, like the father in the parable, using whatever means he can.

Can *Halo* be compared to the parable of the burning house? Is *Halo* upāyic? It might be illuminating to see how effectively we can create an analogy between *Halo* and the parable. While the analogy could never be perfect, it might help us understand *Halo*'s upāyic features. This requires an investigation into the game itself.

The Parable of the Burning *Halo*

The FPS games of the *Halo* series are videogames with two specific purposes: to defeat other players (in multiplayer) or to complete the storyline (in single player). *Halo* is a game of skill—a game of gradually increasing skill levels requiring fine-tuning. The more you play, the more you understand and appreciate subtle improvements in your ability, and the more you learn different strategies and how to implement them. In multiplayer, the game can be an intense duel between players or between teams of players. Each player's score (the number of wins and losses) is tallied and appears onscreen after fragging someone or getting fragged.

The parable described above involves a house filled with hundreds of people. Well, *Halo* is a videogame filled with hundreds of people, at least in online play (though not always all at once). So the game itself (the environment the avatars inhabit) metaphorically represents the burning house.

---

[4] It's possible that the promise of enlightenment itself is a form of skillful means (upāya). Perhaps such a blissful state does not really exist. However, for our purposes, moving closer and closer to such an ideal state might be a good thing in itself—and might itself count as enlightenment. A great king can still be great without attaining the status of *the greatest* king.

But there is a fine distinction to be made here. The avatars are not quite analogous to the sons inhabiting the burning house. Rather, the human beings controlling the avatars from their consoles are the sons, the sons in need of saving. The avatars are actually *Bodhisattvas*, a term we'll explain soon.

In the parable, the sons are promised goat-carts, deer-carts, and ox-carts if they leave the house. What is promised to the users of *Halo*? What is promised is the possibility of winning, mastering the game, whether it's in the form of being the best at multiplayer or finishing all *Halo* single player games on legendary difficulty. The many ways of possible mastery are analogous to the multiple carts promised to the sons. As we've seen, there are subtle increases in skill level a player of *Halo* must undergo. It's the possibility of full mastery of the game that is promised to the players of *Halo* (like being unbeatable on multiplayer), just as the various carts are promised to the sons in the parable.

Master Chief as Bodhisattva: More Buddhism

In Buddhism, a Bodhisattva is characterized by his or her motivation to lead others to enlightenment. A Bodhisattva seeks the enlightenment of all sentient beings, but has postponed her own enlightenment in order to help others reach it. And why should *Halo* gamers be exempt from the jurisdiction of a Bodhisattva? Gamers are, after all, sentient beings, and they need to be reached somehow. *The Lotus Sutra* makes it clear that *all* sentient beings have the capacity to realize enlightenment. What better way than through the assistance of the player's onscreen incarnation, the avatar?

But what's the nature of the relationship between player and avatar? This connection has been qualified in different ways by different theorists. Espen Aarseth suggests that "the user [player] assumes the role of the main character and, therefore, will not come to see this person as an other, or as a person at all, but rather as a remote-controlled extension of herself."[5] That the player will come to see the avatar as an other seems partly correct, but something's missing. The relationship seems more complicated. Bob Rehak sees the player's perception of the avatar as sliding between an intimate extension of self (when the user is playing well) to an

[5] Espen Aarseth, *Cybertext* (Johns Hopkins University Press, 1997), p. 113.

inferior other (when the user is playing poorly).[6] This characterization of the relationship is the one I find most accurate. *And it is the fact that this sliding of perceptions of the avatar is possible that makes the avatar a Bodhisattva.*

The player commonly goes back and forth between identifying with the avatar, Master Chief (or multiple avatars if he uses multiple videogames), and identifying with "who he is" in the real world (his ego). Maybe what the Bodhisattva avatar is trying to get the player to ask herself is "Who am I?" Maybe The Chief wants the player to have a crisis of identity, so to speak, because such a crisis will lead the player to see the true nature of her ego, which is empty in Buddhism.

The true nature of the ego is clarified by the Two-Fold Truth which says that there are two levels of truth, the conventional and the ultimate. At the conventional level of truth are seemingly solid objects like rocks and *Halo 3* game boxes. This is the level at which most of us ordinarily experience the world. At the ultimate level of truth, however, everything is interconnected and there are no true "rocks" or "egos." According to Buddhism, this interconnected level is the *true* state of things. By constantly sliding back and forth between identifying with an onscreen avatar and seeing it as an other, the player might eventually see the true nature of the ego as something that is necessary at the conventional level of truth but ultimately a delusion.

The player might begin to ask herself whether she is the avatar or her real world personality when she is playing as Master Chief. This question itself will open up other questions such as, "Who is my real world personality?" "Is the ego I project onto my avatar any more real than the ego I project onto my real world body?" By thinking and observing along these lines, the player will more easily see that her ego proper may be just as "virtual" as her avatar, and therefore illusory.

At least, we can guess in the context of the analogy, this is what the avatar Bodhisattva hopes to accomplish for the human player. *Master Chief is a Bodhisattva insofar as he represents an incarnation of the player's escape from delusion through the nature of the player's sliding perceptions of himself as the avatar.*

---

[6] Bob Rehak, "Playing at Being: Psychoanalysis and the Avatar," *The Video Game Theory Reader*, edited by Mark J.P. Wolf and Bernard Perron (Routledge, 2003).

The question might arise as to how agency could be imputed to an entity in a videogame. The answer is that Master Chief is a Bodhisattva in that he is that part of the player that the player wishes to become. Because the player is intimately connected with the Chief, the Bodhisattva part of the player is projected onto his avatar. Thus, Master Chief is a Bodhisattva, guiding the player from within (in the sense of being part of the player) and from without (in the sense of being an onscreen entity). So when I wrote above that Master Chief "wants" the player to have a crisis of identity, I meant that a certain part of the player's personality has this want. That is, the player himself has this want without knowing it.

But this is still only the beginning. Once the player sees that his ego is illusory, he still has a long way to go. He's by no means enlightened, nor is he necessarily on the road to enlightenment. He has not even escaped the house yet. But, at the point of true ego-understanding, he has another goal in view: full mastery of the game. This he sees as his ultimate goal at this point.

Whereas in the parable of the burning house the father guides his sons out of the house, the metaphor breaks down when we try to consider who the father would be in *Halo*. The game designers? The best player in the game? However, that the gamer is being guided out by a kick-ass avatar Bodhisattva (Master Chief) makes us wonder if he really can guide players to enlightenment. If players see full mastery of the game as their ultimate goal, once they reach that point, maybe they'll realize that there is something greater to be had outside the game, just as the children realize there is something greater to be had outside the burning house. This greater thing is Buddha Nature, the idea that every living being can reach enlightenment the way the Buddha did. Again, escaping the house is not itself enlightenment. It's only the first step. But it seems like a good thing if Master Chief can even lead them to this point, doesn't it?

The metaphor need not be perfect or exact to illustrate that *Halo* can have upāyic features. By taking a look at the concept of immersion, we can figure out what other upāyic features *Halo* might have.

Immersion, Anger, and Compassion

The first noble truth of Buddhism says that the condition of life is suffering, and the second says that we suffer due to our flaws and delusive thinking. One of the ways we suffer is because we get angry, so mitigating this anger is generally seen as a good thing in the eyes of Buddhism. Let's return to *Halo*'s ability to generate strong emotions in players due to the possible worlds it engenders. This possible worlds/infinite lives scenario can also lead to a strong sense of *immersion* in the game. *Halo* immerses you in the action; you as a player are intimately connected to the gameworld.

Immersion is a well-known phenomenon in videogames. In fact, strong immersion is often cited as the reason why violent videogames are so bad for the youth. If an eight-year-old child kills a Grunt while totally immersed in *Halo: Combat Evolved*, who's to say that that sort of action will not translate to real life? If the child sees the Grunt's life in the game as inconsequential, won't he see life in reality as inconsequential also?

While these are legitimate concerns about videogames, they underscore the fact that people are capable of getting mentally, emotionally, and even physically immersed in videogames (just watch the way someone playing a racing game physically turns their body with every corner they turn onscreen). In the case of the child actually being led to devalue life in general, the immersion clearly leads to a negative outcome. But what if a person's capacity for immersion could be used in a positive way? It seems to be that immersion itself is not a bad thing; like many other things, it is the way immersion is used that is important. One example of a positive use of immersion is Dr. Albert Rizzo's company *Virtually Better* which modified the Xbox game *Full Spectrum Warrior* to create a strong sense of place to help victims of PTSD.[7]

Now, I have discussed the gradual skill level increases necessary to succeed at *Halo*. When you first start *Halo*, this can be very, very frustrating, particularly if you haven't played any other FPS. You can barely figure out how to switch weapons and you have to compete against more experienced players who will not only kill you, but dance around on your avatar's corpse. It's like being a beginning guitar player who is expected to compete with Eric Clapton: it's demoralizing and seems impossible.

Even worse, because you're connected with Master Chief, you are emotionally and mentally invested. Thus every time you lose a duel you can potentially take it personally. Especially when very

[7] As discussed in: Amanda Schaffer, "Not a Game: Simulation to Lessen War Trauma," *New York Times* (August 2007).

nasty, experienced players have poignant things to say over chat like "You suck." In short, at the beginning (and even later too), *Halo* really, really, really makes you mad. As an undergrad, several of my friends were *Halo* players, one of whom had one of the most laid back temperaments of anyone I know to this day. But when he played *Halo* for even fifteen or twenty minutes, he would come away swearing. This anger may be due to many factors in the game and out; but two of the strongest factors with reference to *Halo* are the possible worlds scenario and the immersion, which complement each other.

The beautiful thing about *Halo* is that, once you understand the game itself as provisional—say, after listening to the message of the avatar Bodhisattva (listening to yourself) and understanding the illusive nature of the ego, then mastering the game itself—you can begin to understand your emotional involvement with the gameworld. If the player learns to anticipate this emotional involvement (with anger, for example) then she can begin to work on mitigating it. The player gets to the point where the anger can *almost* be quantified: once a certain event occurs in the game *the player knows how angry it will make her*. If she recognizes it at the right point, she can stop her anger, stop her suffering.

The Dalai Lama, the Buddhist leader of Tibet, discusses the idea that our enemies represent the greatest opportunity for personal growth:

> If we investigate on a still deeper level, we will find that when enemies inflict harm on us, we can actually feel gratitude toward them . . . in order to practice sincerely and to develop patience, you need someone who willfully hurts you. . . . They [enemies] are testing our inner strength in a way that even a guru cannot. Even the Buddha possesses no such potential.[8]

Although this is a quite complex idea in Buddhism involving the development of altruism in the practitioner, the essential point in the Dalai Lama's words is clear enough: our enemies give us an opportunity to develop patience and inner strength—because they make us so angry! The Buddha cannot hate us and behave maliciously toward us the ways that an enemy can. The presence of an enemy with malicious intent can really test our resolve.

---

[8] The Dalai Lama, *The World of Tibetan Buddhism* (Wisdom, 1995), pp. 81–82.

Now, you might be thinking, "Feel gratitude toward the little seven-year-old fuck who pwns me again and again while calling me fuckface?" And the answer is yes, feel gratitude toward even him for providing you with such a great means of improving yourself. It just depends on your motivation: do you want to improve yourself and become a more compassionate and resolute person, or do you want to continue to let seven-year-old fucks get to you?

The Lotus Sutra discusses Devadatta, someone who attempted to kill the Buddha several times. Nevertheless, the Buddha says: "The fact that I have attained impartial and correct enlightenment and can save living beings on a broad scale is all due to Devadatta" (Lotus Sutra, p. 184). Despite Devadatta's malice, the Buddha was able to not only to extend compassion toward him but also to grow and attain enlightenment.

Halo can behave in a similar way. The game gives us the opportunity to deal with hate and anger directly, and we can watch the occurrence of the entire process. By remaining conscious of the process, rather than the process occurring spontaneously as in a heated marital debate, we are better able to control it. (I'm discussing the use of *Halo* after we have acknowledged the possibility of his enlightenment, after we have been shown the light by the Bodhisattva Master Chief and escaped the metaphorical burning house.)

Something else is brought on by the possible worlds/infinite lives scenario in *Halo*: repetition. When you can't beat a checkpoint, but you really want to, what happens? You do it over, and over, and over, until you get it. In Chapter 6 of *The Lotus Sutra*, the Buddha gives predictions for Buddhahood to a few members of the people at an assembly. In each prediction, the Buddha essentially says the same thing, only changing his words slightly. A reader unfamiliar with the Buddhist tradition might wonder why he seems to be reading the same thing over and over. As a Buddhist scholar explains:

> Repetition has a very important function in religious life. To do something repeatedly makes a deep impression on our minds. . . . Anyone who tries repeating Chapter 6 [of *The Lotus Sutra*] with his whole heart will find himself repeating the description of man's ideal state. . . . Through frequent repetition these ideals will penetrate the depths of his mind . . . when it comes to Buddhist practice, we must not shirk repeating everything exactly. Unless one repeats the same thing

> wholeheartedly as often as possible in studying music or in practicing basketball, he will never improve.[10]

Repetition is very important in Buddhism—and other religions for that matter—in coming to a deeper understanding of certain core principles. The importance of repetition also exists in *Halo*. A player does not gradually improve in skill level (or advance to the next checkpoint) unless she practices over and over again, sometimes monotonously.

The importance of repetition in *Halo* is germane to the above discussion of immersion. I contend that, with the assistance of the strong immersion factor in *Halo*, one could potentially mitigate anger and begin to grow compassion. One of the things that allows this to happen is the already existing repetitive nature of the game, the importance of which is to improve one's skill level. But if this tendency to repetition were redirected, say, toward mitigating anger and growing compassion, *Halo*, or similar game, could be used in a very beneficial way.

Halo as a Catalyst for a Buddhism Videogame?

Probably the main objection to seeing *Halo* as upāya is the violence. *Halo* is certainly a violent series of games. But what if the violence is actually necessary? What if the violence itself is upāya in that it appeals to a certain types of living creatures who otherwise could not be reached? Namely, people who like to play violent videogames. If the Buddha indirectly created a *Hello Kitty* videogame (which exists, by the way) it might reach some, but it would not reach those people who want to level a Rocket Launcher at *Hello Kitty* stuffed animals.

But *Halo* is about defeating other players or enemies through skill as much as it's about violence. A monk and poet, Master Kyunyo, discussed the idea that people need to be led to the teachings of Buddhism from a base that is comprehensible to them. He wrote poems designed to cater to a popular audience with the intention of reaching as many people as possible. I might say a similar thing about *Halo*. That some may laugh at the idea of something like a videogame being at all useful for enlightenment is

---

[10] Nikkyō Niwano, *Buddhism for Today: A Modern Interpretation of the Threefold Lotus Sutra* (Kosei, 1976), pp. 90–91.

beside the point. What's important is whether or not people can benefit from it.

Even if you, as a reader, disagree with the specific analysis of *Halo* here, consider the following. What about an enlightenment-oriented videogame in general, maybe using some of *Halo*'s game mechanics as a guide? I can see the Xbox game already: The Dalai Lama's smiling face is on the cover and it is called "Enlighten Yourself," boasting full enlightenment in just under thirty hours of game play! Okay, so maybe that's not the way it should happen. Maybe it should be an expansion for *Halo: Reach*.

Heroic

9
Apocalypse *Halo*

RACHEL WAGNER, TYLER DEHAVEN, and
CHRIS HENDRICKSON

The close relationship between games and religion is nothing new. Game designer Marc LeBlanc reports that players of the ancient Egyptian game *Senet* believed that the game was a sort of divinization oracle that foretold afterlife experiences.[1] In his landmark study *Homo Ludens* (1938), Johan Huizinga also sees an intimate relationship between games and religion. He describes the "magic circle" of play as being "marked off beforehand" just as space is marked off for religious ritual:

> The arena, the card-table, the magic circle, the temple, the stage, the screen, the tennis court, the court of justice, etc. are all in form and function play-grounds, i.e. forbidden spots, isolated, hedged round, hallowed, within which special rules obtain. (p. 10)

All of these "magic circles," he says, are "temporary worlds within the ordinary world, dedicated to the performance of an act apart." Gameplay, then, has rich religious overtones. The *Halo* universe is a perfect example of a magic circle in its elaborate development of an otherworldly experience, drawing players into a visionary journey that invites their full imaginative participation.

Videogames, especially First Person Shooters (FPSs), also resemble a very specific religious form of the magic circle: apocalypses. The adjective "apocalyptic" as commonly used today typically

---

[1] "Tools for Creating Dramatic Game Dynamics," in Katie Salen and Eric Zimmerman, eds., *The Game Design Reader: A Rules of Play Anthology* (MIT Press, 2006), p. 439.

refers to cataclysmic imagery and predictions of the end times. However, the word "apocalypse" has a more specific usage for biblical scholars, identifying a genre of ancient Jewish and Christian texts composed between about 300 B.C.E. and 200 C.E. in the ancient Mediterranean region. These apocalypses exhibit fixed forms and structures, describe events of the end times, adhere to predictable literary patterns, and deal with recurring themes. They also describe otherworldly journeys of visionaries who observe the coming end times and God's violent imminent judgment against evil.

Despite being created some two thousand years after these Jewish and Christian apocalypses, *Halo* fits the definition of apocalypse as articulated by the Society of Biblical Literature Apocalypse Group in 1979:

> An apocalypse is a genre of revelatory literature with a narrative framework in which a revelation is mediated by an otherworldly being to a human recipient, disclosing a transcendent reality which is both temporal, insofar as it envisages eschatological salvation, and spatial, insofar as it involves another, supernatural world.[2]

The *Halo* mythos is rife with apocalyptic imagery and exhibits a *narrative* inevitability that shares features with the notion of *theological* inevitability in traditional apocalypses. Indeed, the formal similarity between *Halo* and traditional apocalypses is remarkable, even if these two end-of-the-world forms appear to be serving different functions for the communities who value them.

God the Programmer

Videogames, like traditional apocalypses, can be viewed as "revelatory literature" with a "narrative framework" about an "otherworldly" location. This framework involves a human recipient and an otherworldly mediator who describes "eschatological salvation" which is located in the future and presents "otherworldly realities" (p. 9). Videogames like *Halo* are similarly structured according to a narrative framework, and invite players to actively enter into a "world" accessible to the player only through the

---

[2] John J. Collins, "Introduction: Towards the Morphology of a Genre," *Semeia* 14:1 (1979), p. 9.

medium of the videogame console. In fact, videogames typically thrive on the imaginative creation of fantasy environments within which players can "really" move and act, and in which they learn about the otherworld.

One of the most important features of ancient apocalypses is their determinism. Apocalypses presuppose history's unfolding as pre-established by God, who could be seen in this case as a sort of cosmic software engineer. Collins argues in *The Apocalyptic Imagination* (Eerdmans, 1998), that apocalypses are "augmented" by "a sense of determinism . . . by affirming that the course of history or the structure of the cosmos was determined long ago" (p. 40). We see this idea portrayed in *Halo* in the device of the Portal, which resides on Earth (and thus is accessible to humans but not to the Covenant). The Portal leads directly to the Ark, in which resides the nerve center of the entire *Halo* array. In this sense, then, humans (and especially Master Chief) appear to be chosen by the Forerunners in antiquity for events that unfold within the game. Humans, it seems, were meant to enact the divine purposes of the Forerunners. They also enact the purposes of the software engineers of *Halo*, who have predetermined to some extent the myth's interactive unfolding in gameplay.

Apocalypses, then, exhibit a sort of theologically-motivated narrative rhetoric. If we think of God as a programmer, then we could say that God has engineered the set of player choices we have as humans, with history revealing the unfolding of his design. Such a sense of predetermination is comforting to the hearers of apocalypses. In videogame theory, this notion is called "procedural rhetoric." In *Persuasive Games* (2007), game theorist Ian Bogost defines procedural rhetoric as those processes that "define the way things work: the methods, techniques, and logics that drive the operation of systems" (p. 3). Bogost convincingly argues that procedural rhetorical claims are "every bit as logical as verbal arguments—in fact, internal consistency is often assured in computational arguments, since microprocessors and not human agents are in charge of their consistent execution" (p. 36). This kind of assurance is akin to the apocalyptic rhetoric of God's certain judgment, his divine procedural rhetoric.

Procedural rhetoric works by creating what Bogost calls "possibility space," which is "the myriad configurations the player might construct to see the ways the processes inscribed in the system work" (p. 42). This sense of "possibility space" could be considered a sort of "covenant" with the player—he or she has agreed to abide by the rules of play and in so doing, has entered into a set of possibilities that are transcribed by the parameters of the game before it even begins. Theological perspectives also demarcate a "possibility space" for believers, who see the world and act in it according to the procedural rhetoric of the belief system.

Games even exhibit the dualism of apocalypses in that both exhibit a marked concern with forces of good arrayed against forces of evil, usually with the assumption of a procedural rhetoric of victory for the forces of good. In *Halo*, human forces oppose the forces of the "Flood," a huge collection of parasites that collectively consume sentient life with sufficient biomass to sustain them. The Flood is a socialist society in which there is no pain, no hunger, and many of life's problems appear to be solved. Unfortunately, the Flood's success is also grounded in the brutal murder of other beings. When viewed as a force of evil, the Flood in *Halo* may be read as a metaphor for unsustainable and rampant contemporary consumerism.

The Flood's uncontrollable exploitation of sentient life can be interpreted as a scathing criticism of industrial greed that heedlessly dominates life for its sole benefit. In this way, then, players are invited to see *themselves* arrayed against the forces of consumerism, as they battle the Flood's literal "consumption" of other living entities in *Halo* and as they return to their own lived daily lives. This kind of metaphorical allusion to contemporary social ills is also a common feature of ancient Jewish and Christian apocalypses, which regularly targeted oppressive regimes like Rome via rich symbolic imagery of beastly and destructive creatures.

Initial contact with the Flood is treated by the Forerunners as a disease instead of a military threat, a mistake that increasingly becomes evident. Once the Forerunners commit to fighting the Flood, they realize that traditional military and naval tactics will not apply. The Flood has, by this time already consumed several cities. Thus, the Forerunners begin to gather and preserve life in a particular place, an installation they call "The Ark." Within it, they deposit life forms as actual creatures or as stored DNA. This sets the stage for the internal dualism of the game: the forces of "good," symbolized by the Forerunners and their human descendants versus the forces of "evil," symbolized by the Flood, analogous to demonic forces in their parasitic consumption of the life-force of others. In both *Halo* and in traditional apocalypses, people enter into the magic circle already convinced that evil will ultimately be defeated and good will win out. In most apocalypses, God and his messianic agents enact this unfolding of history. In videogames, the player serves a messianic function.

Apocalypses, then, could be said to exhibit God's "procedural rhetoric" in their narrative description of the unfolding of history in a way that God has designated, with a certain amount of human "play" within the rules. Videogames are similarly delimited by fixed narrative modes which nonetheless also allow a certain degree of interactivity. But videogames snugly fit within a fixed magic circle of play believed by their users to be fully insulated from the real day-to-day world. Traditional religious apocalypses, by depicting the cosmos as subject to God's rules and shaped by God's own predetermined design, can be viewed as the *ultimate* game, shaped by the *ultimate* procedural rhetoric.

The *Halo* Mythos

Halo's narrative is rife with explicit religious imagery, much of it overtly apocalyptic. Like many traditional Jewish and Christian apocalypses, *Halo* exhibits an interest in both time and space, what scholars of apocalypticism describe as "a temporal and a spatial axis."[3] For traditional apocalypses, the *temporal* axis is revealed in an intense interest in history unfolding: how it began, where humans fit in, and what is to happen in the end times, which the authors believe will take place very soon. The *spatial* axis involves a recurring motif of travel to other worlds, in which visionaries are privy to experiences unavailable to normal human beings. In *Halo*, the player takes on the role of visionary.

The Covenant is comprised of a group of races who together want to "ignite" the "Sacred Rings." In so doing, they will follow the Forerunners (a race of beings who existed thousands of years before *Halo*) into divinity. The Forerunners' eons-old civilization was based on the idea of the "Mantle," alluding to biblical prophetic notions of the prophetic mantle which commits one to a life dedicated to social justice in the name of God. The Forerunners saw it as their sworn duty to protect and perpetuate life in the *Halo* galaxy, which is also understood as our own galaxy a few hundred years from now. Thus, as players we are drawn into the mythos of

[3] John J. Collins, "The Jewish Apocalypses." *Semeia* 14:1 (1979), p. 25.

Halo and invited to see it as our own. The Forerunners successfully protected life in the galaxy until the invasion by the Flood. This could be an allusion to the biblical stories about life before Noah (and thus before the biblical flood). In both cases, Forerunners (or biblical forefathers) were originally dedicated to the maintenance of creation. In *Halo*, the appearance of the Flood event kicks off the story that unfolds in the games.

The Forerunners create installations called "rings" across the galaxy. These are the first "Halos," a last-resort weapon intended to destroy potential host biomass and thereby destroy the Flood by starving it. As the war with the Flood continued to devolve into chaos for the Forerunners, they gathered themselves together and ignited the Halos, obliterating all sentient life (including many of their own life forms) within three galactic radii of the center of the galaxy, while preserving survivors as remnants in the Ark. This effectively contains the Flood for the time being. The Forerunners, however, kept samples of the Flood alive for research purposes—a move that was later seen to be a terrible mistake. It's not difficult to see analogies to the biblical story of Noah here, as in that case too survivors are gathered into a single stronghold to withstand the onslaught of a flood that destroys all other life.

After the rings are ignited as Halos, the surviving Forerunners disperse life via the use of mechanical drones equipped with the DNA of life forms and the materials needed to reseed life. These drones are dispatched to protected worlds that the Flood cannot access, creating new small pockets of life. After this, the Forerunners leave the galaxy completely. Perhaps this was a move of self-preservation: if the Halos had to be reignited, the Forerunners would be out of the blast radius. Millennia pass.

At this point our own history is integrated into the *Halo* mythology. Hundreds of years in the future from our present time, *Halo* depicts humankind as spreading across space and colonizing various worlds, a movement that echoes the biblical accounts of the spread of ancient Israelite tribes throughout Canaanite territory as they similarly establish settlements and with God's sanction destroy those who resist them. The primary governmental force in *Halo* is the UNSC (United Naval Space Command). As humans colonize, they repeatedly encounter resistance, leading the UNSC to supersede local authority and, like the ancient Israelites, kill insurrectionists if necessary. Successful human colonization comes to a halt when humans encounter the Covenant at "The Harvest," a colony that humans had previously taken over. In response, the Covenant obliterates the human inhabitants there and proceeds to destroy additional human settlements. When game-time of *Halo* initializes, the Covenant has already destroyed all human colonies outside of Earth. The secret of Earth's location is closely protected by the Cole Protocol, a defense system which works for some twenty-seven years. In 2552, Earth is discovered.

The Covenant worships the Forerunners as gods. The "covenant" they make is to ignite the rings (Halos), which the Covenant believes will set off a "Great Journey" to being divine. However, the rings were in fact created to annihilate life, a notion that the Covenant denies in their arrogant hopes for divinity. This kind of hubris obviously echoes the story of the Tower of Babel in Genesis, in which humans build a structure that they believe will enable them to reach the heavens and become god-like in so doing (Genesis 11). Humanity understands that igniting the rings would actually enact an apocalyptic destruction, and thus one of the game's primary themes comes into focus: modern secularism vs. blind religion. The Covenant represents blind religion with their actions and hopes, while humanity accentuates the merits of modern secularism. In this way, the dualism of *Halo* contrasts with the dualism of typical Jewish and Christian apocalypses, which celebrate a monotheistic worldview against all others.

So why does the Covenant hate humanity enough to wish to annihilate them? Humanity, as revealed by the Robots (Sentinels and Oracles) created by the Forerunners, is actually descended from the Forerunners. Humans are viewed as heretical for their embrace of the concept of modern secularism, a crime viewed as all the more heinous for their divine origins. The Covenant, not descended from the Forerunners but worshipping them, want to destroy humanity because humanity's divine ancestry could enable them to supersede and undermine the power exercised over the Covenant by the Covenant's leaders, the Prophets (leaders of all the races of the Covenant).

Havoc on the Earth

This situation sounds remarkably like the situation described in a little-known version of the biblical flood mythology. Fragments of the story appear in the Genesis account, but are fleshed out in the *Book of Enoch*, an ancient Jewish apocalypse with narrative layers as old as 300 B.C.E. One of these oldest sections is called *The Book of the Watchers*, and relays the experiences of the visionary Enoch, the great grandfather of Noah. From an angel, Enoch learns the story of angels who descend to Earth, teach humans about technology, weaponry, and herb healing, then mate with human women and give birth to "Watchers," or giants who themselves want only to consume human resources, eventually devolving into cannibalism. It is Enoch's job to petition to God for the Watchers' forgiveness, a task that he fulfills but which does not result in success for the Watchers, who are then judged and destroyed by God. This little known variant of the reason for the biblical flood likely lies behind Genesis 6 and the "sons of God" who mate with "daughters of men" and give birth to the "Nephilim," the "mighty men that were of old, the men of renown" (Genesis 6:1–4).

The flood in Genesis can then be read as God's solution to the problem of the Nephilim, creatures that are part divine and part human, much like the humans in *Halo*. However, in *Halo* the Covenant represents the consuming force, whereas in Genesis it is the divine-human entities, the Nephilim, who wreak havoc on the Earth. Thus, the *Halo* mythology borrows from but problematizes the Enoch account, suggesting that consumerism itself is the enemy, and that humans have the ability to stop it, albeit by violent means. *Halo*'s revisions also deny that any supernatural force can rectify the problem of the Flood and instead identify the Flood as its own sentient force, implicitly suggesting that *any* entity causing such destruction should not be worshipped but be utterly destroyed. This reading suggests an indirect but powerful critique of traditional theology, suggesting that the biblical flood was a brutal force enacted by a vicious God.

The sinister association of biblical divine forces with the evil forces in *Halo* continues in the game's depiction of the "Prophets" as agents of the Covenant who seek to destroy humanity out of fear of sublimation of their own power and beliefs. Ironically, only humans in *Halo* can activate Forerunner technology, while those with a sacred "Covenant" find themselves helpless. This is the point at which the games situate us: humanity is on the brink of destruction. The Covenant's threat is real and dedicated. The Covenant has obliterated every other human colony besides Earth. Without help, humans will surely be destroyed. The game unfolds with the player taking on a messianic role within the *Halo* universe, seeking to use a combination of skill and nerve (and weaponry, of course) to lead a force against the Covenant as they descend upon Earth. The Master Chief leads a force defending the planet and chases the Covenant off the planet and back to the Ark.

Apocalyptic Themes in *Halo*

Apocalyptic literature flourished during the two centuries before the Common Era and the two centuries after. This era was popular for apocalyptic literature for a reason: the peoples who produced it felt oppressed by their Greek and Roman overlords and sought a means of coping with their inability to prevent their own persecution. For some, writing and telling stories about the destruction of their enemies helped them to deal with an intolerable situation by enabling them to imagine God's imminent intervention. Accordingly, Christian and Jewish apocalypses from this period describe the hope for a divinely-ordained messiah to intervene and defeat their enemies and predictions of divine judgment to come against their persecutors (as well as vivid images of the punishment to be eked out by God against their enemies).

As the Society of Biblical Literature definition of apocalypse indicates, the hope for this judgment is typically relayed in the form of a vision mediated by an otherworldly mediator and depicting an otherworldly journey in which the visionary sees the future and possibly also the places of reward and punishment to come. Because the authors of these visions hoped for divine intervention very soon, there is typically also an intense interest in relaying of events of the coming end times. Visionaries often identify themselves with ancient religious figures to lend credibility to their experiences.

Master Chief the Messiah

The religious allusions in *Halo* are reinforced by the player's role as a messianic agent of deliverance. In the beginning of the third game as Master Chief is falling to the Earth, Cortana says:

> They let me pick. Did I ever tell you that? Choose whichever Spartan I wanted. You know me. I did my research. Watched as you became the soldier we needed you to be. Like the others, you were strong and swift and brave. A natural leader. But you had something they didn't. Something no one saw, but me. Can you guess? Luck. Was I wrong?

Cortana's choice is an indication of the special qualities that make up the figure who is to become known as Master Chief, Spartan 2, and John-117.

John-117 fits the mold of what biblical scholars call the "Davidic messiah." Based on the much-admired rule of King David, Jews writing apocalyptic literature some one thousand years after David's reign hoped for another ruler like him, an "Anointed One" or king who would reunite the kingdom of Israel and free them from oppressors. Some of the most poignant celebrations of the hoped-for David messiah appear in the prophetic oracles of Isaiah (7–11) and in the Psalms (2, 45, 89). As a type of Davidic messiah, John-117 is known as the "Master Chief" because he is the head of the Spartans, responsible for putting down the insurrections in the colonies and fighting against the Covenant. And like King David, he is responsible for uniting the colonies and maintaining order. The Davidic messiah is alluded to repeatedly in Jewish and Christian apocalyptic literature as a figure expected to return in the end times and destroy Israel's oppressors. Master Chief is the hoped-for deliverer of the Humans in *Halo*.

Master Chief was born with the name of "John" on Eridanus II in 2511. As a young boy, he was kidnapped by Dr. Katherine Halsey and inducted into the Spartan II training program. Master Chief receives the designation "117" when he arrives at the Reach Colony for training. The title "John-117" seems to be evocative of biblical passages from the Gospel of John. If read as John 1:17, the name evokes a passage regarding Jesus's relationship to Moses: "For the law was given through Moses; grace and truth came through Jesus Christ." This passage could be read as alluding to Master Chief as the bringer of "grace and truth" and the freer from the law of the "Covenant." This reading is evocative if also deeply problematic in its suggestion that the Jewish covenant associated with Moses, like the Covenant in *Halo*, is a consuming force to be resisted and destroyed. It is also possible to read the name as referring to John 1:1-7.

This reading is much more suggestive and rich since it explicitly associates Master Chief with the disciple John and suggests the crucial role of both figures as witnesses to coming salvation. The most poignant verses suggest John's divine purpose:

> There was a man sent from God, whose name was John. He came for testimony, to bear witness to the light, that all might believe through him. (John 1:6-7)

The passages preceding allude to Christ as the "Logos," the word of God that is made manifest in the world as the principle by which God created the universe. To associate Master Chief with the appearance of cosmic light through these allusions to John's gospel show John-117 as a keeper of divine forces, one worthy to serve as steward of the Rings in the *Halo* mythos.

In his childhood training, John-117 is quickly noticed for several unique traits, including his preternatural ability to predict on which side a coin will land. He is a natural leader, has great luck, intense determination, and refuses to give up on any struggle. These qualities are enhanced by obvious physical strength which is augmented further by the "Spartan II Augmentation Procedures." He becomes swifter and his height is enhanced, making him effectively a "giant," perhaps another allusion to the "giants" or "watchmen" in the Book of Enoch, and hinting at John's character as both human and divine. Master Chief, then, is a savior, a messiah, and a giant.

The role of the Arbiter carries the stigma of both heretic and messiah in the *Halo* universe. This tradition began when the original Arbiter observed that the Prophets' Covenant was established for control over his planet and people. The Arbiter acted against the Covenant, and the Prophets decided that his punishment would extend past his death. Since then, the rank had been given to a disgraced commander as a way to atone for his failures.

In *Halo 2*, the player enacts the Arbiter as he seeks redemption for his failure to kill the Master Chief. The Arbiter eventually learns of the greater threat presented by the Prophets, as well as the Flood, and chooses to side with humanity. He fulfills the definition of an arbiter, a judge who impartially decides or resolves a controversy, as well the function of a co-messiah alongside the Master Chief.

Judgment of the Players

In traditional apocalypses, visionaries look forward to rewards for the faithful and punishment for the wicked as enacted by God. The visionary simply watches, delivers information, visits places, and shares insights. The real action is performed by God and his messianic agents, which in Christian apocalypses also sometimes include Jesus as a sword-wielding, fire-breathing entity, and in Jewish apocalypses may include military leaders on the model of King David, prophetic leaders, or even priestly figures who enact divine purification. As Michael Stone notes in *Jewish Writings of the*

Second Temple Period (Fortress Press, 1984), although apocalypses are generally driven by an expectation of the end times and judgment, "the advent of the end *does not depend* upon human action" (p. 383). Collins agrees, arguing in *Encounters with Biblical Theology* (Fortress Press, 2005) that "The great majority of Jewish apocalypses are quietist in the sense that the world will be changed by divine intervention rather than by human action" (p. 137).

The occasional apocalypse does depict human beings enacting judgment under God's guidance, but it is quite rare. Furthermore, in all traditional apocalypses, *God* not humans is in control of salvation, and will intervene to end his people's suffering by destroying their enemies. In videogames, agency in salvation is not situated with God but squarely with the player, who may rely upon guides for assistance but ultimately enacts salvation by himself or herself, often in dramatically violent form. Even in *Left Behind: Eternal Forces* (2006), a videogame with the larger assumption of God in charge, it is up to humans to enact God's will on Earth. There are no supernatural agents to assist.

The player's role as agent of deliverance is even more evident in FPSs like *Halo*, in which the player identifies as a messianic character in a virtual world of secularized dualisms, single-handedly saving humanity through the brutal destruction of its enemies. In *Halo*, the Master Chief plays an important role in the enactment, or prevention of enactment, of the rings. In game one, he prevents the firing of the ring. In *Halo 2*, the player plays as the Arbiter (an important figure in the Covenant leadership), and must kill Tartarus to prevent him setting off the ring. In game three, the player again takes on the role of Master Chief, this time igniting the ring in order to destroy the Flood infestation, thereby saving the galaxy. Of course, gameplay throughout involves the player fighting enemies by using weapons (Battle Rifles, shotguns, Rocket Launchers, Plasma Grenades) and operating artillery vehicles (scorpion tanks, all-terrain jeep-like vehicles called "warthogs," and hovercraft like the "hornet").

Indeed, Master Chief is defined by his ability to effectively and efficiently use any kind of weapon with finesse, adding to his messianic function. The Forerunners and Cortana also serve as sorts of "supernatural agents," but they are very limited in their ability to help the Master Chief. The Forerunners play no direct role in the game's immediate unfolding apart from forces set in motion long before humans ever appeared on the scene. As in *Halo*, all FPSs celebrate the use of weaponry as a means of defeat of enemies; it's part of the genre. However, the role of the player as agent of deliverance marks these new contemporary apocalypses as concerned with humanity's own role in saving itself.

Otherworldly Mediators

Otherworldly mediators are a familiar feature in apocalypses, escorting the visionaries through what might otherwise be treacherous otherworldly terrain, interpreting for them what they see, and reassuring them about God's purposes. In the *Book of the Watchers* (Enoch 1–36), in 3 Baruch, and in 4 Ezra, a seer acquires privileged heavenly knowledge through questions asked of an otherworldly mediator. The visions and information gained in these heavenly tours is then kept as a secret by the visionary, who relays this secret information in the apocalyptic text he writes down for posterity.

In *Halo*, players are aided by Cortana, an artificially intelligent computer who explains the backstory and strategies appropriate for the player as he or she assumes the role of the Master Chief. Cortana is modeled on the doctor who was the original head of the Spartan 2 project, responsible for the genetic development of the Master Chief (the player's role). She has no physical form, but portrays herself holographically. Cortana teaches players how to move around and how to use programs for targeting. Cortana also reveals information about the rings several times throughout the games because she is uploaded into the rings' network. Cortana serves several critical functions; she can act as a tactical navigator in unfamiliar areas, hack encrypted enemy communications networks, and generally keep the player informed about what to do and where to go.

In the *Halo* books, Cortana reveals to the reader secret information in the form of the personal history of John-117, the Master Chief. In a sense, then, the *Halo* books themselves can be seen as a sort of apocalyptic text, offering secret insights unavailable to the player in the games alone. Another way in which secret information appears in the game is in the form of objects like the thirteen "hidden skulls" in *Halo 3*, a collection of secrets in the game which, when discovered, affect gameplay in sometimes unpredictable ways, as in the removal of the HUD (heads-up display) on the screen. These objects unlock achievements and generally make gameplay more difficult, creating prestige for players and amassing points for them in ways that raise their status among their real life peers.

The entity 343 Guilty Spark also acts as an otherworldly guide in *Halo*, answering questions from Master Chief, Cortana, and the Arbiter about the Halos' true purpose. Guilty Spark, referred to as an "Oracle" by the Covenant, is a floating Forerunner construct designed to guide any human to activate the Halos. Guilty Spark assumes that the Reclaimer (its name for the current human trying to activate the Halos) already knows the Halos' purpose, and will dutifully carry out their deadly activation. Guilty Spark also knows the Forerunner's secrets, and Cortana learns these when she is inserted into the control room's mainframe.

These technological mediators call attention to an important distinction between traditional Jewish and Christian apocalypses and *Halo* as an apocalyptic videogame. In *Halo*, artificial intelligence—not an angel—tells us how to navigate the new worlds in which we find ourselves. Players of *Halo* realize that the universe the games depict is fictional. Nonetheless, societal warnings about the dangerous future of an unthinking hyper-technologized world may have real merit, especially as we watch the devastating effects of the BP oil spill in the Gulf Coast. Perhaps *Halo*'s handling of artificial intelligence shows that today we more commonly associate the idea of revelation with technology than with divine forces. Yet still we're fascinated with stories about saviors, especially interactive stories in which we get to *be* saviors. Perhaps it's a truism to suggest that we need not believe in God in order to long for understanding of the human situation. And it may be easier today to imagine wisdom coming from technological sources than divine ones. One might even say that *Halo* suggests that our belief in the divine is in some ways being implanted by our "faith" in technology.

Otherworldly Journeys

As John J. Collins explains, an "otherworldly journey" in traditional apocalypses takes place "when the visionary travels through heaven, hell or remote regions beyond the normally accessible world." Revelation, he says, "is usually predominantly visual," a claim that is all the more interesting for the importance of vivid graphics in contemporary videogames.[4] Also like in videogames,

[4] John J. Collins, "Introduction: Towards the Morphology of a Genre," *Semeia* 14:1 (1979), p. 6.

traditional apocalypticists depict the otherworldly realm as a place that can be entered into as a "temporary world" formally distinguished from surrounding space and time.

Take, for example, Enoch's description of his ascent into the heavens, described in terms that sound remarkably like the design for their own videogame:

> the vision clouds invited me and a mist summoned me, and the course of the stars and the lightnings sped and hastened me, and the winds in the vision caused me to fly and lifted me upward, and bore me into heaven.

In heaven, Enoch sees "a wall which is built of crystals and surrounded by tongues of fire" and "a tesselated floor (made) of crystals." On the ceiling, he sees "fiery cherubim" (I Enoch 14). Later, an angel gives Enoch a tour of otherworldly locations, including the "firmament of heaven," a "region at the end of the great Earth" and a "deep abyss" filled with fire. The angel with him explains to him the meaning of the vision, and its relationship to God's purposes in the coming end times (I Enoch 18). As Collins notes, in apocalypses "heavenly geography" of this sort is typically described in vivid detail, relating it to beliefs about God's order and power over creation (Collins "Introduction," p. 9).

What Collins calls "heavenly geography" appears often in *Halo*, in the lush and varied geography of the rings, a few of which Master Chief visits. In addition, if you play the third game of *Halo* on the most difficult "legendary" setting, you see Master Chief at the end of the game stuck in half of the ship, the only bit remaining after a cataclysmic explosion. If you win the game, it ends with a vision of the ship descending to a planet infused with symbols that the astute player will recognize as associated with the Forerunners, implying a sort of return to divine origins. Thus, the trope of journeys to otherworldly places is a core feature of *Halo* play, inviting the player to see himself or herself as a visionary traveling around the *Halo* universe, gathering important information, completing crucial tasks, and defeating enemies. Some people even view the virtual world *itself* as a glimpse into a world or "reality" not limited in the same way as our physical world: a place where bodies do not decay, where fantasies can be fulfilled, where our actions have deep and meaningful impact. The player in this case *is* the apocalyptic visionary.

The End Times

Videogames are "temporal" in their explicit division of gameplay into levels and time-limits, mimicking those apocalypses that divide time into epochs or stages before the final end. For example, in "The Apocalypse of Weeks" in I Enoch, time is divided into ten periods of "weeks," with history reaching its climax in the seventh week (the author's own time) and looking forward to the eighth week (in which judgment of the wicked will take place). The expectation of an imminent end characterizes many apocalypticists' messages of impending judgment of the wicked and rewards for the just. Time in apocalypses is typically presented as moving inexorably forward toward its imminent end.

An effective videogame is similarly characterized by what designer LeBlanc calls the dynamics of "dramatic inevitability, the sense that the contest is moving forward toward a conclusion." According to LeBlanc, if a game's contest appears "as if it will never conclude—or not conclude any time soon—then it has no sense of urgency, and the dramatic tension is dispelled." In both apocalypses and videogames, involvement depends upon "our level of emotional investment in the story's conflict: the sense of concern, apprehension, and urgency with which we await the story's outcome."[5] Whereas in apocalypses the periodization of time creates tension, in videogames other techniques are used, such as the technique called the "ticking clock."

The ticking clock, says LeBlanc, "stands as a constant reminder that the game will end, and soon." The ticking clock features of a game conveys "a sense of forward motion: as time runs out, the players feel propelled toward the conclusion of the contest." One way to enhance this experience is to utilize an actual countdown. Another is to give a sense of dwindling resources, "quantifiable assets within the game state that deplete over the course of play and are never replenished." Ticking clocks are "nonreversible processes" or "changes to the game state that can't be undone" (pp. 446–454). These project a sense of linearity into an experience that is moving inevitably toward a fixed outcome.

Time in apocalypses can also be viewed as cyclical. As Aune states, an apocalypse "anticipates a cataclysmic divine intervention

---

[5] Marc LeBlanc, "Tools for Creating Dramatic Game Dynamics," in *Game Design Reader: A Rules of Play Anthology* (MIT Press, 2006), pp. 453, 443.

into the human world bringing history to an end, but thereafter a renewal of the world in which Edenic conditions will be restored."[6] However, Flannery-Dailey suggests another model for understanding time in apocalypses: the "spiral model." Time is linear in its movement toward the end of time, but it is also cyclical "in that it is characterized by a regular succession of events that begins again repeatedly at the starting point."[7] The repetition is not perfect, since previous events are not repeated but "recapitulated" through symbolic interplay.

Mark Wolf says something similar about videogames in *The Medium of the Video Game* (2002). Videogames exhibit "repetition" in "cyclical or looped structures of time, which in some ways combine notions of movement and stasis" (p. 77). Of videogames, Wolf claims that the repetition generates a sort of familiarity that engenders confidence, so that "Learning the patterns of behavior and working around them is usually itself part of the game." In videogames, players must learn the spatial structure through repeated plays until they experience "a sense of the temporal loops" and so that "their timing, linkages, and other structures" will help them successfully navigate the space (p. 81). According to Wolf:

> Repetitions, cycled images, consistent and repeating behaviors, revisited narratives branches, and the replayability of many of the games themselves create a sense of expectation, anticipation, and familiarity for the player. They encourage the player to find the underlying patterns which allow him or her to take control of the situations encountered, and this assured orderliness may well be an important factor in the allure that videogames have for many people. (p. 82)

The ticking clock in *Halo* typically precedes some sort of cataclysm. The player thus has a stronger stake in the outcome of the story, having to complete tasks with the added impetus of urgency to prevent the end of the game, but more importantly, to save the world. Instead of offering a simplistic timer counting down, *Halo* repeatedly depicts increasing levels of chaos and systems derailing all

---

[6] David Aune, "Understanding Jewish and Christian Apocalyptic," *Word and World* 25:3 (2005), p. 237.

[7] Frances Flannery-Dailey, "Non-Linear Time in Apocalyptic Texts: The Spiral Model," *Society of Biblical Literature Seminar Papers* 38 (1999), p. 235.

around, with the need for imminent escape. In addition, there is literally a countdown timer in the last level of every *Halo* game. In the first and third game, you must escape the Halo before you are destroyed by it. In the second game, you must stop the activation of one of the Halos by killing Tartarus (a Brute minion of the Covenant) and thwarting the firing of the ring.

The urgency and danger created via the ticking clock in the different levels in *Halo* are akin also to the journey through multiple heavens in Jewish *merkavah* (or "chariot") literature and the hazards that visionaries typically encountered in them. In such visions and journeys, the seer must "negotiate with heavenly beings," including being "threatened by dangerous angels."[8] To ascend through the heavens and indeed to make it out alive at all, the visionary must know the right incantations, the appropriate actions, and must exhibit the right kind of piety. Levels of ascent also appear in *The Ascension of Isaiah* and also in *The Book of Enoch* which includes Enoch's "ascent to heaven" and "his guided tour of remote places, where he sees such things as the chambers of the dead and the places that have been prepared for final judgment."[9]

In addition to the player's movement through increasing levels of play, the idea of ascent is also quite literally indicated in *Halo* through the dream of the Covenant to "ascend" into divinity, which they mistakenly believe will happen through activation of the Halo array. This idea of "ascent" as a mode of entering a new world is also distinctively gnostic, as the gnostics believed that secret knowledge could enable them to ascend to a state of unity with the divine. In gnostic apocalypses, ascent is the entire goal of the visionary, who instead of viewing the punishment of one's enemies, is treated to a vision of eventual reunification of all things in the godhead. However, the Covenant's own drive to ascend to divinity in *Halo* contrasts with such traditional gnostic views in that instead of achieving enlightenment, they instead are damned for their ignorance. Indeed, the only thing they effect is their own destruction, and thus their quest for wisdom is a profound failure. The gnostic ideal of unity is in fact best achieved by Cortana and

---

[8] Paulo Augusto de Souza Nogueira, "Celestial Worship and Ecstatic-Visionary Experience," *Journal for the Study of the New Testament* 25:2 (2002), p. 180.

[9] John J. Collins, *Encounters with Biblical Theology* (Augsburg Fortress Press, 2005), p. 138.

Master Chief in their ability to recognize the true function and intent of the rings, the equivalent of gnostic wisdom.

Halo enables players to replay games at four different levels of difficulty, with each level offering greater challenges and occasional new experiences and insights. While the campaign mode reveals the story, the online multiplayer mode invites the player to compete with or cooperate together with fellow players for virtual victories, which afford the players higher online rankings and community status.

Speaking of traditional apocalypses, Nogueira points out that the process of gaining access to heavenly worlds through religious ecstasy is not easy: It "demands technique." The recitation of proper formulas such as the *kedusha* appears in apocalyptic liturgies in *Revelation* and *The Apocalypse of Abraham*.[10] Salen and Zimmerman observe in *Rules of Play* (2004) that games too require skills, some of which are consistent with those described in ascents: "visual scanning;" "auditory discrimination;" "motor responses;" "concentration;" and "perceptual patterns of learning" about the system of the game (p. 315). Salen and Zimmerman remark that to play a game is "to experience the game: to see, touch, hear, smell, and taste the game; to move the body during play, to feel emotions about the unfolding outcome, to communicate with other players, to alter normal patterns of thinking." Journeys to other worlds, whether in videogames or in traditional Jewish and Christian ascent literature, require intense concentration and developed techniques.

False Identity

Writing under someone else's name is an exceedingly common practice in ancient Jewish writings. A number of reasons for the adoption of pseudonyms have been offered by scholars, including Stone's argument that writing pseudonymously evokes "an aura of antiquity and participation in a tradition of great status and authority."[11] By writing in another's name, authors can "claim that they possess a tradition of learning inspired by God but not deriving its

---

[10] Paulo Augusto de Souza Nogueira, "Celestial Worship and Ecstatic-Visionary Experience," *Journal for the Study of the New Testament* 25:2 (2002), p. 181.

[11] Michael Stone, "Pseudepigraphy Reconsidered," *Review of Rabbinic Judaism* 9 (2006), p. 9.

authority through the Mosaic revelation" (p. 10). Players of *Halo* create their own pseudonym, registered to their Xbox Live account, in order to participate in a tradition of virtual skirmishing and rising in both ranking and ability.

In *The Method and Message of Jewish Apocalyptic* (1964), D.S. Russell identifies another reason for pseudonymity: an experience that he calls "contemporaneity," which refers to the author's identification with the ancient personage whose name he adopts and so shares the same visionary experiences and receives the same divine revelations (p. 136). In other words, the author experiences the same things as the person he's writing about and writing as. The apocalypticist in this way could see himself as an extension of the ancient seer's personality (p. 138). Such language resonates with contemporary discussions about players' identifications with avatars.

Thus, one could argue that contemporaneity, as a form of identity play, is a very basic element of ritual, of games, and of apocalypses. The player in *Halo* primarily enacts the personality and actions of the Master Chief, but occasionally plays the role of the Arbiter (in the second game). The player "contemporaneously" enacts the tasks of the Master Chief, the messianic figure in the game, through pivotal firefights that amount to the salvation of humanity from the Flood. In so doing, the player also *becomes* a sort of visionary, experiencing the game *as* a vision.

Apocalyptic Angst

So are there any common characteristics when one compares ancient fans of apocalypses and contemporary fans of videogames? One possibility is the *Sitz im Leben* or "situation in life" of the people typically drawn to these forms. David Hellholm has suggested that the Society of Biblical Literature definition should include the statement that apocalypses are "intended for a group in crisis with the purpose of exhortation and/or consolation by means of divine authority." Devotees of apocalypses, then, are typically feeling overwhelmed by forces beyond their control and are driven by a desire for certainty, assurance, and a sense of empowerment.

The life-situation of traditional apocalypses is well known, characterized by the experience of oppression and suffering at the hands of Greek and Roman overlords. In some ways, the life-situation of today's videogame players is similar, at least in spirit. Marc

Fonda points to the disasters in recent decades, including "natural calamities, abortion, the Gulf War, political correctness, the AIDS epidemic, 9/11, as well as political and economic instability throughout the world." Fonda says that the anxiety caused by these events may cause "those of us in the West" to suffer from "disaster syndrome." We have "become stunned, withdrawn, passive, suggestible" and we are experiencing "diminished mental capacity" as we have trouble "perceiving reality correctly."[12] Maybe some contemporary game players, like the ancient apocalypticists, feel a loss of control and purpose, and turn to games for the certainty games like *Halo* offer in telling us who is "good," who is "evil," and what to do about it.

Fonda outlines what he sees as "characteristics common to both millennial movements and postmodern thought," including the claim that adherents to both "suffer from a specific degree of angst caused by the recognition of impending doom of civilization as they know it." The hope of apocalypticists is for a "revitalization" that emerges out of a need "to reduce the stress and anxiety that confronts people when their society is no longer capable of providing an effective means of doing so." Thus, in today's society, Fonda sees examples of secular apocalypticism in "feminist thought, a perceived environmental disaster, scenarios regarding plenary destruction, and certain Internet subcultures."

Halo, too, can be seen as a form of "secular apocalypticism." Despite the obvious religious imagery in *Halo*, casual players themselves are not likely to see their gameplay as a religious activity, even if they might indeed feel overwhelmed by angst in their daily lives and experience the game as a temporary oasis of moral certainty. Furthermore, the transformation of traditional religious imagery within a *game*—especially within the context of a fantasy-driven and violent First Person Shooter—suggests that *Halo*'s commentary on religion is more scathing: *this* apocalypse is not literally expected to arrive by anyone playing the game. Accordingly, judgment is merely a performance of virtual doom, a ritual acting out of contemporary angst with no ultimate payoff.

However, some dedicated groups of hardcore gamers play for hours on end, for reasons that may transcend the game itself.

---

[12] Mark Fonda. "Postmodernity and the imagination of the Apocalypse: A Study of the Genre," <http://www.religiousworlds.com/fondarosa/dragon.html>

Bungie's ad campaign for *Halo 3* and *Halo: Reach* included inspirational phrases, calling the player to "Believe" and "Remember Hope." Multiplayer online battles reinforce competition and advancement, while the core themes of the game's campaign include war, duty, sacrifice, and heroism. The game's widespread impact is a cultural phenomenon, and this is perhaps due to its function as a form of "secular apocalypticism" for the modern age masses who crave epic, meaningful experiences within the safe virtual domain.

Videogame Apocalypses and Secularism

Halo and apocalypses both exhibit a sort of procedural rhetoric. They both involve otherworldly mediators who help the player-visionary understand the experiences and succeed in the mission, usually involving the sharing of secrets acquired through the journey. Both can be viewed as instances of the "magic circle" of games, in which areas are marked off for "play," in the sense that new rules apply within the demarcated space. Both offer a vision of transcendence, suggesting there is more to life than our daily experiences. Both present a dramatic sense of time's passing, creating expectation and urgency in the awareness of the approaching end of time. Both invite player-visionaries to see themselves as identified with great figures from another time or place, to see their own identities fused, at least for the time of the "play," with these figures, to experience what *they* experience and see what *they* see.

There are distinctive similarities between apocalypses and FPSs like *Halo*. But what do we make of the differences?

The element of secularism marks the most distinctive feature of videogame apocalypses. Indeed, the challenges and anxiety associated with postmodernism are quite distinct from those experienced by early Jews and Christians suffering under Roman rule. Death in videogames is temporary, not permanent—thus salvation is also temporary. Worlds visited are transient. Enemies defeated are not real. When one turns off the game and returns to one's daily life, the same hardships, the same problems, the same doubts remain. Apocalypses may have offered early Jews and Christians comfort precisely because the "game" they invited us to play was infinite, so the rewards of "winning" had some lasting consequences, and so could offer real comfort in daily life. The popularity of fabricated apocalyptic visions of the sort encountered in today's videogames mark both the appeal of the genre and also its ineffectiveness in times of generally accepted moral relativism.

Hearers of traditional apocalypses could find comfort in God's approaching judgment of the wicked and rewards for the righteous. Videogames can certainly also be viewed as looking imaginatively forward to a judgment, but this experience may take shape in many different forms of dualisms, most of which are presented in a fantasy framework. In one game, the enemy is a group of aliens; in another it is people from another country or religion; in another, it is monsters or children or soldiers. The dualisms do not contribute to an overall ordered view of the cosmos, but rather offer only a temporary sense of order and satisfaction, within the programmed world of each game. Even in games that purport to represent real events and impose a rigid dualism on them, as in various videogames about current military engagements, the satisfaction is cheap. One's so-called enemies will simply produce another videogame in which *you* are portrayed as the enemy.

The complexities of morality in a globalizing world make easy dualisms difficult to maintain beyond the "magic circle" of play, but they also suggest that we should think carefully and deliberately about what we believe and why we believe it. Perhaps the ancient apocalypticists also saw their own otherworldly journeys as play, but it seems likely that if they did, they utilized the elements of play to make much larger claims about their own certainty of meaning in the cosmos, and their own hope that God would intervene soon to prove them right. Today, it seems, things are a bit more complicated and we have to work harder to figure things out for ourselves.

10

The Plasma Grenade Is the New Razor Blade

MICHAEL JENKINS

Bullets are flying, grenades are going off in the distance, but no one has seen you. You're sneaking around the back. You've got a full clip and an itchy trigger finger. This is what you live for. This is what gives it all meaning. As you peer around the corner, you see a Covenant standing with his back to you. This is the perfect opportunity. You saunter up and pull the trigger on your Mauler, execution style. As he falls to the ground, all becomes right with the world. That is, all is right until you hear that tink of a bouncing grenade. With that you are stuck back at a loading screen.

This is the beginning of our love-hate relationship with the *Halo* series. We live for the moment in a deathmatch where we get the winning kill or in capture-the-flag where we save the game. The problem is that those moments are so few and far between. Most of the moments we experience are filled with pain and suffering. We're the ones who are getting slaughtered. We're the ones who are getting killed over and over, and most of the time it's because of teammates who just can't work together. We end up doing most of the work ourselves, fighting all the odds, and getting slaughtered for it.

However, that's part of the reason we enjoy the game. If *Halo* were too easy, we would simply move on. As much as we crave those moments of victory, they are meaningless without the challenge. This is why we crank it up to hellfire nightmare legendary difficulty or continue to join games even when we consistently get put into failing teams. The challenge is what makes the game. However, it's also the challenge that's at the heart of our use of *Halo* as a tool for self-injurious behavior (SIB). But before we go too far, let's look into what self-injurious behavior is.

Nerdrage and Me

Jennifer J. Muehlenkamp, a clinical psychologist with a focus on SIB tells us that "Superficial/moderate self-injurious behaviors are characterized as repetitive, low-lethality actions that alter or damage body tissue (such as cutting or burning) without suicidal intent. Superficial/moderate SIBs have a unique set of symptoms" and "are viewed as a type of morbid self-help."[1]

This gives us a beginning definition of SIB and a few important points about it. The first is that SIB results in *physical* damage. This is one point which I will contest. Another point is that SIB is always meant to be non-fatal. The action is meant to cause pain and suffering, not to end your life. The final point, which ties into the second, is that the action is often performed as a form of self-help or self medication.

If we simply stopped here, the closest we could come to SIB and *Halo* would be if there were some electro-shock feedback or we beat ourselves over the head with the controller anytime we died. However, if we take more time to look at what SIB actually is, we can see whether there are any more subtle characteristics that can allow *Halo* to be a tool of SIB.

Two psychologists, Matthew K. Nock and Mitchell J. Prinstein, argue that SIB can be broken down into positive and negative reinforcement types. A positive reinforcement would be one that brings a desirable stimulus. A negative reinforcement would bring the removal of an undesirable stimulus. "*Automatic-negative reinforcement* refers to an individual's use of SIB to achieve a reduction in tension or other negative affective states" (for example 'to stop bad feelings').[2] In other words, someone who actively performs SIB is doing so to stop feeling a certain way. They are using the SIB as a form of relief. For people who play *Halo*, this would be akin to using it to blow off steam. Pulling that trigger, throwing that nade, it all makes us feel better. We *enjoy* watching things go boom and enemies dying. Tapping into that warrior nature relaxes us.

---

[1] Jennifer J. Muehlenkamp, "Self-Injurious Behavior as a Separate Clinical Syndrome," *American Journal of Orthopsychiatry* 75:2 (2005), p. 324.

[2] Matthew K. Nock and Mitchell J. Prinstein, "A Functional Approach to the Assessment of Self-Mutilative Behavior," *Journal of Consulting and Clinical Psychology* 72:5 (2004), p. 886.

In *automatic-positive reinforcement*, individuals engage in SIB "to create a desirable physiological state" (for example, 'to feel something, even if it's pain'). In other words, rather than serving the purpose of removing feelings, SIB may also function as a means of feeling generation. Here, the SIB participant is trying to find something to feel, to chase the numbness or loneliness away. She wants *some* feeling regardless of what it is. One way in which this is done is to use the pain to *replace* the feeling she's trying to escape from, to give her something else to focus on.

In our situation, *Halo* might be used to generate these feelings. We may get on and die repeatedly to replace the loneliness or depression with anger. Sure, we're going to get fragged a lot in any deathmatch, but the adrenalin is worth it. Sure, the match may be way one-sided because the team we joined is just awful. Driving that Warthog or dying repeatedly at the same stupid spot may be the most frustrating thing we've done lately, but it's still something other than wallowing in our own loneliness. It gives us something *else* to be angry and frustrated about. It changes our focus.

In contrast, social reinforcement functions refer to the use of SIB to modify or regulate our social environment. *Social-negative reinforcement* refers to an individual's use of SIB "to escape from interpersonal task demands (for instance, 'to avoid punishment from others' or 'to avoid doing something unpleasant')." This falls much more into the realm of escapism. The SIB participant uses this behavior to either inflict harm on herself which she feels she deserves or, once again, find something else to focus on instead of a difficult situation she is stuck in. *Halo* can be used the same way. We don't want to do any homework or deal with chores. We don't want to deal with parents or nagging spouses. We use *Halo* to avoid all these things, to enter into a realm where they don't matter, where all that matters is who pulls the trigger first.

Finally, "Social-positive reinforcement for SIB involves gaining attention from others or gaining access to materials (for example 'to try to get a reaction out of someone, even if it's negative' or 'to let others know how unhappy I am')." This is often a result that comes *after* the SIB has occurred. That is, the SIB participant wants someone to see the wounds and to respond. She wants *some* kind of interaction with other people and feels this is one way to gain it. It doesn't matter whether the interaction is praise or blame. She simply wants *some* reaction or attention.

Anyone who's ever played a *Halo* match online, with the headset plugged in, knows that there's plenty of interaction, most of which is definitely not praise. We've even coined our own term for this "interaction"—nerdrage. You turn on the game, you log into a match, and you find nerdrage. You do well, you kill all the other team, capture the flag (and so on) and you get nerdrage either from the other team and your "cheating" or from your team and your "kill stealing." You do poorly, and you get nerdrage from your team about being a noob. And the language. You get twelve-year-olds who put drunken sailors to shame. Voluntarily putting on that headset has to be some form of SIB simply because of the language.

Pull The Pin. You Know You Want To

In all this, we begin to see how SIB can overlap with *Halo*. Many gamers use *Halo* as an outlet to relieve stress or to escape whatever drama is happening around them. It can be a form of relaxation. Any gamer knows that a game like *Halo* can constitute a form of escapism. It's a place we can go that's not *here*. It's the place to go and release that tension and anger. It's the place we go to have some control—and nothing says control like running crap over with a Warthog and using a nice heavy machine gun on anything that remains. However, simply because both SIB and *Halo* are outlets to relieve stress does not mean that it is a form of SIB. It simply means that it can be a form of relaxation.

The problem arises when we are willing to go through such hell, so many respawns, and so much frustration just to reach that release. We have all tried to play games on "super easy" mode before. We have even tried to play deathmatches with bots with their settings turned down "just to kill lots of stuff." However, this rarely gives us any enjoyment. Unless we're playing *Halo* for the story, we want more than to just yawn our way through it. We want life and (virtual) death situations. The pain and suffering in *Halo*, just like in SIB, is what makes the game so appealing.

Remember Me?

Though these four divisions give us a broad understanding of what SIB is and how it's used, we should look at a few of the motivations a little more closely. The first is that of driving away loneliness. Possessing loneliness, in and of itself, does not make you a contender for SIB participant of the year. As social creatures, it is natural for us to feel lonely when a companion (just anyone won't do) is not around. However, what concerns us with SIB and loneliness is the extent we go to drive it away. As we saw, being willing to put up with random nerdrage is an argument for SIB. However, there are other ways to use *Halo* to drive off loneliness.

One way for us to do this is to join a clan, a forum, some community to give us something we feel like we belong to. We may know the strife, the flame wars, the drama that comes with it, but we *need* somewhere to go to be less lonely. Once again, it's not the search for the connection with other people that can place *Halo* in the realm of SIB. It's the acceptance, the sheer reveling in the flame wars and strife that goes on in the community that seems to place gaming there. As one poster on an SIB forum said, "I think my greatest fear is to be forgotten. A teacher I had last year doesn't even remember my name—it makes me think that no one remembers me. How do I know I exist? At least I know I exist when I cut."[3] In these self-made communities, among the strife and flame wars, we try to make our mark on the (our) world, and we're willing to go to great lengths to do this very thing.

Still, there are some major discrepancies. One arises when we consider the standard understanding of SIB. Typically, SIB methods are those such as "cutting, burning, hitting, severe skin scratching, and interfering with wound healing." It's most commonly acted out on the arms, legs, chest, and other areas on the front of the body. Some argue that this is simply for easy access while others argue it's because those areas are easily concealable. "It is also common for an individual who engages in repetitive acts of SIB to identify himself or herself as a cutter or burner, establishing a sense of unique identity as a result of his or her behavior" (Jennifer Muehlenkamp, pp. 324–25).

If we consider this, we can see how it can be argued that *Halo* can't be a form of SIB because of the "physical damage" clause. Dying in *Halo* or losing a match doesn't result in physical harm. We don't bleed when Master Chief gets shot, and we don't feel the impact when we ram a Warthog into a wall. There's a line between fantasy and reality that keeps us separate. However, this becomes

---

[3] Janis L. Whitlock, Jane L. Powers, and John Eckenrode, "The Virtual Cutting Edge: The Internet and Adolescent Self-Injury," *Developmental Psychology* 42:3 (2006), p. 407.

complicated when we consider two things: how influential technology is and our connection to it.

No One Knows Who Threw that Nade

The psychologists Janis L. Whitlock, Jane L. Powers, and John Eckenrode, maintain that adolescents use the Internet primarily for social reasons. "The Internet has become a virtual meeting place where teens hang out with their peers to pass time. Many adolescents reportedly prefer being online to other media, including the telephone, TV, and radio" (p. 407). To support this claim they go on to state: "Computer access and use among adolescents have grown exponentially over the past decade." More than eighty percent of American youth twelve to seventeen years of age use the Internet, and nearly half log on daily.

While the Internet is not the same as *Halo*, there is a connection. They both promote the same kind of environment and usage. We can turn it on, plug in, and silence the rest of the world. They give us a place to go where we cease to be ourselves and can become our handle or avatar. They both have their own unique social setting with its own set of acceptable behaviors. At the very least, the Internet is what has allowed *Halo* to become such a praised multiplayer game. It has supplemented its growth and changed the way we view it and interact with people through it. The list of similarities and connections can go on and on.

However, if we keep the similarities we listed in mind, we can begin to see how influential technology such as *Halo* can be. When we log on to *Halo*, we have the chance to interact with other people. We are no longer sitting alone. We meet with friends, strangers, and potential friends to play and interact. We say and hear things that sometimes influence others. We are no longer isolated when we play. This gives us a place to develop and learn about ourselves. Whitlock, Powers, and Eckenrode also argue that "chat rooms and similar venues in which adolescents share experiences anonymously may provide a safe forum for less socially adept adolescents to practice social interaction" (p. 408).

This anonymity is where the connection to SIB begins. The idea is that because *Halo* allows a certain level of anonymity, it allows the player to express herself in ways that are not normally socially acceptable. The easiest example is, once again, the language. Most things said while playing, like the infamous Chuck Norris jokes that haunted us for so long or a discussion by grown adults over which *Twilight* character is the best, are only acceptable over something that provides this anonymity like *Halo*. This anonymity also allows us to participate in SIB without ever being discovered. It allows us to act out these behaviors without the risk of discovery and in a more socially acceptable way. Sure, some people will say that anyone who plays *Halo* is a loser. However, even this label seems somehow more socially acceptable than those who bear the scars of SIB. Getting killed over and over in *Halo* allows the same self-medication without the risk of accidentally causing serious harm or being discovered.

My Avatar and Me

The second consideration is the bond we develop with our avatars. As we spend more and more time playing *Halo*, we tend to identify and begin to empathize with our virtual avatars. Simply look on any Internet forum and see how many flame wars erupt when Master Chief is mocked (or what came about when a *Halo* character appeared in *Dead or Alive 4* but was not Master Chief). This bond allows us to empathize and "feel" what they feel. If we simply look at reading or watching movies we can see how this is true. We cry when a character gets hurt or dies. We wish them the best through the stories and always hope it turns out a particular way. We rarely watch a movie or read a book completely indifferent to the characters. As we progress, we form a connection with the characters. The same thing happens as we play *Halo*. We begin to form a bond with the character. We begin to see that character as a manifestation of ourselves. We got the kill. We died at a certain spot.

However, this doesn't change the fact that Master Chief is still a virtual character and cannot be harmed in the way a real life human being can. To participate in SIB through *Halo* we must find other ways to inflict this punishment and find relief. That is, we can't simply cut our avatars and feel the pain. We must use alternate methods to punish ourselves and find that sweet release. We do this by constantly queuing up for losing games. That is our self-punishment. Our sweet release comes when we actually win. This is the endorphin rush that physical cutting causes. We just have to work a little harder to get the "medication" into our system.

This idea that emotional harm is also a form of SIB is supported by the fact that more than thirty-three terms have been used to represent SIB, some of which include "suicidal behaviors and indirect forms of self-harm, such as risk taking, promiscuity, and drug abuse, in their definition." An expanded definition such as this would allow a much broader range of activities to be accepted as SIB. They would not have to be behaviors that resulted in direct physical harm. Not all risky actions, such as sky diving, result in physical harm. Not all promiscuous actions result in physical harm either. However, some can, and with definitions that vary this much, the idea that "mental harm" is another form of SIB is not a far stretch. If we accept this, we see how *Halo* can fit right in. It would qualify as an "indirect form" resulting in mental harm and not physical. Some people may even argue that driving a Warthog so often is self-injurious.

Maybe I'm just "special," but I seem to spend more time with my Warthog upside down, exploding, or stuck on something than actually driving it or firing the gun. I'm really not sure why anyone lets me drive anything anymore, and don't even get me started on flying the Hornet. All I do is die. Talk about voluntary self-injurious behavior. My co-op partner had to do that whole part himself. Yet, I continued to play the game. I didn't stop when it became infuriating. I was willing to put up with the pain and—I hate to admit it—shameful carnage of my repeated death to continue until I found a place of sweet release. I don't think I'm alone in having my own "special moment" in the game where I die over and over and over. Most players will find that moment, each differing based on particular skills, especially those of us who start with legendary mode.

Who? Me?

All these things point to psychological consistencies between SIB and playing *Halo*. Each gives the participant a purpose beyond simple entertainment. Each fulfills a need. We play *Halo* to do more than entertain ourselves or pass the time. We play it to help relieve loneliness, hopelessness, or some other feeling. We go there because it provides a haven. It allows us to find others like us without all the social pressure. Both SIB and *Halo* have some meaning behind the actions involved. This is one of the main reasons *Halo* can fall into the category of SIB. It can be used both to reinforce destructive patterns and as its own destructive pattern.

"Estimates of SIB have ranged from 400 to 1,400 cases per 100,000 annually," reports Jennifer Muehlenkamp. This number, however, fails to consider the rest of us, those who do not use physical self-injuring to self-medicate. It might end up being much, much higher. Does this mean that everyone who plays games has some masochistic personality? Not hardly. Does it mean that some do? That seems clear enough. Maybe next time you sit down, headset on and controller in your hand, you should consider why you're playing the game. You might end up realizing you're just like the rest of us, and that we all need a little self-medication from time to time.

11

Playing with Fantasies in the Spartan (Sub)Consciousness

PATRICK TIERNAN

You sit down to another afternoon of videogame play, lost in an electronic world of post-apocalyptic proportion. Equipped with your Spartan Laser, you form an alliance with United Nations Space Command (UNSC) forces who relish the opportunity to seek out and destroy the insurgency of Brutes.

Now hit the pause button—literally and figuratively. To what extent is your gaming fantasy real? So you've kept current on your electric bill and your Xbox is still under warranty despite the "red ring of death," but what about the implications of encountering this new reality which has you as Master Chief John-117? You are the stoic military figure ordained to vanquish the Covenant forces and ensure the preservation of humankind. It all sounds slightly idealistic to say the least, as the last of a genetically enhanced soldier project. Yet when we immerse ourselves in *Halo* we encounter a world not of our making with a storyline script written for us. It is a journey that brings us along in the search of what it means to be an individual.

When we say "I'm playing *Halo*" we must ask if this refers to the individual at the helm of the controller or the digitized figure on the screen. How real is the act of playing a videogame? To what extent can a game role allow us the space to behave in ways that would otherwise be socially inept, or at worst inhumane? Are fantasies an acceptable means of escaping our own reality? In examining these questions, let's consider what we perceive to be real and what is experienced as fantasy, what influences the person we are becoming and what we project as our ideal self.

Playing with the Future

When we play *Halo*, what exactly are we doing? We may often refer to the ways in which playing a game is a form of release from the mundane and pedestrian markers of existence. We play as an escape from the stress that makes commitments on our time and to indulge some fantasy of ours that transcends our everyday life. However, when we play a videogame, it's the creator's fantasy that we choose because of its allure. The cultural theorist Johan Huizinga says the following:

> Summing up the formal characteristics of play we might call it a free activity standing quite consciously outside "ordinary" life as being "not serious," but at the same time absorbing the player intensely and utterly. It is an activity connected with no material interest, and no profit can be gained by it. It proceeds within its own proper boundaries of time and space according to fixed rules and in an orderly manner. It promotes the formation of social groupings which tend to surround themselves with secrecy and to stress their difference from the common world by disguise or other means.[1]

Several ideas can be taken from this passage as they apply to the battlefield, such as the Blood Gulch. First, there is the acknowledgment that playing a game does not garner any form of material or financial benefit (although many rogue *Halo* competition circles may beg to differ on this point). Second, there is a set parameter of time and space which provides the storyline for the game. The expansive timeline of the *Halo* series underscores this point—from the origins of the Forerunners as the pre-eminent species of the universe to the twenty-sixth-century conflict with the Covenant—that there is a defined history to which all players are accountable, to be aware of your origins as well as your destiny is imperative in the world of the UNSC.

The last point is perhaps the most intriguing in that Huizinga contends there is a social value in play; the multiplayer function in *Halo 3* is an example of this group dynamic. To ponder the intricacies of weaponry, taxonomy of Covenant legions, and moral implications of preserving or destroying all sentient life in the known universe is, to say the least, an exhaustive feat for one to

---

[1] Johan Huizinga, *Homo Ludens* (Beacon Press, 1950), p. 13.

contemplate. Nevertheless, this is exactly what makes the *Halo* enterprise one of the most commercially successful games in First Person Shooter (FPS) history. By allowing its players to differentiate themselves from the everyday world in a dynamic storyline, *Halo* invites us to become part of a competition for the ideal representation of its protagonist John 117. We imagine what it would be like to embody the legend of the UNSC alliance! Like the Pillar of Autumn's first encounter with the *Halo* ring, we have experienced a new level of reality which our language reflects as experience. The figurative nature of this is captured in statements like "You killed me" or "Take the elevated position and cover me." In a subtle way, words can capture our imagination through unique modes of awareness.

Play as a form of escapism can also be classified as *mimicry* in which one assumes another identity where

> it can consist not only of deploying actions or submitting to one's fate in an imaginary milieu, but of becoming an illusory character oneself, and of so behaving. One is thus confronted with a diverse series of manifestations, the common element of which is that the subject makes believe or makes others believe that he is someone other than himself. He forgets, disguises, or temporarily sheds his personality in order to feign another.[2]

They say imitation is the sincerest form of flattery and this is no truer than when we assume the role of the Spartan commander. As a cultural icon, John-117 has been the hit at numerous Halloween parties across the globe and even took over the John Harvard statue in Harvard Yard to resemble the Master Chief during a 2007 MIT prank celebrating the release of *Halo 3*. The *Red vs. Blue* phenomenon is another example of the popularity it takes for granted in certain Internet circles. While most people playing videogames do not explicitly mimic the character they are navigating, there is a way in which players try to one-up their friends who participate in the same storyline like getting the plasma sword in multiplayer mode or debating over who drives the Warthog in co-op mode. All of these contribute to the notion of mimicry where we engage in the play of the moment. Caught in this free play while interfacing

[2] Roger Caillois, *Man, Play, and Games*. (Shocken, 1979), p. 19.

with an electronic storyboard allows us the imaginative space to ponder what it would be like to stand in the military boots of another. While we may not think we somehow leave our "true self" out of imaginary play, it is intriguing to consider what we mean when we use "I" statements as conscious individuals aware of ourselves in the world.

When the Screen Stares Back

The psychoanalyst Jacques Lacan believed the human psyche could be divided into three concepts—the real, imaginary order, and symbolic order. The real refers to a pure state of nature before our birth. He describes it as a state of fullness or completeness that is marred by the entrance into language; to name it would only impose limitations. This state is comparable to the era of the Forerunners where life was innocent, blithely unaware of the cataclysmic disorder that lay waiting. Lacan was often quoted as saying "the real is impossible" and to some extent there is truth to this claim since without the Forerunners' activation of the Halo Array, the ensuing narrative would have no relevance. This is not meant as a truism but rather as a way of perceiving the original state of the *Halo* worldview.

The imaginary order corresponds to what Lacan called the "mirror stage" where an individual is capable of seeing herself as a new manifestation. He states that

> this development is experienced as a temporal dialectic that decisively projects the formation of the individual into history. The *mirror stage* is a drama whose internal thrust is precipitated from insufficiency to anticipation—and which manufactures for the subject, caught up in the lure of spatial identification, the succession of phantasies that extends from a fragmented body-image to a form of its totality . . . to the assumption of the armour of an alienating identity, which will mark with its rigid structure the subject's entire mental development.[3]

The central idea embedded in this order is that it is primarily narcissistic, being completely enamored with oneself. The anticipation

---

[3] Jacques Lacan, "The Mirror Stage as Formative of the Function of the I as revealed in Psychoanalytic Experience," in *Écrits: A Selection* (Tavistock, 1977), p. 4.

Lacan refers to here is the setting for the fantasies of desire. To fantasize about what we can become is an intriguing ontological dilemma because it questions what we understand by the nature of reality. I don't necessarily believe I am an incarnation of John-117, but I may pretend, posture, or project myself onto the world of that character. For Lacan, a young child experiences anxiety in the mirror stage when he realizes his body is separate from the world and his mother (insert your favorite Freud joke here). This continues throughout our adult life as we seek to fill that void with physical and material desires. We may also maintain a fantastical image of ourselves, what Lacan called the "ideal ego," by emulating people and figures that reflect our deepest desires. Consider the mystique surrounding Master Chief whose identity is veiled in myth but retold in militaristic narratives. His reflective helmet shield conceals his true identity, allowing any FPS player to project her own identity onto this blank slate.

The final aspect of the psyche is the symbolic order which is primarily about desire. This is the way we enter into a world of language to describe our unconscious desires. It should be noted that psychoanalytic theory deals with those unconscious thoughts, feelings, and experiences that influence an individual's beliefs and decisions. Our past in many ways shapes our present. For example, consider how *Halo: Reach* serves as a prequel where the figure of John-117 emerges from this narrative. There is an inherent tension among these three realms of the psyche in which we struggle to discover ourselves while at the same time reach out to know others—those friends we play the game with and the characteristics of the characters we emulate in the game itself. This is what Lacan means by the function of the symbolic order. It is not so much attaining the object of our desire as it is the act of fantasizing about it that is paramount for understanding this psychological position. As most gamers will attest, it is not actually becoming Master Chief that is appealing but the thought of what it may be like that is the source of this attraction. As a case in point, our psyche allows us the opportunity to imagine the act of taking out the Prophets in an epic battle to preserve the human species. Fantasy is not the same as actually living out the desire to become a savior (most individuals would call this neurosis). The fact that *Halo* takes place in the 26th century is significant here insofar as it is undoubtedly beyond the realm of wishful thinking—as opposed to a setting in say 2050 where one could make reasonable predications about the state of humanity and technology. So how does all this relate to how we perceive ourselves and others?

Does the Covenant Have a Personality?

Carl Jung was a seminal figure in the field of psychoanalysis who developed what he called archetypes, universal models that influence subsequent figures and ideas.[4] Part of the commercial success of *Halo* could be attributed to the way in which its characters act as personas that could represent individuals we encounter in our own lives. We may know someone with the solemn confidence of Master Chief, the religious commitment to the mystery of the divine like the Forerunners, or the sagacious leadership and intelligence of Cortana. While these figures are specific to this particular videogame, in their totality they embody characteristics that we discover in many of our twenty-first-century relationships. Jung notes that the concept of the archetype comes from the universality of characteristics or themes that continually emerge from different forms of literature; they tend to be reaffirmed by our dreams and fantasies. In one respect, the characters encountered in *Halo* are not novel to our everyday experience but are merely re-imagined in a futuristic storyline.

While there are numerous archetypes in his writings, I will describe a few. The *persona* is our public image, our "mask" that the world sees. According to Jung and his philosophy of the individual unconscious, we may believe what we pretend to be. This resonates with me whenever I hear my students discussing *Halo* strategies as if they had life and death consequences! The *animus* and *anima* are the gender aspect of our persona for men and women, respectively. Together they are called *syzgy*, referring to the unity and complementary nature of these dynamic identities.

We could make the argument that Cortana and Master Chief symbolize this archetype of interdependence but more importantly it shows how an overwhelming number of *Halo* players are men who identify with the aggressive, stoic, and defiant male persona of Master Chief. Nevertheless, their interdependency is witnessed by being "alone together" in a life pod as they make the

---

[4] Carl Jung, *Man and His Symbols* (Doubleday, 1964).

voyage home after the final battle where they are presumed dead at the end of *Halo 3*. Finally there is the archetype of the *self* which is described as the ultimate unity of our conscious and unconscious identities, a perfection of personality that is only attainable in death. There is tension between this archetype and the persona of Spartan soldiers exemplified by the fact they are never listed as "Killed in Action" to preserve the awe of their military efforts.

These Jungian archetypes provide us with a framework for exploring the types of personalities we put forth, both in the public square and within the confine of our own conscience. The Brutes and dignified Elites signify how archetypes are presented as antagonistic forces in the mission of Master Chief. There are universal traits that we associate with specific relationships in our everyday lives—social friends, work colleagues, family members, and those outside our developing network of connections. This Jungian analysis of archetypes transcends particular personalities and allows us to generalize human nature in terms of the characters we encounter in the grand narratives of history. For example, the hero serves as another archetype grounded in *Halo* which allows for the conflict between a protagonist and antagonist in a climactic ending requisite for any storyline! By highlighting these universal norms of personalities, we can begin to see the social allure of seeing ourselves as part of the UNSC struggle because we are able to identify with its parallels to human history. Jung's perspective on human nature is helpful in our analysis because the psyche—our collective memories and fears, fantasies, and desires—is the culmination of a lifetime of experiences.

There Is No "I" in *Halo*

So what can we say about the psychology of videogame play? The twenty-first century has provided us with novel opportunities for connecting with people from around the globe. The advent of online gaming is no exception as players now have the capability of working with each other rather than in opposition. Although this may be a weak assertion—namely, that games like *Halo* create opportunities for social interaction—there is a sentiment that technology now allows us a new sense of freedom to behave and project in ways that were once a fantasy. Social profiles need not be accurate and even our pictures are substituted with avatars that may or may not resonate with our personality. In this sense, the eighteenth-century philosopher George Berkeley was right to say that to be is to be perceived. Objects that are judgedd to be true do not refer to external ideas or forms but merely reflect the qualities apprehended by the individual perceiving.

A *Halo* player's perception of the reality portrayed in gameplay may manifest itself into a social ignorance—or at worst, apathy—toward genuine conflict in the world—strife in the Middle East and Africa, for example. While *Halo* may not necessarily amplify this disconnect between the television screen and national news outlets, it could have an adverse effect in the extent to which we seek to escape from the violence and unimaginable tragedies that mar our world. Moreover, the individualistic nature of gaming may unintentionally foster stereotypes about the fabric of our stoic male culture. Strength, aggression, and conflict are guised as hero worship in the figure of Master Chief who stands as the paradigm of the male fantasy. It should come as no shock that many if not most readers of this chapter are likely to be males in the standard marketing demographic of 18–35 years of age. *Halo* projects a narrative that could be viewed as a reinforcement of stereotypical "boys will be boys" aggression albeit within the confines of your own home. When you lose a mission as Master Chief, it becomes privatized within the confines of your living room.

But the implications do not end with the individual and her perception of reality. The French paleontologist Teilhard de Chardin wrote about the evolution of the universe into what he called the "noosphere," a realm where all of humanity would participate in a unified identity. This conclusion is called the Omega (referring to the last letter of the Greek alphabet) and points to this coalescence of consciousness which will lead us to a new state of peace and planetary unity:

> To be fully ourselves it is in the opposite direction, in the direction of convergence with all the rest, that we must advance—towards the 'other'. The peak of ourselves, the acme of our originality, is not our individuality but our person; and according to the evolutionary structure of the world, we can only find our person by uniting together. There is no mind without synthesis. The same holds good from top to

[5] Pierre Teilhard de Chardin, *The Phenomenon of Man* (Harper and Row, 1959), p. 263.

> bottom. The true ego grows in inverse proportion to egoism. Like the Omega which attracts it, the element only becomes personal when it universalizes itself.[5]

Deep, isn't it? To truly understand ourselves is to grow in relationship with others. The globalization of economics, justice, and social mores exemplifies this increasing interdependency of our world. Some have viewed the Internet as the harbinger of this convergence coming to fruition, as technology has given us the ability to connect and communicate in ways unfathomable even a generation ago. In the context of what we've discussed here, we may entertain the idea of unconsciously participating in this evolving connectivity. This idea of the noosphere, albeit esoteric by design, could be the social antidote to the individualism and stoicism that the *Halo* culture dramatically amplifies.

The Challenge to (Dis)connect

When we immerse ourselves in the electronic world of videogame play, we unconsciously imagine what it would be like to put on the mask of another. The potential danger lies in form of the medium we engage—in this case, our Xbox. When we begin to play there is potentially never a compelling need to end the role playing, save that of going into work or attending class. Like a movie or song on a continual loop, videogame players sometimes struggle with the figurative and literal ability to disconnect. Framed as a metaphysical question, we must consciously return to our true self by being reminded—however deceptively childish it may seem—that it is only a game. This doesn't negate the fact that we bring a myriad of emotions to the *Halo* universe. We may feel the compulsion to play after a tiresome day on the job or after a difficult exam for school as a cathartic means of relieving stress or anxiety. On the surface, most would agree this is nothing more than an example of leisure at its finest hour. Nevertheless, the moral question lingering is when and how this form of escapism begins to control us, when the player becomes the played. However, many also play as a means of connecting with others through a shared experience: with all its eccentricities sometimes gaming is merely an opportunity to socialize with and against a familiar backdrop.

I began the chapter with the statement "I am playing *Halo*" as a way of framing the conscious act of entering into the videogame narrative. A subtle inversion of this line "*Halo* playing am I" can serve as a summary of the philosophical tenets described above. While resisting the temptation to make a Yoda joke about grammar, we can see that "playing" focuses on the mimicry detailed in *Halo* whereby imitation allows the psychological space to explore new realities in an embodied character quite apart from our typical mode of existence. The first person singular of "be" is "am" which implies the ontological question of reality. If I am merely mimicking Master Chief, then that still leaves us asking about the nature of our ego. The "I" may never entirely become "that which it plays" but it does raise interesting questions about the state of our (sub)consciousness when we engage the stark realism of twenty-first-century videogames, as opposed to, say, *Pong*. In the "I" we encounter the problem of self-knowledge which is why we have the tendency to identify with certain characters and the real qualities they embody, albeit in a twenty-sixth-century setting. Consequently, when we say we are playing *Halo* we just might be saying more about how we project ourselves onto the backdrop of a fantasy world.

Like the final creature caught in Pandora's Box, at the end of our analysis we are left with hope. Intended to heal the wounds of the soul and body in the infamous Greek myth, hope is a residual theme throughout the *Halo* franchise. Not merely wish-fulfillment, hope stands in contrast to the threat of nihilism in a world fraught with confusion. Escapism then can be a healthy outlet if the individual is capable of returning to what is truly real. The fantasy of playing the role of Master Chief is only surpassed by the potential reality portrayed in the game itself. The cataclysmic battle over natural resources and technology serve as a reminder that there are genuine threats to civilization on Earth. So while entering this mental arena may not lead to the detriment of our psyche or dramatically impact our outlook on life, it might just be enough to make us reflect about who is in control the next time we hit the start button.[6]

---

[6] I am grateful to Michael Bonina, colleague and *Halo* aficionado, for his suggestions on earlier drafts. Much of the ontological speculation in this chapter about Master Chief comes from him. Thanks also to Michael Frost for his constructive feedback, insights, and philosophical banter about the psychology of videogame play. Lastly, I want to recognize my students Daniel Clavijo, Patrick Norton, and Mitch Hanna, who served as videogame consultants by reviewing my work when they should have been finishing their homework.

12

What's Wrong with Camping?

GALEN A. FORESMAN

Campers are the scourge of multiplayer in First Person Shooters (FPS). The Flood, the alien parasite bent on infecting all sentient life and the central cause in the extinction of vast highly intelligent civilizations, has nothing on these annoyances. Campers are detestable cheaters lacking any complete set of quick response motor skill functionality necessary for honest reticule assassination. They are, in a word, pathetic.

The camper is a player who camps out in a particular position in a multiplayer game that gives her a strategic advantage over other players. The advantage may be defensive positioning, a very useful item drop, or something as simple as the element of surprise. Depending on the type of multiplayer match being played, a camper's strategy and positioning might change and probably should. This creates a variety of types of camping, each lending themselves to an equally diverse set of evaluations. These evaluations range from "expected" and "legitimate" forms of camping that include acts like guarding the flag in capture-the-flag matches to more notorious forms of camping like spawn camping, where campers position themselves to eliminate players immediately upon starting or respawning into a game. Given camping's variety and often polarized evaluation, it is perhaps one of the most hotly contested issues in any multiplayer FPS, so much so that camping has become a central issue in game design.

In competitive multiplayer, first person shooters are dominated by two types of players: those that just said "Amen" to the introduction to this paper, and those that were immediately angered or frustrated by it. The latter group is made up of those that are themselves campers, or those that take a more moderate approach to their overall evaluation of gaming strategies.

But, as we'll see, the debate about camping is dumb. The vast majority of arguments against camping come from a notion of fair play that has little to do with playing fair at all, but lots to do with being a loser.

Equivocation

Equivocation occurs when a person shifts between the meanings of a word without indicating that they are doing so. Used cleverly, equivocation in humor or artistic allusion can enrich a work. Master Chief John-117 may simply be the generic name given to the protagonist of the *Halo* series, or John-117 was cleverly chosen because of its allusion to the chapter and verse of the New Testament book John 1:17, an apt contrast to the Covenant dogmatism. Intentionally chosen or coincidence, the ability to equivocate on the origin of John-117 allows for a variety of possible interpretations and story arcs.

Equivocation, unfortunately, is not often encountered in such positive forms. Instead, equivocation often happens in conversations with self-proclaimed know-it-alls who appear to be talking about one thing, but when questioned, shift their position as though they were talking about quite another. Suppose, for example, someone were commenting on the awesome power of the pistol in *Halo*, and you, knowing a thing or two about the evolution of the pistol in the *Halo* series—and eager to call out this obvious phony—pressed them on whether they were referring to the M6D or the M6C. If such a conversation were actually to occur like this, and it easily might if you were talking to someone who had only played *Halo: Combat Evolved*, then your line of questioning would be homing in on this phony's equivocation of the type of pistol he or she was referring to.

It's very common to assume you understand what someone means, and it is even more common to do this when you think they're wrong about something they just said. Suppose that instead of asking the phony which pistol they were referring to you simply argued with them about their claim that the pistol had "awesome power." You point out to this phony that the pistol is only powerful sometimes, and other times the pistol feels like a worthless lump of crud in your hands. Had you taken this approach to the conversation, you might argue for several pointless minutes and waste valuable breath citing five to ten good examples of how the pistol simply is not all that powerful. And to top it all off, the phony can maintain their facade of fan-boy superiority by concluding the discussion by saying they were only talking about the pistol from the first *Halo* game (leaving off *Combat Evolved* entirely from the title!). Because you jumped into the debate without first getting clarity on what this phony meant you allowed someone to talk as though they knew a whole lot more than they actually did. And unfortunately, as soon as you point out how they're wrong, they can always claim they were only talking about the M6D, not the M6C.

So while equivocation can be used in some really interesting and artistic ways, it's often also used more nefariously. Those that are ignorant of the truth can use equivocation to retroactively change the meaning of what they said, and those that are interested in manipulating people's beliefs might use equivocation in their arguments. For our purposes, we want to be clear that we are not equivocating in some way when we evaluate the act of camping and those individuals that love to camp. In order to do this, we will need to be clear about the types of camping we are discussing, and we will need to be clear about the criteria we are using when we evaluate camping.

Camping and Strategy

Camping occurs in several different contexts, and so before we say anything derogatory (or I should say, anything *else* derogatory) about the camper, we must be clear about the type or types of camping we find offensive. Let's try a definition. As I said at the outset, campers are those individuals who position themselves in strategic locations during competitive multiplayer games. Of course, camping isn't simply being strategic in placement, since every player worth their salt attempts to be strategic in how they move about the map. No, camping is different than simply being strategic in positioning yourself in that once a camper finds a strategic location, they pretty much stay there the entire game, or until it's clear that the strategic advantage of the positioning has been compromised.

Despite the open hostility towards campers, to anyone who uses their brain when they play a game this sounds more or less exactly like how you would want to play an FPS, particularly one that was militarily inspired. After all, soldiers in battle don't run willy-nilly around a battlefield. They often position themselves in strategic locations, and I have no doubt that when and if wars could be safely won by remaining in these strategic locations, there is no reason to move out of them. Moving around the battlefield is dangerous, and so it is a matter of taking a calculated risk when soldiers are given orders to move. In competitive multiplayer, like that in the *Halo* series, moving around means taking certain risks. The primary difference between these cases—and we should not gloss lightly over this—is the fact that soldiers in battle are risking far more when they move around than a person playing a game. The risks and advantages of moving are always balanced against the risks and advantages of remaining where you are. If staying where you are presents a very strategic advantage and doesn't present a very large risk, then you should stay where you are. If, on the other hand, moving proves to be the most strategic thing to do in light of the foreseeable risks, then a person should move.

So when camping out provides a strategic advantage, then it seems like a very reasonable thing to do, almost like the smart thing to do! But camping is also something that we do with good reason, and that reason is to achieve some goal that we have in an FPS. When we start mixing reasons with goals, then we're on the brink of making evaluations or judgments. Hence, when we describe an activity like camping and we talk about *why* people camp, it is virtually impossible to do this without incorporating some sort of evaluation. Since our goal here, ultimately, is to evaluate camping, then the reason why a person camps seems to be a perfectly appropriate place to divide up the types of camping.

Camping, Context, and Evaluation

The context or situation in which a player camps determines in part the strategic advantage that camping gives a player. Camping in a particular context is more or less a good idea or a bad idea depending on the degree of advantage granted by the position balanced against the risk of remaining in that position. In capture the flag, camping out by your team's flag makes it more difficult for the other team to get your flag, and so it's usually a good idea. In a king-of-the-hill type game, where players earn points by remaining in certain locations for as long as they can, clearly camping out in those locations is a good idea. Alternatively, we can see how camping is a very bad idea when it does not serve to help you achieve your goals, like winning the match. If everyone on a team during a capture the flag match camped out by their own flag, then they would never get the other team's flag. If both teams did this, then neither team would ever come into contact with their opponent. If you never even see the other team and you never get their flag, then you really can't win.

This goes to show that camping's worth or value is wrapped up in the context within which a player camps, and so must our evaluations of camping. Good camping, at its core, involves smart playing given a particular game context, and consequently, bad camping involves dumb playing in a particular game context.

Why then all the bad press for campers? If a person is taking advantage of a strategic location given the game type, then it seems as if camping is the laudable thing to do. It is, after all, the smart thing to do. Campers should be raised up and held on high as our intellectual superiors! Who cares if it slows down the pace of the game? So what if this leads to stalemates in some game types like capture the flag? Stalemates aren't caused by anything inherently wrong with camping, are they? It's perfectly fine and smart if a few people do it, right?

Unfortunately, players do not always understand when camping makes sense and when it doesn't, and this lack of strategic camping is the cause of much angst. Furthermore, camping may prove to be what is called a "dominant strategy" in some game types like slayer (deathmatch) or team slayer (team deathmatch). A dominant strategy is a strategy employed by a player of a game, because it is the best strategy regardless of what the opponent chooses to do. Dominant strategies and the problems they pose were first systematically discussed by game theorists in applied mathematics, but dominant strategies and game theory are as old as war, economics, and politics. They have been discussed by philosophers for thousands of years, and it applies equally in those cases as it does to competitive multiplayer in FPS.

Suppose there are only two people playing a competitive round of slayer. The strategy to sit and wait for your opponent to appear so that you can surprise and frag them seems preferable—strategically speaking—to the alternative, which is to run around looking for them.[1] Your opponent is faced with the same choice, after all,

[1] Similarly, if you get separated from someone you're trying to find, and they

and while you're running around looking for them, they may be lying in wait to frag you. As a result, two smart players following their individual dominant strategy will camp the whole match and never see the other person. In this case, camping actually undermines the goal of the game, which is to achieve the most frags. By being the best strategy to win the match, it also prevents either player from achieving the goal of the game.

Let's put this into a little perspective. You now know that in order to play a game of slayer at least some of the players must not camp. But you also now know that those who are moving around the map are putting themselves at risk. Putting those two thoughts together implies that some players must risk themselves in order to keep the game going. Ultimately, legitimate frustration stems from those individuals who are trying to play the game, are thereby forced to take risks, but who are forced also to compete with individuals who do not see the bigger picture or who do not care. Those that camp benefit from those poor saps who run around the map to achieve a greater good. The tension and hostility between campers and non-campers in a slayer type game—in its purest theoretical form—is a tension and hostility between egocentric free riders[2] and those that are working to keep the game going. It is a matter of fairness and getting what you deserve.

Spawn Camping

Now, of course, it is the way of the philosopher to shoot for the most theoretic and often esoteric explanation of a problem possible, even when a simpler explanation is readily at hand (Occam's Razor out the window!). Even Socrates who claimed regularly to speak like the common people, rarely made his point without making some mind-bendingly complex arguments. However, if we want to call campers to the mat, and truly make a mockery of their behavior, then we will do well by our argument to make the strongest case possible against the fairness of camping. We certainly can't do this if people don't understand what we're talking about, and admittedly, talk of game-theoretic and dominant strategies was probably over the heads of those campers who end up

are trying to find you as well. Isn't it better for at least one of you to stay in the same place, so that you can fix your chances of running across one another?

[2] "Egocentric free riders" is an academic way of saying "selfish jerk."

ruining what would otherwise be a good match. It certainly didn't change the minds of those we most need to eliminate from our games. We need a simple example.

Spawn camping is probably the clearest example of what we would want to call an unfair or unsportsmanlike form of camping. We've seen how camping can be legitimate in some forms, and so instead of muddying the waters of debate by equivocating on the types of camping we might not like, we can focus on this obvious example. Spawn camping occurs when the camper's strategic location allows them to frag opposing team members shortly after they have entered or re-entered the game. Entering the game or re-entering the battle after you have been fragged is often referred to as spawning, hence the name. The camper's position has been strategically chosen because they know this is where the opposing team spawns, and thereby makes them relatively easy targets.

This type of camping is thought of as unfair, since it doesn't allow the spawning team an opportunity to fight back. This strategy can be so dominant and prevalent in certain game types that if players are intent on spawn camping, then it takes a change in game design to prevent it. The issue we're looking at here is basic to the question of whether games *should* be designed to prevent this behavior. We can't simply assume that they should. We need to explain why this is unfair and what problems come from it. Since spawn camping can occur in any type of game and it is advantageous to do it in virtually all types, the question as to whether or not this is a good or bad way to play is a significant philosophical issue.

Determining the standing of spawn camping is a matter of evaluation, and evaluation is the process of making a determination about the value or worth of some thing or action. Oftentimes people refer to this as giving an "opinion" about the thing or action in question. Tragically, that term has an unfortunate history in our educational system, which trivializes the importance of these evaluations. Children are taught from elementary school on that there is a difference between facts and opinions, and that facts are things that can be proven true or false while opinions cannot. The result of this logic is that opinions are often thought of as things we cannot argue about, since we can't prove them to be true or false.

As you might expect, the *truth* is actually far more complicated than this. Proving something to be true requires an entire theoretical framework, including criteria for what counts as evidence. At best these frameworks, like those foundational to scientific reasoning, have been proven practical or reliable. Of course, if that is our standard—being practical or reliable—then opinions and evaluations are equally justifiable, since they are at their core practical, and when done well, reliable. It's good enough for our purposes if we grant that evaluations, judgments of value, or determinations of value are considered better or worse depending on the reasoning that supports them. Making a claim that spawn camping is wrong, unfair, or unsportsmanlike depends on whether or not those descriptions aptly apply. And this requires an argument and reasoning to prove that those terms do *in fact* apply.

We've already seen that people often equivocate when they make evaluations. Terms like "right," "wrong," "good," "bad," "fair," "unfair," "sportsmanlike," and "unsportsmanlike," are evaluative words. They describe things much like any other way of describing something. For example, if I say that a table is two yards long and one yard wide, then I have described that table. Anyone I'm speaking with who understands what a yard is and what a table is now has a better idea of the table I'm talking about. If I say the table is white and good for writing on, then anyone I'm speaking with who understands what white is and has an understanding for the process of writing, now knows even more about the table.

You could, of course, disagree with me about any of these things I've said about the table. You might, for example, measure the table, and show me that the table is not actually two yards long. In which case, my original description of the table would have been inaccurate. When a way of describing something does not fit the way a thing actually is, in this case the table, then we have inaccurately described the thing in question. This happens in the sciences when a thing or event is described inaccurately, just as it happens in evaluations.

How does this all matter for evaluating spawn camping? Well, the problem we want to avoid is making an evaluation based on criteria that are unclear or not shared among most other users of the words. We can argue about the length of the table, because we actually agree on what a yard was. In the same way, we can argue about whether or not spawn camping is good and fair, or bad and unfair, provided that we share some understanding of what those words mean. In this way, we avoid equivocating, and we can have a substantive discussion. The upshot of all this intellectual effort is that we can stop acting and thinking like the children who often dominate us in online battles.

Covering Values

Covering values are the values we employ when we make a comparison between two or more things. Typically, a covering value is used to compare two things that are similar in some ways but different in others. For example, the expression, "You're comparing apples and oranges," is a good example of when a covering value might be used. Even though apples are different than oranges, that doesn't mean we can't compare them. Further, it doesn't imply that we can't decide one is better than the other. What it does mean is that when we do make a determination that one is better than the other, we must be very clear why and how we made that determination. When we evaluate two things so that we can make a comparison to determine which is better or worse (or if they are the same), we use some set of criteria to determine the "pros" and "cons" of each thing we are evaluating. Once we have our lists of what's good about a thing and what's bad about a thing, we then use those lists to compare. For apples and oranges, we can compare these fruits using a covering value, and we can determine that one fruit is better than the other with respect to that particular covering value.

So suppose I decide that oranges are better than apples, and you disagree. To understand our disagreement, and to determine if I have correctly assessed the apple and orange, we must first unpack the covering value I used to make the comparison. Let's say that you ask me why it is that oranges are better than apples, and I respond that oranges are more acidic and juicier than apples. I have just listed two criteria for evaluating these two fruits. My covering value for the comparison is comprised of these two things. Based solely on the criteria I have set out to make the comparison—acidity and juiciness—I am correct that oranges are better than apples.

Two different things might occur to you at this point: 1. acidity and juiciness are not the only things good about a fruit, or 2. acidity and juiciness are not relevant to how good a fruit is at all. If either of these things are your objection to my assessment of the orange and apple, then you're objecting to my use of the covering value that evaluates based on those criteria. You are not actually objecting to the aptness of my evaluation. In other words, you haven't objected to whether or not I was correct in describing the orange as juicier or more acidic. The important thing to learn from this is that you can agree with how I applied my evaluation, but disagree that my evaluation accurately captured what it means to be a better fruit in those circumstances.

How does all this matter for spawn camping? Well, deciding whether or not spawn camping is something that someone should or should not do in a game depends on how we evaluate it compared to the alternatives. In other words, when we choose to spawn camp over playing the game in another way, we have essentially evaluated spawn camping as better than the alternative. To make this sort of evaluation, we need a covering value. The question now is: What covering value are people using when they make that choice, and is that the covering value that ought to be used?

From the outset, when we talked about types of camping we did so with regard to the strategic advantage that camping provided. And if camping didn't provide any advantage, then it wasn't worth doing. In that context, we assumed that the criteria for what made camping good was whether or not it led to winning the match. Although we weren't being explicit about it from the start, it turns out that the covering value we employed was one that measured how well a particular action in an online match helped us win. Hence, when camping caused the game to fall apart because all the players camped and no one came out of hiding, we decided camping was bad because the consequences were that no one could win. Similarly, spawn camping will be evaluated based on the results it produces.

Well, what are the results of spawn camping? It's an easy way to rack up kills, and if you're playing slayer or team slayer, then that's certainly the path to victory. In other game types, spawn camping is advantageous because it keeps your opponents busy and away from their goal, in which case, spawn camping again puts you on the path to victory. So by all accounts, spawn camping is an effective strategy for winning matches. It might even be the most effective strategy, in which case, it is the smartest way to play. Rather than disparaging the spawn camper, we should do our best to be more like him.

At this point, you may be experiencing a bit of discomfort.

ResPwn

Can this be right? We agreed from the outset that spawn camping was unfair and we agreed—for those of us who understood the argument—that the problem with camping in general was that it led to unfair situations in which some players were forced to take risks simply so that the game could be played. Doesn't the same argument apply to spawn camping? It would be nice if it did, because then we would have a good argument against spawn camping. Unfortunately, there's an important difference between camping somewhere on the map, and camping at an opposing team's spawn point. Care to hazard a guess as to what that difference is?

Our covering value evaluates based on how effective a particular strategy is for winning a game. If everyone camps in a generic way—with no spawn camping—then no one actually goes out in to battle and no one wins. Since this proves a very ineffective strategy for winning, we had to conclude according to our covering value that this is a bad thing. On the other hand, if everyone tries to spawn camp, then players being victimized don't actually get to play. They spawn into the game and are immediately fragged. In which case, regardless of the type of game you are playing, the first team to successfully spawn camp has rendered the other team impotent to do anything, and so, game over. Spawn campers win, and the only game in town from here until the end of time is spawn camping. Notice the difference? Spawn camping, regardless of the situation, actually has a winner. It does not undermine our achieving of the goal, which is to win the game.

What we can conclude from this is that if your goal is to win and it doesn't matter to you how you achieve that goal, then you're actually being foolish if you don't spawn camp. According to our covering value, which is the same covering value we used before to evaluate camping in general, spawn camping is the best thing to do.

Turnabout's Fair Play

So you might have thought from the introduction that this was a chapter on the evils of spawn camping, but now you've stumbled over my conclusion in support of spawn camping. You might say that I've been doing a little camping of my own, and while I've been waiting, since it took you so long to get here, I thought of some counter-objections to the objections you're only just starting to form. So let me start by telling you what you're about to say to me in rejection of my analysis, and I'll conclude by telling you how right you are, so that I can frag you in the back at the end.

I think there are two major lines of argument to be used here. The first is that winning by any means necessary is not an appropriate way to win, and the second is that the act of spawn camping really undermines the type of game that is supposed to be played.

I'll start with the second objection first, since I think it is the better of the two objections to spawn camping. If I sit down to play a game of capture the flag, domination, or king of the hill, then I have done so with certain expectations about how those games are played. The rules that guide those games have been constructed—at least they were intended—so that I am forced to think about more than simply fragging my opponent as many times as possible, and I have chosen to play them, because I did not want to play slayer or team slayer. Call me weird, but I like a little diversity. The problem with spawn camping is that it can completely eliminate the elements of the game I enjoy. While one team is effectively pinned down by spawn campers, the team that has successfully spawn camped may proceed to complete any other goals of the match unobstructed. The game strategy shifts back to the same old slayer strategy, and camping is the only game in town. If this is your objection to spawn camping, then we are in agreement.

Oh no, wait, we aren't actually in agreement. The game type hasn't changed just because one team uses a stregy that is so effective that the other team can't retaliate. The rules are still the same, and one team followed those rules to victory. Just because your team fell victim to the strategy doesn't mean it wasn't a good way to win. Nor does it mean you were playing a different game. It just means one type of strategy works for a variety of game types.

As for the first objection, which I have for the sake of confusion dealt with second, the fact that someone does not like the way in which another person played the game—provided they played within the rules and did not force a shift in game type—does not appear to be anything more than saying, "I don't like that. It's not the way I do things." This is a variation of, "you should win by being good at aiming and shooting, and spawn camping is a cheap way to win."

It's difficult to know quite how to reason with a person like this, since they're being totally unreasonable. This game is a game like any other, because it has rules that lead to having a winner. If you're not breaking the rules, then what is the difference in terms of fairness between your dying after I move my reticule over your character and your dying because your character was moved into my reticule? It's true that one may take more skill than the other, but just because skill is involved doesn't mean things are suddenly more fair. Skills take time to develop, time that appears to be wasted on middle-schoolers, high-schoolers, and socially awkward college students. How is it fair that they have all that time to develop their skills? It isn't really.

The idea that these games should be won or lost based on skills is almost always argued for by people with those skills, and the notion that camping or spawn camping is a perfectly legitimate way to win is often argued for by those smart enough not to waste their time developing those skills. As for fairness, that's a concept trotted out primarily by the losers.[3]

---

[3] Special thanks to Sam Butcher, the greatest gamer I know. And apologies to Chris Metivier, who hates campers and whose copy of *Halo 2* I have yet to return.

Legendary

13
Sandbox Confrontations

SHANE FLIGER

At the heart of every *Halo* game and every player's experience is warfare. It takes different forms, to be sure—the *boots-on-the-ground* First Person Shooter (FPS), the *command-tent-presence* Real Time Strategy (RTS) game—but it lies at the core of every experience crafted in Bungie's gameworld.

Humanity launches latter-day spears and explosives, and in return the Covenant lets loose with bolts of energy from more starkly advanced plasma-based weaponry. While the series has expanded into table-top strategy games and numerous other genres of gaming it remains, at its heart, a series based on the immersion that only First Person Shooter gaming can provide. With the gun raised from the bottom of the screen and the HUD laid over the television screen, the player steps into a futuristic battlefield and fights for the salvation of humankind.

In the four FPS games within the *Halo* library, the player takes on the role of two vastly different human protagonists. The main protagonist, the Master Chief John-117, is a Spartan-II super-soldier clad in powered armor. He appears as the central figure in the main trilogy—*Halo: Combat Evolved, Halo 2*, and *Halo 3*—as such, most of the plot is witnessed through his golden visor. The second human protagonist is the Rookie, an Orbital Drop Shock Trooper (ODST) who recently survived the near-annihilation of his unit and got assigned to another squad just prior to the game's opening. Appearing in *Halo 3: ODST*, the Rookie's story takes place simultaneously as the Chief's during the time frame of *Halo 2*.

These two playable characters are the primary human instruments by which the player experiences war in the Bungie sandbox.

Each represents a differing aspect of that conflict, and by examining both an astute player can glean much about the nature of war itself.

Knight Errant + Walking Death-mobile = Master Chief

> You are the Master Chief—all that remains of a classified military project to build a series of genetically enhanced super-soldiers. *You are humanity's last and best hope* against the Covenant—but you're woefully outmatched, and survival is not guaranteed.
>
> —*Halo: Combat Evolved* Instruction Booklet (emphasis mine)

While appearing at first to be yet another hot-off-the-shelf character from the Hero Factory, the Chief is much more than one more faceless character waiting to be controlled by the gamer. He carries significant importance to the plot as well as any study of warfare in Bungie's creation. An in-depth look at his armor, weapon, and voice-acting showcases Bungie's hero as a moral representative for Just War Theory as much as a hero found in any epic tale.

Just War Theory, as put forward by philosophers Aristotle and Cicero and later by theologians St. Augustine and St. Thomas Aquinas, deals with the justification of how and why wars should be fought. Just War Theory is broken into three areas:

1. *Jus Ad Bellum*—the rules that govern the justice of war
2. *Jus In Bello*—the rules that govern just and fair conduct in war, and
3. *Jus Post Bellum*—the rules that cover the responsibility and accountability of warring parties after the war.[1]

Due to *Halo 3* closing with the end of the Human-Covenant War, the final area is problematic to explore in Bungie's gameworld. The first two, however, prove excellent areas of exploration in regard to the Chief and the conflicts he participates in.

From the moment that the Master Chief steps out of the cryogenic chamber in *Combat Evolved*, he is immediately understood to

---

[1] "War," *Stanford Encyclopedia of Philosophy*, <http://plato.stanford.edu/entries/war/>.

be something more than human. Clad in pearlescent green MJOLNIR armor and gazing out from a golden visor, at first glance he has more in common with the alien foes boarding the *Pillar of Autumn* or the Scorpion tanks in the cargo bay than the fellow humans desperately defending the ship. The technicians running the diagnostics on his armor chatter nervously in the face of the Chief's silence, uneasily sharing space with such an imposing figure. Even while the Chief heads toward the bridge unarmed, he still shrugs off plasma bolts from Elites and Grunts that make other soldiers shout out in pain.

The MJOLNIR armor is one of the most defining markers of the Chief, and calls forth images of both medieval knights and modern machines of war. This mixture is key, as it helps reveal the sterile yet idealized nature of warfare that the Chief represents throughout the *Halo* games. With the full helmet and armor, comparisons to medieval knights are inevitable.[2] Just as with those chivalrous knights of medieval lore, the Chief fights for a just cause: the avoidance of extinction. This ties directly into a key requirement of *jus ad bellum*, the set of criteria that determine if entering a war is justifiable: the possession of *right intent*.

The general concept of *right intent* is that a nation waging a just war should be waging that war for justice and not for self-interest or warmongering. This raises a potential issue: *how would the conflict portrayed in Halo not be based in self-interest, when the whole game is about surviving?* This question raises a good point, but once the scale of the conflict is taken into account the point becomes moot. The Covenant has been waging a genocidal campaign against humanity for well over thirty years, and the species' collective back is against the wall. The Chief, then, is fighting a war where his self-interest cannot overwhelm the larger case of justice—the preservation of the species—due to the intrinsic connection between the two. During the conflicts in the main trilogy, the Chief is central to the climaxing events of a war spanning more than three decades. Given that knowledge, there is little doubt that the war is justified despite the Chief's self-interest.

After all, this is the survival of the human race we're talking about! Even absolutist pacifists would be hard-pressed not to pick up a weapon when faced with utter extinction, and that is the exact fate that the Chief fights to deny.

---

[2] Indeed, with the introduction of the energy sword in *Halo 2* the comparisons made themselves!

Combined with the allusions to medieval knights, the Chief's MJOLNIR armor represents military technology with an utter lack of subtlety. While lip service may be given to the fact that the Chief's armor is green and thus based on camouflage on some level, the sheer fact that it is pearlescent negates any real use for that property. As previously mentioned, when the Chief steps out from the cryogenic tube in *Combat Evolved* or climbs up from the impact crater in *Halo 3* he more closely resembles the material of waging war than his fellow soldiers. This difference allows the player to be one step removed from the action at all times, as they experience warfare through the visor of energy-shielded armor as opposed to the helmet of a regular soldier. This is especially notable in *Halo 3*, as the markings on the glass of the helmet are superimposed on the player's television HUD.

Moreover, the sounds and visuals created by the MJOLNIR armor are clear parallels to unmanned military drones and other front-line technology. Much of this information—red arrows depicting the direction of incoming fire, for instance, or the slow whine of recharging shields—is absorbed by the player subconsciously during the game. In practice, the gauges and meters are no different than a fighter pilot's instruments or the gas gauge on the vehicle parked in the garage. They allow an individual to read information about their surroundings without directly experiencing it, fighting a war without the full tactile force of the conflict. Plasma bolts are absorbed by the armor's energy shields while the baseline Marines next to the Chief shout in pain when each landed shot burns through skin and body armor.

The power of the MJOLNIR armor that the player wields as the Chief is an excellent example of another condition of *jus ad bellum*: the end being proportional to the means used. At the opening of *Combat Evolved*, the Chief's goal is simply to survive. As the trilogy moves forward, the end goal continues to rise in importance—not only does the Chief need to ensure humanity's survival against the religious zealotry of the Covenant, but also has to defend it from the all-consuming Flood parasite recently released. Against enemies such as these, the power unleashed by the MJOLNIR armor against obviously weaker enemies such as Grunts or Jackals ceases to present a moral issue. Indeed, even the similar shielded armor worn by the Elites (and later Brutes) is less effective than the armor worn by the Master Chief. By the end of *Halo*

3, the only enemies that seem equal to the Chief are the Brute Chieftains and Flood Pure Forms.

If one invokes the principle of proportionality, however, the perceived inequality of force shows itself as false. The Covenant has razed humanity's colonies and slaughtered untold billions of souls. Single Covenant carriers decimate entire battle groups of human starships. When inserted into this larger backdrop, the military superiority of the Chief's MJOLNIR armor shows itself as totally within the bounds of proportional force. The one-on-one inequality tilted in the player's favor during firefights is vastly outweighed by the larger inequality in manpower and technology tilted in the enemy's.

Silence of Master Chief

Keep your head down! There's two of us in here now, remember?

—Cortana to Master Chief, "The Pillar of Autumn"

Another key component to examine when considering the Master Chief and his role in Bungie's war-focused sandbox is the element of voice that surrounds him. First and foremost, the Chief is a mixture of a pure silent protagonist and a voiced character. Silent during gameplay sequences, the Chief is fully voiced during the cinematic sequences. Outside of the cinematic sequences, the Chief is the silent straight man to the surrounding characters. Ostensibly done in order to allow the player to more fully immerse themselves into the role of the Chief, it also showcases a principle of *jus in bello*, the justice of war: the principle of responsibility.

The best example of this comes in *Combat Evolved*, during the missions involving the quite possibly rampant AI Monitor 343 Guilty Spark. Abducted to Halo's Library, the Chief is told by Spark that the installation must be activated in order to contain the Flood outbreak. Having just experienced the parasite firsthand in the previous mission, the Chief readily agrees to help and proceeds to fight his way through the Flood-infested Library. The Chief reacts to the most visible threat—the Flood—and lacks the knowledge to understand exactly what Spark means by "containment protocols." By lacking the knowledge that activating Halo's defenses will result in the mass murder of billions, the Chief stands his moral ground in ignorance instead of knowledge. His silence during gameplay reinforces the Chief's decision to activate Halo's defenses. He is totally focused on the task at hand, and believes it to be the correct one.

Once achieving the Index from the Library, Spark teleports the two of them back to Halo's Control Center. After being confronted by an irate Cortana and informed of Halo's true nature, the Master Chief faces another aspect of the principle of responsibility: the morality of obeying orders. He has been ordered to activate Halo by Spark, with the threat of death hovering in front of him in the form of Sentinels. Equally, he has been ordered by Cortana to prevent Spark from firing the ring and slaughtering billions of individuals needlessly. The principle of responsibility asserts upon soldiers that they must remember that they will one day become civilians again, and must be prepared to do so without the guilt of war crimes.

The Chief sides with Cortana, fending off the Sentinels and instigating the endgame of *Combat Evolved*. He bears, however, the responsibility of the Flood outbreak on *Halo* while he attempts to destroy it. The Marine casualties (as well as those of the Covenant) are squarely on his shoulders for deciding not to immediately activate the ring. The Chief is placed in the unenviable position of weighing the cost of those lives against the innocent lives that would be sacrificed to stop the Flood. Again, the moral status of ignorance comes into play. Now that he has been given all of the information regarding Spark's "containment," the Chief can no longer claim ignorance. He must knowingly sacrifice those billions in order to contain the Flood, and the Chief chooses to disregard Spark's order in favor of his own moral compass. By doing so, he reveals even more strongly the idealized warfare that Bungie has crafted around him. He is able to make that decision, as opposed to having a superior simply issuing an order. His internal morality is what drives his decision, reinforcing the sense of an idealized warrior.

Master Chief's Weapons

I need a weapon.

—Master Chief to Sgt. Johnson, "Cairo Station"

The final key component to be considered when examining the Master Chief is the weaponry that he is depicted using. While able to wield almost any weapon in the game, the in-game cinematics always depict the Chief armed with a version of the game's Assault Rifle.[3]

---

[3] In *Halo 2*, the Assault Rifle was removed in lieu of the Battle Rifle. While the difference in gameplay was substantial, the difference in symbolism was minor.

Even when the player starts with different default weaponry, such as the *Combat Evolved* level "Truth and Reconciliation," the cinematic directly before gameplay shows the Master Chief shouldering an Assault Rifle. The Assault Rifle's single-mindedness—a weapon meant to dominate, not undermine or strike from shadows—mirrors the Chief's own determination and the gamer's focus on achieving the objectives of the given mission.

In terms of gameplay, the Assault Rifle is often eclipsed by other weaponry. Why, then, would Bungie insist on continually depicting the Chief preferring it? First, the Assault Rifle is first and foremost a human weapon. It clearly marks the Chief as a human, when his armor and size differentiate him so much from the other humans encountered in the game. Second, it showcases the abilities that the Chief can bring to bear on the battlefield. An average soldier can be given an outstanding weapon and perform spectacularly, in-game and out-of-game. An outstanding soldier can get the job done with a toothpick, and that is what the Chief represents.

The Assault Rifle becomes a part of the Chief's symbol, as synonymous as a lightsaber has become with Luke Skywalker. This matches the Chief's role in the fight for humankind's survival, as the player is repeatedly forced into both small-and large-scale battles against enemies. This ties into the idealized symbol the Chief becomes over the development of the trilogy, as the Assault Rifle clearly marks him as a front-line fighter. The Master Chief stands as a bulwark upon which waves of hostile aliens and parasites break. Under the player's control, the Chief turns into both unstoppable force and immovable object; inspiring tenacity in NPC (Non-Player Characters) cohorts and terrified scampering in enemies in equal doses, he immediately controls whatever battlefield he steps onto. Throughout Bungie's trilogy, the Master Chief exists as a fundamental example of the strengths of Just War Theory.

A Less Idealized Soldier for a More Desperate Time

This Marine was recently transferred from the 26th MEF, part of a Rapid Offensive Picket that suffered near-annihilation at New Jerusalem, Cygnus. *Like most ODSTs, his actions speak louder than words.*

—Bungie.net summary of the Rookie (emphasis mine)

When compared to the Master Chief, the ODST known as the Rookie seems like a young child who is trying to step into his father's *too-big-to-fit* boots. Appearing in the expansion *Halo 3: ODST,* the Rookie seems at first to be a lackluster replacement to the towering figure of the former protagonist. Indeed, on first glance the Rookie shares more in common with the NPC soldiers fighting and dying beside the Master Chief than with the Chief himself! One can easily imagine the Rookie being inserted into the main trilogy only to serve as a tutorial for the danger of the Flood or some other death-causing threat. The decision by Bungie, then, to make him the central protagonist for *Halo 3: ODST* is a remarkable one on many levels. Not only does the Rookie challenge the validity of the gamer's conception of a "hero," he also challenges the representation of Just War Theory that the Chief follows through on in the main trilogy.

Absolute War and Total War

A highly-trained but baseline human, he lacks the physical and chemical upgrades that the Chief possesses as a Spartan-II as well as the MJOLNIR shielded power armor. As such, he (and through him, the player) experiences the full tactile experience of war in a way that the Chief cannot. When subjected to an enemy melee attack, for instance, the Rookie goes flying while the Master Chief can typically go toe-to-toe with most enemies. He is also alone for a majority of the game, as gameplay revolves around finding clues to trigger flashbacks in order to establish the fate of your ODST squad. By looking at the Rookie through the same criteria that we used to examine the Chief, it quickly becomes clear that he represents a vastly different conception of war: a mixture of absolute war and total war.

As put forth in the book *On War* by Carl Von Clausewitz, absolute war can be defined as the deployment of all a given society's resources and citizens into the machine of war.[4] Clausewitz held that absolute war was caused by three reciprocal actions:

1. an utmost use of force, where each State continually upgrades the force used to grasp the advantage over an enemy

[4] Carl von Clausewitz, *On War* (Penguin, 1982).

2. the aim to disarm the enemy, so that the defeated enemy will comply with the victor, and
3. an utmost exertion of powers, where both the strength of available means and the strength of will are measured, compared to the enemy's, and increased accordingly.

These three reciprocal actions function as a continuous circle, as each side continues to raise the level in response to the enemy. Clausewitz described this as an unachievable absolute in order to serve as the bedrock for his more nuanced theories. Yet Clausewitz never imagined a war of the likes that humankind has found itself embroiled in during the twenty-sixth century. The Covenant and the United Nations Space Command, with advances such as faster-than-light space travel and an end goal involving the possible extermination of a species, are at least partially engaging in Clausewitz's "logical fantasy."

Total war, however, is not just a synonym for absolute war. The phrase "total war" simply describes the lack of any restraint when it comes to how a given war is conducted. This lack of restraint is most typically experienced with a war's noncombatants, as a nation engaging in total war will likely make no distinction between soldier and civilian. Germany's supreme general during World War I, Erich von Ludendorff, wrote extensively on the topic of total war. He claimed that "War is total; first, because the theater of war extends over the whole territory of the belligerent nations. In addition to this diffusion of risks, total war also involves the active participation of the whole population in the war effort."[5] Humanity has a long history of engaging in "total war" campaigns, and as such the Covenant's modus operandi isn't totally new to the humans of that conflict.

Rookie and Chief

> Course, from what we can tell, the Super isn't exactly in fighting shape. Seems the Covenant have knocked a few screws loose. Won't be a problem. *ODST's are used to working in the dark.*
>
> —Gunnery Sgt. Buck, *Desperate Measures* ViDoc (emphasis mine)

---

[5] Edward Mead Earle, *Makers of Modern Strategy: Military Thought from Machiavelli to Hitler* (Princeton University Press, 1943).

The first clear example of this new mixture of war that the Rookie represents is his armor. While clearly manufactured by the same military apparatus that crafted the Chief's MJLONIR armor and bringing to mind the same similarity to machines of war, it altogether lacks the similarities to medieval knights that the Chief carries. The armor is matte black and grey, not pearlescent green. With its harsh angles and dark coloration, the helmet more closely resembles a death's head than the fighter-pilot-inspired helmet of the MJLONIR armor. Instead, the Rookie's armor suggests a much more modern parallel—so-called "deniable operations," such as those performed by special operations teams. This depicts the Rookie as not only obviously human (something the Chief struggles with), but as the type of soldier that is often ordered to do the type of actions that win wars but are morally questionable. The Rookie is fighting for the same end goal that the Chief is, but he is not a shining paragon of military virtue. He is not fighting battles that will shape the face of the galaxy or involved in the breaking of a religious hegemony. The Rookie is simply fighting to survive, to reclaim whatever possible out of a wreck of a mission.

In terms of function, there are two major differences that mark the distinctions between the types of warfare the Chief and Rookie engage in. The strongest difference is the lack of energy shielding in ODST armor.[6] As such, the Rookie lacks a key component of protection that is fundamental to the Master Chief. He (and the player) are exposed to a higher level of danger in every firefight because of it. The Rookie must be continually aware of his surrounding in the wreckage of New Mombasa, because a stray sniper shot would not simply deplete an energy shield. This continued tension showcases that the Rookie experiences the full tactile nature of war, as well as a requirement to strike from the flanks of the enemy. Referring back to Clausewitz's third reciprocal action, the Rookie's limitations of armor force him to adopt tactics fueled by subterfuge and not moral strength.

The second difference is the lack of a motion tracker in the HUD of the armor's helmet.[7] It subconsciously feeds information in

---

[6] In terms of gameplay, the introduction of "stamina" is meant to make up for the lack of shielding. Incoming fire depletes this stamina before actual health is depleted, but it is obvious the Rookie is still physically under fire during this period.

[7] A motion tracker does exist in *Halo 3:ODST*, in a manner of speaking. By opening the VISR database, the Rookie can see a top-down tactical map of the area

the middle of firefights, letting the Chief plan his attack and subsequently execute it with efficiency. The deeper issue that the motion tracker conveys is that, as part of a Just War, the Chief can morally judge who are combatants and who aren't. He is utterly confident both in who his targets are and his ability to dispatch them. In comparison, the Rookie has Visual Intelligence System, Reconnaissance (VISR)—an enhanced-vison mode that enables his HUD do two things. First, it enhances the ambient light on the streets of New Mombasa. This reinforces once again the fact that the Rookie is forced to strike from shadows in order to establish a superiority of force against the Covenant. Secondly, and more importantly, it outlines friendly contacts, enemies, and important objects with varying colors. This reinforces that the Rookie is involved in a "total war" campaign, as he has to visually identify his targets instead of relying on a sense of moral strength to justify his actions.

Silence of the Rookie

Hey Rookie, you out there? Respond, that's an order!

—Gunnery Sgt. Buck, "NMPD HQ"

Unlike the Master Chief, the Rookie is a true silent protagonist. He never speaks throughout the entirety of the *Halo 3: ODST* campaign, responding to questions with body language or direct action.[8] His silence only reinforces the loneliness that inhabits the city—while the Rookie works to establish what happened over the span of time he was unconscious, he has no friendly contacts to respond to. This lone-soldier reality, made much more poignant due to his limitations of equipment, showcases the total war environment he has dropped into. He literally has nobody to call for support: no AI companion speaking in his ear, no alien sidekick to help spring traps or cover his back.

He steps into a situation where the only option is to treat every living creature as a possible threat. It could be argued that Vergil,

---

with Covenant soldiers marked on it. This fails to be a one-to-one equivalent, however, due to the Rookie's inability to use it while moving or fighting.

[8] Given the Rookie's experiences before the events of the game, the possibility of post-traumatic stress disorder is a compelling reason for his lack of speech. It would give yet another reason to support the Rookie representing a darker view of war, as well. Delving into this idea, however, is beyond the reaches of this essay.

the Superintendent-class AI inhabiting the city itself, serves a similar role as Cortana does to the Master Chief. This comparison falls short when push comes to shove, though, since Vergil can only speak through signs and machines. He lacks the emotional complexity of Cortana, and cannot satisfy the position of a fully-capable teammate.

The other noteworthy consequence of the Rookie's silence comes during the climax of the game. After being reunited with both Dare and Buck, the Rookie suddenly has teammates who speak freely during firefights and more quiet moments. The primary impact this has is to make the battlefield much, much *noisier*. After an entire night of silence, of hiding and striking from shadows in order to establish superiority of force, the Rookie is thrust into a cacophony of taunts, orders, and status updates. The effect is disorienting. The player struggles along with the Rookie to establish that clear focus of the previous hours. The Rookie is not the Chief, however, and clearly is meant to function as a part of a team. He eventually finds that the total war the Covenant has been inflicting can be turned back around much easier with teammates, regardless of the additional voices now surrounding him.

> You've been solo since we dropped? Fighting on the surface? Unless you spent all night hiding in your pod, you must know your stuff. Show me.
>
> —Captain Veronica Dare to Rookie, "Data Hive"

As with Master Chief and the Assault Rifle, Bungie made the decision to equip the Rookie with a signature weapon. In all of the cinematics in *Halo 3: ODST*, the Rookie is shown wielding the M7S, a sound-suppressed caseless submachine gun. First handed the weapon by a fellow ODST, the Rookie can continually find more ammo for it in the many supply caches throughout the city. Like the games that feature the Master Chief, the Rookie can wield any other weapon prior to triggering a cutscene and still be shown with his respective default weapon. The fact that the Rookie's default weapon is a silenced version of a mid-range weapon is just as telling as the choice of the Assault Rifle for the Chief.

From a gameplay perspective, the M7S is arguably far more useful in-game than the Assault Rifle. It gives the Rookie the ability to engage smaller patrols of Covenant troops without alerting others nearby. Similarly, it possesses a remarkable ability to strip the armor from the Brutes that the Rookie encounters. The rather limited range of the submachine gun calls into focus two things. It showcases the type of conflict that the Rookie typically experiences, which underlines the seriousness of the threat due to his lack of shielding. In addition, it also suggests the tactics that Bungie had in mind when crafting the character. He is not intended to thunder across an open area, whacking Grunts with the butt of his rifle then trading shots with a Brute captain; he is meant to strike from the flanks, mercilessly hitting the enemy where they are weak.

The M7S has become just as synonymous with the Rookie as the Assault Rifle has with the Master Chief. More than just helping to represent a character, however, it erodes some of the moral strength which the Chief had been endowed with. As central of a character as the Chief is, he could never successfully "finish the fight" if troopers such as the Rookie were unwilling to face a more morally ambiguous battleground.

> What can I say? It was a hell of a night.
>
> —Gunnery Sgt. Buck, "Coastal Highway"

The core of Bungie's *Halo* universe is warfare. By offering two vastly different human protagonists, the game developer challenges players to decide which version they respond to most vividly. The Master Chief's Just War Theory calls forth martial posters and representations of real-life soldiers as moral combatants, waging the good fight with clear consciences. In stark opposition, the Rookie's mixture of Absolute War and Total War conjures images of embedded journalists and the harsh reality of urban warfare. The two combine to create a more realistic portrayal of warfare than either one could do separately, and leave players with a more complete vision of the differing efforts required to snatch victory from the maw of defeat.[9]

---

[9] I thank Luke Cuddy for his incredibly helpful revisions, as well as my parents, Richard and Kathleen for their support. Additionally, this chapter would not have been possible without the author's personal shipboard AIs—Lindsey Render, Tim Weaver, and Jennifer Klimczak—as well as the numerous other friends who spent so much time corpse-humping and trash talking over *Halo*.

14
What Would Foucault Think about Speed Runs, Jeep Jumps, and Zombie?

FELAN PARKER

> The game is worthwhile insofar as we don't know what will be the end.
>
> —-Michel Foucault, *Technologies of the Self*

Have you ever played *Halo* in a new way, different from the way it's meant to be played? Maybe you've done a speed run, and tried to complete *Halo 3* on legendary difficulty as fast as you can. Or maybe you've done some jeep jumping, gathering as many frag grenades as possible under a Warthog and trying to blast it over the archway in "The Silent Cartographer" in *Halo: Combat Evolved*. Perhaps in *Halo 2* you participated in a multiplayer Zombie match, using a set of rules made up, perfected and enforced by your fellow players.

If you have, you're not alone. These novel ways of playing *Halo* are forms of "expansive gameplay," the phenomenon of videogame players adding rules to a game in order to refine, enhance, or otherwise change their experience of it. Not only are speed running, jeep jumping, Zombie and other similar games-within-games loads of fun, they can be linked to the philosophy of Michel Foucault, one of the most (if not *the* most) influential French philosophers of the twentieth century.

Foucault's idea of *aesthetic self-fashioning* is a remarkably similar process to the examples described above. Put simply, aesthetic self-fashioning is about developing rules to live by—a personal ethics—that allow you to become whatever you want to be, and to live in whatever you consider to be a worthwhile manner. For Foucault, the range of possible selves available to a person is strictly limited by the historically-specific institutions and structures that govern their societies and their lives. People are not, in this sense, free. The historical context into which I have been born makes me who I am—I cannot be anyone else, and if I try I will be ostracized or punished by society. However, Foucault contends that in between the rules and limitations of existence, there is space for what he calls aesthetic self-fashioning, which counter-intuitively involves *adding* optional rules to the rules that already govern life. For example, acknowledging that the university cafeteria serves nothing but crap, I can choose to instead eat a strict diet of healthy, organic foods brought from home, and in this small way transform not only my body, but my experience of the world, as well. By imposing these personal rules, individuals can regain control over who they are—in the same way that players can add new rules to *Halo* and gain control over their experience of the game.

There's an uncanny surface resemblance between Foucault's conception of aesthetic self-fashioning and the phenomenon of expansive gameplay, which I'll explore in more detail below: individuals and players, within the historically-specific constraints of lived existence and the rules of a game, impose additional, optional rules, and in doing so gain some measure of power or control over themselves and their experience.

Of course, it would be foolish to simply read meaning into this resemblance uncritically, but it is difficult to ignore. Foucault spent much of his career breaking down certainties and singularities, so it would be profoundly un-Foucauldian to present only one way of pursuing this resemblance. Instead, I'm going to explore the convergences (and divergences) between these two concepts from several perspectives.

First, expansive gameplay can be understood as an explanatory metaphor or model of Foucault's concept of aesthetic self-fashioning; second, expansive gameplay can be understood as an actual example of aesthetic self-fashioning and liberation from constraints; and third, expansive gameplay can be understood as a kind of *simulation* of aesthetic self-fashioning, allowing players to experiment with ways of constructing themselves in the real world on a smaller scale. What does it mean to add rules to *Halo*, and what does this have to do (if anything) with the aesthetic self-fashioning Foucault describes?

Aesthetic Self-Fashioning

Foucault's earlier work on the institutions and discourses of the human sciences, madness, prisons and discipline, and sexuality establishes how structures of knowledge and power—what he sometimes refers to as "games of truth"—constrain, dominate and *constitute* human beings as subjects, determining the range of existential possibilities open to them. For Foucault, knowledge and truth are not universal, and have taken many forms in different historical eras. Knowledge controls minds, determining what is commonly accepted as true and legitimate in a given historical context, while power relations enforce the official laws and unwritten rules that govern human bodies and behaviour.

There's no escaping this omnipresent structure, sometimes referred to as "Power-Knowledge," for it is always already there, *making people who they are.* Power-Knowledge can never really be challenged or changed, because everything people are, everything they know, everything they believe, and everything they can do emerges out of their positioning within these structures—without them, individuals would be so fundamentally different that existence would be rendered incomprehensible. This seems like a pretty dire situation—not only am I powerless to change the structures that dominate my life, I don't even have control over my self or who I am. However, in his later work on sexuality and subjectivity,[1] Foucault argues that *within* these constraints, individuals can engage in specific kinds of practices that are in some sense liberating.

As individuals, people are subjected to power, but are nevertheless constituted as active subjects that can use the power available to them to transform their selves and experiences. Although they are restricted by Power-Knowledge, people are not brainwashed automatons—they are more-or-less thinking, acting subjects who can learn to harness the very human powers of thought, imagination and desire within the limits of our historical context to gain a measure of control over themselves and their lives. This later turn toward the self as the third component of his philosophy (Power-Knowledge-Self) is intended by Foucault to "show people

[1] See Michel Foucault, *The History of Sexuality Volume 2: The Use of Pleasure* (Vintage, 1985) and *The History of Sexuality Volume 3: The Care of the Self* (Vintage, 1986).

that they are much freer than they feel," to articulate spaces of freedom, and to search for alternative ways that people can construct themselves.[2] "Individuals . . . constitute themselves as subjects of the moral code of their culture that simultaneously provides a field where it is possible to re-create oneself" (p. 154). Through an ethical and aesthetic practice of self-fashioning, Foucault argues, life can become a work of art. Foucault never specifies what life as a work of art should look like, because he does not believe in a singular, fixed ideal. Rather, each individual determines for himself or herself, based on constant, rigorous self-examination, what they will become, and how.

According to Foucault, modern subjectivities are limited and *fashioned* by many different forces, but the right attitude or approach to life can challenge this limitation. The key question therefore becomes how individuals can intervene in this process by engaging in *further* fashioning of the self, in order to move beyond their historical contexts. Foucault outlines four elements of aesthetic self-fashioning: the *ethical substance* is the specific part of the self that is "worked on;" the *mode of subjection* is the reason or motivation for engaging in self-fashioning; *ethical work* is the particular means, tools or activities by which change occurs; and finally the *telos* is the goal, the ideal or the aspiration of the process, which is constantly changing over time as the self is re-fashioned again and again (pp. 141–42). So, if physical exercise is for some people a form of aesthetic self-fashioning, the ethical substance would be the body, the mode of subjection would be a recognition of the body as something that can be improved, the ethical work would be the exercise itself (jogging, lifting weights), and the telos would be the goal of a fit body.

To engage in aesthetic self-fashioning is to exert power on *oneself*—that is to say, impose rules and disciplines on the way one lives—in the same way that an artist exerts power on his or her materials in order to make a work of art. These "tactics by which we live in the world" allow people to "reinvent ourselves as subjects, better fitted for living with the self and with others."[3] These rules are not about what you do, but rather *how to be*. They are

[2] Pirkko Markula-Denison and Richard Pringle, *Foucault, Sport, and Exercise: Power, Knowledge, and Transforming the Self* (Routledge, 2006), p. 138.

[3] Geoff Danaher, Tony Schirato, and Jen Webb, *Understanding Foucault* (Sage, 2000), p. 131.

things you don't *have* to do, but you do anyway to make life better. Playing the last level of *Halo 2* on legendary with all the lights off and the sound cranked to high isn't necessary, but it certainly makes for more exciting experience!

In cultivating a relation to the self, it is possible to cultivate relations to and a responsibility for others, making aesthetic self-fashioning a fundamentally social practice. The fashioning individual must look both inwards at the self and outwards to others at all times in reflecting on his or her situation. The care of the self and of others intensifies social relationships that already exist, having been constituted by Power-Knowledge. Taking care of oneself and knowing oneself are key, linked parts of this process.

Individuals must come into the knowledge that they are constituted, through active contemplation, identification, acknowledgement and problematization of their situation. Foucault's version of the self is a malleable material open to stylization, not a singular, universal, transcendent "true self" to be unearthed (this is not about "unlocking your true potential" in the manner of self-help books). There is no fixed end point to the process of aesthetic self-fashioning. Whenever a goal is achieved or a person becomes what he or she desires to be, the process must begin again and new goals must be determined in order to continue transforming the self. Throughout an individual's life, he or she must pay close attention to, learn about, test, improve and transform himself or herself in order to construct these new ways of existing.

Gilles Deleuze sums it up nicely: "It's no longer a matter of determinate forms, as with knowledge, or of constraining rules, as with power: it's a matter of *optional rules* that make existence a work of art, rules at once ethical and aesthetic that constitute ways of existing or styles of life . . . the will to power operating artistically, inventing new possibilities of life."[4] Personal rules of conduct transform selves and experience, allowing individuals to build (and rebuild) new possibility spaces that exist within the limitations of Power-Knowledge, by using whatever power they have been allowed to possess by those systems. Something as simple as riding a bicycle to work, cutting across parks and through alleyways instead of following the main roads, can become a practice of aesthetic self-fashioning. When reflected upon, this practice highlights

---

[4] Gilles Deleuze, *Negotiations, 1972–1990* (Columbia University Press, 1995), p. 98.

the limitations of everyday existence (in this case, the structure and rules of a city) and creates new ways of navigating and living within these limitations by imposing new rules about where and how to travel. The point of all this is not the kind of systemic change of an idealized Revolution (Foucault, in his later work especially, seems to think this kind of change is either impossible or would be catastrophic); rather, Foucault's modest ideal at the end of his career is a life-long, constant process of revolutionary change in (and between) individual people—life as a work of art-in-progress.

Expansive Gameplay

As noted above, expansive gameplay is a term I coined to refer to the phenomenon of videogame players creatively or pragmatically imposing additional rules on themselves and the game in order to expand, refine, reinvigorate or otherwise enhance their gameplay experience.[5] By adding rules to a game, the player acts within digitally fixed rules, but not necessarily in alignment with the intended or implied ways and goals of playing the game, which sets expansive gameplay apart from straightforward strategizing.

A relatively simple example of expansive gameplay is "role-playing" a game character according to an ethical code, a style or a personality—refusing to murder or steal and choosing friendly dialogue options as a "good" warrior in a fantasy world, or insisting on using certain favourite strategies in favour of others in spite of potential rewards, for example.

Expansive gameplay is different from related practices such as modding (manipulating an existing game to create a new version or an entirely new game, such as *Halo*'s "Forge" mode) and machinima (the use of videogames to create animated narratives or imagery, such as *Red vs Blue*, the popular web series using in-game footage from *Halo*). Unlike modding and machinima, expansive gameplay takes place entirely *within* the fixed rule-based system of the videogame. The player doesn't "break" the rule-based system, he or she *expands* it from within by adding new, optional rules, hence "expansive" gameplay. This phenomenon can take many

[5] For a more in-depth discussion of expansive gameplay as a concept and as a form of emergent gameplay, see: Felan Parker, "The Significance of Jeep Tag: On Player-Imposed Rules in Video Games," *Loading . . . Journal of the Canadian Game Studies Association* 2:9 (2009).

forms, and is not limited to any one genre or type of videogame. Presumably due to its widespread popularity, the *Halo* series has been an extremely rich site for expansive gameplay, yielding a diverse range of examples.

One of the most popular forms of expansive gameplay is "speed running," which imposes a quantifiable goal—rapid completion—on top of the existing, fixed rules of a videogame. In essence, a speed run is an attempt to successfully complete a game (or part of a game) as fast as possible. Video recordings of top times are shared and compared in online communities such as Speed Demos Archive (http://speeddemosarchive.com) that establish a social space for verification, competition and encouragement (after all, a record speed run isn't much good without bragging rights).

Although older games like *Super Mario Brothers* and *Doom* are popular choices for speed running, examples can be found for virtually any well-known game, and the *Halo* series is no exception. A website called High Speed Halo (http://www.highspeedhalo.net) is dedicated to *Halo* speed runs, and compiles statistics and videos of standard speed runs as well as other variations with additional or alternative rules. "Pacifist" runs require the player to complete the games, or specific levels, as fast as possible without killing any enemies (no small feat in an action-oriented game like *Halo*). "Zero Shots," similarly, are completed without using guns or other ranged weapons—only close-combat melee attacks and hand grenades are allowed. All speed runs posted on High Speed Halo are expected to be completed single-player (unless otherwise stated) on the hardest difficulty setting, in order to ensure an equal playing field for all competitors. Needless to say, the rules of speed running and derivative forms of expansive gameplay are not inherent in the *Halo* games: these additional victory conditions are imposed and enforced entirely by individual players and speed run communities.

A famous example of expansive gameplay in a multiplayer context is known as "Zombie," which was originally cultivated by players of *Halo 2*. The game begins as a timed round, and requires each player to be equipped with a shotgun and an energy sword (a powerful close-range melee weapon), and two teams. One player starts on Team A, as the Zombie, and uses the energy sword exclusively. All other players start on Team B, and use the shotgun exclusively. If the Zombie kills a player on Team B, that player must manually switch teams, joining the Zombie on Team A and now using the energy sword exclusively. In keeping with the zombie theme, this is known as "infection." (Evidently, these rules are inspired by the conventions and "rules" of zombie horror in fiction and other videogames.)

The game ends either a) when there are no players left on Team B, because they have all been infected (zombies win); or b) if the time runs out and there is still at least one player left on Team B (surviving humans win). Zombie was subsequently integrated as an official game mode called "Infection" in *Halo 3* due to its popularity—one of several examples of expansive gameplay being appropriated by game developers in "official" fixed game modes.

"Jeep jumping" in *Halo* involves players using grenades and other explosive weapons to launch the in-game Jeep-like vehicle, the M12 Warthog, as high as possible (or sometimes in an attempt to clear a specific obstacle). The classic challenge is to clear the massive rocky archway on the beach in "The Silent Cartographer" level of *Halo: Combat Evolved*,[6] but jeep jumping can take place in many different areas throughout the series. In some cases, videos and screen-captures are then posted. Unlike speed running, jeep jumping is less of a quantifiable competition and more of a performance, evaluated mainly on aesthetic grounds. (In fact, many of these videos are edited and set to music.) Nevertheless, the performance proceeds according to a specific set of rules imposed on the fixed rules of the game, designed to produce a specific range of entertaining, and frequently hilarious, possibilities.

Expansive Gameplay as Metaphor

Philosophers are no strangers to game-related explanatory models—indeed, it would not be out of the question to suggest that the game, the roll of the dice, and the strategic move are privileged metaphors in a fairly wide range of philosophical work. Although he does not cite specific games, Foucault himself returns to the general metaphor with some frequency, as indicated by the epigraph to this paper and the aforementioned concept of games of truth.

Games of truth are the systems of rules that govern various institutions (such as the asylum, the school or the prison) and create the accepted truth within those institutions. Everyone is positioned

[6] Check out <www.warthog-jump.com/> for one classic example.

by and within these systems of rules, and they produce or constitute everyone's subjectivity. Describing networks of power and knowledge as games—that is to say, as rule-based systems—certainly seems an effective way of explaining how people are constituted as subjects (players) within those networks (games). The university classroom, for example, can be seen as a game of truth: an assemblage of institutional structures and hierarchies (power relations), accepted ideas and ways of thinking and seeing the world (knowledge) that produces a specific version of truth in its subjects, the students.

For Foucault, entirely free choice cannot exist, because people are always already within the constraints of Power-Knowledge. However, if the rules of the game (society) determine the possibility space of experience, and the range—however limited—of available options, then people can add more rules (aesthetic self-fashioning) to change and refine that possibility space (making life into a work of art). Think about someone who carefully considers and meticulously arranges every aspect of their lives, from the way they look, to the food they eat, to the home they live in, the people they spend time with and so on. It would not be uncommon to call this person's life a work of art, and he or she would appreciate life and enjoy it as such. If people are all players within the fixed rules of the game of existence, then the most effective path to some kind of liberty is to refuse to be content with "playing the hand we are dealt," and to play it with *style* and engage in what Foucault calls "practices of liberty" or "practices of freedom." This is an accurate, if simplistic, description of *both* expansive gameplay and aesthetic self-fashioning, but it's worth pushing the metaphor further.

Can Foucault's four elements of aesthetic self-fashioning described above (the ethical substance, the mode of subjection, ethical work and telos) be explained in terms of expansive gameplay? Consider speed running in *Halo*. The ethical substance, in this case, is the player's skill and reflexes: his or her ability to play the game as rapidly and as efficiently as possible. While an ordinary single-player game of *Halo* involves a variety of different "substances," including reflexes, aim, spatial awareness, resource management (in terms of ammunition and health points) and so on, expansive gameplay highlights certain aspects (and reconfigures them) as the substance to be refined and improved. The mode of subjection is more difficult to explain in game terms, but presumably would involve an awareness of (or boredom with) the limitations of the game, and a desire to expand or transform the experience and difficulty of gameplay with a new challenge.

The ethical work of speed running and other examples of expansive gameplay are the imposed rules noted above (the new goal of rapid completion), and the establishment of the community necessary to engender competition. The ethical work produces the desired change in experience; different sets of imposed rules produce different changes. And what is the telos of speed running? As in any competition, the telos is constant improvement, successfully achieving increasingly more difficult goals, whether this takes the form of a new personal best or a world record.

Foucault's aesthetic self-fashioning is in some sense an "expansive" ethics, based on similar principles and operating in an analogous manner to expansive gameplay. By imposing additional rules onto the structure of existence, the possibilities of life can be worked upon and expanded in the same way that gameplay can be enhanced beyond the fixed rules of the game. Neither concept is (necessarily) subject to a transcendent universal ideal, as the goals and parameters of these practices can be endlessly reconfigured in order to produce different results for different individuals. This metaphorical compatibility, however, could easily be challenged. There's always a quandary in relating philosophy to art and other cultural objects.

What's to be gained in straightforwardly "using" videogames to explain philosophical concepts, or in uncritically applying philosophical concepts to videogames? Neither strikes me as particularly interesting. To engage Foucault's theory with concepts derived from *Halo*, or to engage *Halo* using Foucault's concepts, should require that both the theory *and* the games are transformed in the process. Nevertheless, as an explanatory model for aesthetic self-fashioning, expansive gameplay in *Halo* is surprisingly satisfying, and indeed the tenets of aesthetic self-fashioning are surprisingly useful in explaining the practice of expansive gameplay.

Expansive Gameplay as Practice of Freedom

At what point does expansive gameplay cease to merely resemble aesthetic self-fashioning and become an *actual* practice of freedom? Perhaps the metaphor described above is satisfying precisely because expansive gameplay is more than an explanatory model, and is in fact an example of Foucault's system of ethics in practice. The rules of *Halo* and other videogames can, after all, be seen as very real parts of the systems of power and knowledge that constrain experience and constitute people as subjects. Can expansive gameplay therefore be seen as a "real" site of resistance?

First and foremost, not *all* practices of self-fashioning are genuinely practices of liberty. There is nothing inherently freeing about jogging—it has to be framed in a certain way to be liberatory. However, *any* discipline or activity can in theory become ethical work when approached with the right attitude, so what differentiates some practices from others? The discussion of Foucault's philosophy in sport and exercise studies is useful here. According to Pirkko Markula and Richard Pringle, the "sporting self" that adheres to a personal code or mandate within the larger moral codes of sport (and the rules of the game in question, of course), can in some cases be seen as a form of aesthetic self-fashioning. It's like the old adage: it doesn't matter whether you win or lose, *it's how you play the game*. When an athlete is concerned with the process and experience of training and playing (which is about his or her relation to himself or herself and to other players), rather than simply the outcome of the game (which is mandated by the "official" rules), he or she is stylizing their sporting life in a way that can be described as aesthetic self-fashioning. It is clear, then, that playing videogames might also be part of a process of aesthetic self-fashioning.

A key component of Foucault's philosophy is the problematization of the self, as constituted by systems of Power-Knowledge, which develops when people test and ponder the boundaries of those systems. In other words, the individual must recognize (or "verbalize") and grasp the societal rules that produce their subjectivity and self in order to self-fashion as an ethical being within those rules. Understanding how the game works, and how it constructs and positions the player, is fundamental to a practice of freedom within a game. Foucault often says that power produces its own opposition. By creating a field (however tiny) in which individuals are not completely helpless (a space of possibilities), restrictive systems allow them to recognize their boundaries and to act freely within those boundaries. Expansive gameplay in videogames, therefore, can be seen as genuine aesthetic self-fashioning, but only in contexts where the rules of the game are actively recognized and problematized.

An ordinary multiplayer game of Zombie in *Halo 2* doesn't necessarily indicate a Foucauldian ethics in practice, because presumably no such questioning occurs (indeed, the socially imposed rules of Zombie are so formalized it seems decidedly unlikely). However, acting within one's means as a player in ways that highlight or challenge the real-world games of truth of which *Halo* is part and parcel just might count. Take, for example, the Pacifist Run described above. The *Halo* series is unquestionably dogmatic in its glorification of violent, male military heroism, and war for survival against foreign, alien beings—that's a big part of what makes it so thrilling. Completing the game without killing anyone while deliberately bearing this glorification in mind, therefore, could be seen as a practice of freedom. Saving humanity without firing a shot makes an interesting point. By the same token, the performance-based expansive gameplay of jeep jumping, if approached from a certain standpoint, could become a meaningful appropriation of fictional tools of violence and domination to create a spectacle that can only exist within the rules of the game, but embraces an aesthetic completely different from the game's intended heroic interpretation.

Are these effective or productive forms of aesthetic self-fashioning? Do they allow individuals to make life a work of art? Well, probably not, because as I have argued, Foucault's ethics depends entirely on the specifics of a given situation. A major problem with interpreting expansive gameplay as a practice of freedom is that it is far too tempting to simply declare "it counts as self-fashioning if you really mean it," and leave it at that. In reality, most of the time expansive gameplay in *Halo* is not particularly introspective or thoughtful (even though it *could* be in theory) and is in no way part of an ongoing process of critical reflection and self-fashioning.

For Foucault, the difference between a reactionary politics that ineffectually rages against "The System" and an actual practice of freedom is that the latter recognizes and comprehends that subjectivity is fully and irrevocably constituted by the very system that is being critiqued. Furthermore, this way of understanding expansive gameplay relies on a conception of games as being entirely part of the larger system of Power-Knowledge, and many theorists of games and play would be very hesitant to commit to such a statement. The relationship between games, culture, and social reality is much more complex, with games and other art forms existing in an in-between space that is not entirely real *or* entirely imaginary.

Although aesthetic self-fashioning in or through videogames is possible in certain hypothetical instances, approaching expansive gameplay as a general cultural phenomenon from this perspective seems ill-advised.

Expansive Gameplay as Simulation

Finally, I propose a hybrid option. If expansive gameplay as metaphor glosses over some meaningful aspects of the relationship between systems of rules in reality and systems of rules in games, and expansive gameplay as an actual practice of freedom presumes equivalency between these systems, then the notion of simulation represents in my view an appealing middle ground. From this perspective, videogames simulate the kinds of systems that are experienced in reality, in games scholar Ian Bogost's sense of simulations as systems of simplified rules or principles that reference real-world systems.[7]

My somewhat unconventional use of the term 'simulation' doesn't refer only to the representation of specific real world processes. *Halo* simulates gunplay, driving, running and so on, but what's important here is that games also simulate the form of rule-based systems *in general*. Game rules are a special class of rules that reference and emulate the kinds of rules people live with in the real world. Expansive gameplay can thus be understood as more than just a metaphor: as a simulation, it is inexorably linked to real-world practices and serves a similar function to aesthetic self-fashioning, but on a different scale. Reality is not just a game, and games are not entirely "real." Games are like scale models that simulate, adapt and recontextualize the systems of reality.

According to this conceptual framework, expansive gameplay takes place within a simulation of real-world systems of rules, and so, as a practice, it too is neither wholly real nor wholly imaginary. As such, it can be understood to have a meaningful-but-not-equivalent relationship to aesthetic self-fashioning, in the same way that games have a meaningful-but-not-equivalent relationship to reality. The rules of games like *Halo* constitute a culturally and socially demarcated (but not completely isolated) space for the pleasurable exploration of rule-based systems.

---

[7] Ian Bogost, *Unit Operations: An Approach to Videogame Criticism* (MIT Press, 2006), pp. 96–97.

In the "safe" possibility space between the fixed rules of a game, which is analogous to the real space between the limitations of Power-Knowledge, players can *practice* (in both senses of the term) ways of refining lived and played experience. Although the specific strategies of expansive gameplay (playing through *Halo 3* without killing any enemies, or using the game's explosive weapons in an aesthetic performance) don't really translate into the real world, and hardly count as making life a work of art, the *forms* that these strategies take very much do. As noted above, imposing new rules on existence and re-purposing available tools are entirely consistent with Foucault's notion of aesthetic self-creation.

The active contemplation (or at the very least, the implicit acknowledgment) of the rules and possibilities of a videogame that is so fundamental to engaging in expansive gameplay can be seen as a small-scale, simulated version of the problematization Foucault insists is necessary for aesthetic self-fashioning. Expansive gameplay emerges from the exploration of a game's rules and the spaces for play that they constitute, just as practices of freedom emerge from the exploration and contemplation of the self as constituted by the rules of society. As a group of players explores the basic multiplayer modes in *Halo 2* and experiments with different combinations of weapons and game modes, the rules and possibility space of the game become apparent, and are reconfigured into the expansive gameplay of Zombie.

Players' relations to themselves and to other players, and the idea of transforming these relations, are inevitably considered in the course of expansive gameplay. As players develop ways of refining their in-game experience, expansive gameplay can (perhaps) help them to problematize real-world rules and systems and to cultivate the inward and outward-looking critical stance necessary for aesthetic self-fashioning.

This is the utopian view. The gloomier interpretation is that expansive gameplay actually *replaces* real-world practices of freedom, by allowing individuals to fashion and produce themselves in a straightforward, entertaining, and harmless manner that has minimal impact on their real-world experience. Expansive gameplay allows people to enjoy the illusion of liberty while their real lives remain unchallenged and unchanged.

In either case, thinking of expansive gameplay as a simulation of sorts is a productive way of understanding it as a cultural phenomenon. When considered as analogous to aesthetic self-fashioning (but on a smaller scale and at a remove from the real world), an interesting relationship between the two practices becomes apparent. The kinds of strategies and forces that can be employed by an individual constituted by and existing within a system of rules, and the way in which these practices are cultivated and produced through the active contemplation of spaces of possibility, helps draw connections between the playful, "safe" exploratory practice of expansive gameplay and the more substantive transformations enabled by a rigorous, real-world practice of Foucauldian self-fashioning.

So next time you're trying to beat a record speed run of Floodgate, blasting a jeep across Blood Gulch, or pwning n00bs in a round of Zombie, consider the relationship between expansive gameplay and Michel Foucault's philosophy of aesthetic self-fashioning. Reflect on the structures of Power-Knowledge that determine who you are and the possibility spaces available to you, and think about ways of taking control of your lived experience, just like you've taken control of your played experience of *Halo*.

15

Would Cortana Pass the Turing Test?

SHEROL CHEN

Artificial Intelligence (AI) has its beginnings in philosophy and has been adopted by a number of communities of thought today. The *Halo* series presents potential layers of application for better AI as it relates to interactive experiences. Through Cortana, *Halo* gives a common example of Artificial Intelligence in science fiction. In fiction, there are countless examples of what AI could be. In reality, however, there are a number of less obvious applications, most of which are far from being practical.

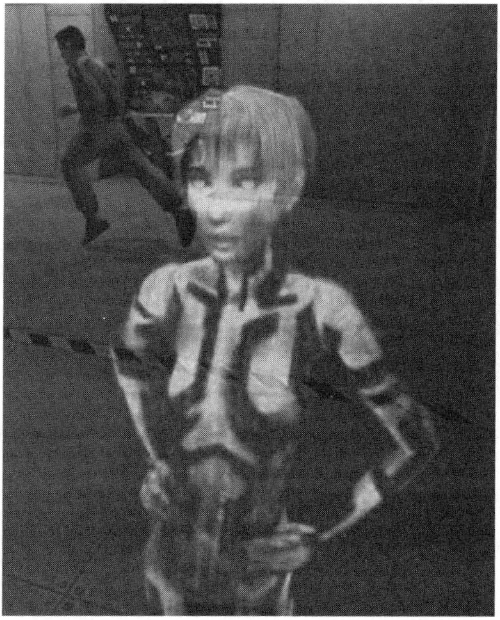

*The AI Cortana stands in the Pillar of Autumn (*Halo: Combat Evolved, *2001).*

So, where else do we find AI or the lack of AI in a game like *Halo*? This all depends on the community you ask. If you're talking to the AI Summit at the Game Developers Conference, then the AI is the path finding and combat strategies of Non Player Characters (NPCs). Game AI, experienced as alien combat strategies for you to thwart, is the only aspect of *Halo* where the actual practice of Artificial Intelligence is appropriately applied. While psychologists and cognitive scientists are interested in the user-end perceptions and experiences from the challenge of First Person Shooters (FPSs), there's also the emotional engagement and overall fun that a player has. I've interacted with lead AI developer for *Halo 2* and *Halo 3*, Damian Isla, in a few different sorts of settings, from AI conferences, to game conferences, to conferences on Disney Cruise Ships. Not only has Damian made practical many of the advancements in game AI, he's actively pursuing those things not yet feasible now at Moonshot Games <http://www.moonshotgames.com/>. In 2002, he co-wrote an article on "New Challenges for Character-Based AI for Games" for the Association for the Advancement of Artificial Intelligence, where he describes opportunities to realize believability in NPCs. If you want to know more about AI in *Halo* from a reliable source, I'd suggest starting with that article.

*Combat visualization for NPC AI in Halo games (*Halo* GDC talks, 2002 and 2008)*

Making NPCs better at FPS games is a given, but current AI research in game technology also aims to create characters that exhibit unscripted intelligence, stories that can intelligently construct themselves, and mechanics that can assist or achieve the game designers' goals of an, otherwise, unattainable end experience. To give insight into the pursuits of what is not yet possible, it's important to understand the overall experience and the limits that consumers take for granted. Areas of research such as Game Studies, Expressive Intelligence, and Serious Games enable more intentional means for application and analysis of interactive experiences or development processes. Through an understanding of the technology, we are able to realistically expect what is impossible, or, at the very least, not settle for less than what is currently possible. By focusing on common problems in the history of AI and their relation to believability in videogames, this chapter will ask the question of what would make *Halo*, as defining as it is, more than just a well-thought-out franchise.

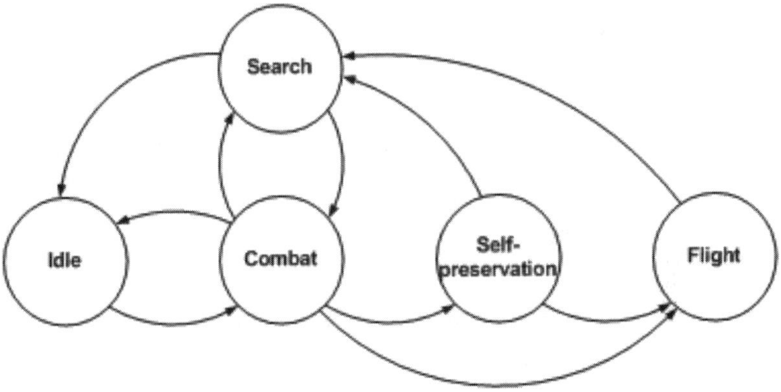

A Visualization of Actual AI in Practice Today (Handling Complexity in Halo 2 *AI, Damian Isla, GDC 2005)*

What Is Artificial Intelligence?

Cortana is a clear fictional example of an Artificially Intelligent existent. So, what isn't Artificial Intelligence? Well, humans aren't AI, because they're naturally intelligent, and plasma rifles aren't AI because they aren't intelligent. In the realm of science fiction, Artificial Intelligence takes the form of machines that believably emulate human behaviors. In real life, applications of AI are far less dramatically compelling. In the widely used AI textbook *Artificial Intelligence: A Modern Approach* Russell and Norvig introduce four primary pursuits of AI:

Some definitions of AI. They are organized into four categories

Systems that think like humans.	**Systems that think rationally.**
"The exciting new effort to make computers think . . . machines with minds, in the full and literal sense" (Haugeland, 1985) "[The automation of] activities that we associate with human thinking, activities such as decision-making, problem solving, learning . . . " (Bellman, 1978)	"The study of mental faculties through the use of computational models" (Charniak and McDermott, 1985) "The study of the computations that make it possible to perceive, reason, and act " (Winston, 1992)
"The art of creating machines that perform functions that require intelligence when performed by people" (Kurzweil, 1990) "The study of how to make computers do things at which, at the moment, people are better" (Rich and Knight, 1991)	"A field of study that seeks to explain and emulate intelligent behavior in terms of computational processes." (Schalkoff, 1990) "The branch of computer science that is concerned with the automation of intelligent behavior" (Luger and Stubblefield, 1993)
Systems that act like humans.	**Systems that act rationally.**

First, the AI textbook distinguishes between being rational and being human, with primary emphasis on rational AI. Currently, human behavior and thought do not provide much practical application to today's relevant scientific pursuits. The AI that we see in science fiction is not only a non-priority for scientists, but seemingly more unattainable than current AI research endeavors.

The study of AI as rational agent design therefore has two advantages. First, it is more general than the "laws of thought" approach, because correct inference is only a useful mechanism for achieving rationality, and not a necessary one. Second, it's more amenable to scientific development than approaches based on human behavior or human thought, because the standard of rationality is clearly defined and completely general. Human behavior, on the other hand, is well-adapted for one specific environment and is the product, in part, of a complicated and largely unknown evolutionary process that still may be far from achieving perfection (Russell and Norvig, p. 12).

Now to distinguish between thinking and action, what it means to think humanly has its own area of academic pursuit in cognitive science and philosophy of mind. The textbook calls this the "cognitive modeling approach." Experientially, however, it only matters that Cortana, in her *actions*, has believable human behavior, with no regard to how accurately her thought process matches the *thinking* of human beings. This test for believability was famously published by Alan Turing, known as the "Turing Test."

Can Machines Think?

In his paper, Alan Turing posed the question "can machines think?" He thought the answer could be tested empirically. Turing took a common party game, the imitation game, and used it to test for intelligence. The Turing Test has had a number of criticisms since Turing first published it,[1] such as Searle's Chinese room[2] or French's seagull test argument[3] (both of which will be discussed in more detail soon). Jack Copeland defends Turing by pointing out that he never proposed a formal definition for consciousness, rather Turing was merely testing for evidence of intelligence.[4] As quoted below, Turing was not trying to contest what defines intelligence, nor was he claiming that he could create intelligence; rather, he was proposing a test of whether or not computers could feign intelligence.

> I do not wish to give the impression that I think there is no mystery about consciousness. There is, for instance, something of a paradox

---

[1] Alan Turing, "Computing Machinery and Intelligence," *Mind* 59 (1950).

[2] John Searle, "Minds, Brains, and Programs," *The Behavioral and Brain Sciences* 3 (1980).

[3] R.M. French, "Subcognition and the Limits of the Turing Test," *Mind* 99:393 (1990).

[4] Jack Copeland, "The Imitation Game: Alan Turing and Artificial Intelligence," (2007).

> connected with any attempt to localize it. But I do not think these mysteries necessarily need to be solved before we can answer the question with which we are concerned in this paper. (Turing 1950, p. 5)

In an earlier article[5] Turing created a fundamental architecture for future computing, the "logical computing machine," and established that any computable operation can be performed on such a machine. This is known today as the Turing machine, forerunner for computers as we know them in this century. As an extension of the Turing machine, Alan Turing described the type of machine that would be interrogated in the imitation game as the digital computer, a machine that is intended to "carry out any operations which could be done by a human computer" (Turing 1950). Systems evaluated through the Turing test are the first applications of artificial intelligence, or more specifically, the first instantiation of the believable agent.

Believable Intelligence

As Copeland argues, thought experiments that counter-argue the appropriateness of Turing's test are moot, as they refute a claim that Turing was not trying to make. Chinese rooms and seagulls, however, provide a means of analysis of experiences in games like *Halo* through widely discussed thought experiments from the philosophy of mind community. First, in his own words, Turing describes the inspiration for the Turing Test, the Imitation Game:

> The new form of the problem can be described in terms of a game which we call the "imitation game." It is played with three people, a man (A), a woman (B), and an interrogator (C) who may be of either sex. The interrogator stays in a room apart front the other two. The object of the game for the interrogator is to determine which of the other two is the man and which is the woman. . . .
>
> We now ask the question, "What will happen when a machine takes the part of A in this game?" Will the interrogator decide wrongly as often when the game is played like this as he does when the game is

[5] Alan Turing, "On Computable Numbers," *Proceedings of the London Mathematical Society* 2 (1936).

> played between a man and a woman? These questions replace our original, "Can machines think?" (Turing 1950, p. 6)

How does Cortana do it? Does she have electrodes that are modeled after our neurons? History tells us, maybe, but probably not. Take artificial flight. If birds are capable of natural flight, then does this mean that artificial flight is most appropriately an exact physical replication of birds? No, we, of course, don't rule it out as possible, but it is evidently not the only way, as the Wright brothers have demonstrated. The Turing Test doesn't ask how Cortana is able to behave humanly; it asks whether or not she behaves humanly. As far as Master Chief is concerned, the constitution doesn't change the experience.

In 1956, John McCarthy called together a community of researchers together at Dartmouth University. This summer research project coined the area of Artificial Intelligence, creating AI labs at Carnegie Melon, MIT, Edinburg University, and Stanford. Early conversational AI systems such as ELIZA, Parry, Hacker, Sam, and Frump were developed from research projects soon after. Current conversational agents are developed for the Loebner Prize Contest, held every year, as a direct application of Turing's test.

Just because It Acts Intelligent, Doesn't Mean It Is

In response to Turing, Searle said that performance does not constitute intelligence. For example, imagine there is a Chinese room as Searle describes:

> Suppose that I'm locked in a room and given a large batch of Chinese writing. Suppose furthermore (as is indeed the case) that I know no Chinese, either written or spoken, and that I'm not even confident that I could recognize Chinese writing as Chinese writing distinct from, say, Japanese writing or meaningless squiggles. To me, Chinese writing is just so many meaningless squiggles. . . . Suppose also that after a while I get so good at following the instructions for manipulating the Chinese symbols and the programmers get so good at writing the programs that from the external point of view—that is, from the point of view of somebody outside the room in which I am locked—my answers to the questions are absolutely indistinguishable from those of native Chinese speakers. Nobody just looking at my answers can

> tell that I don't speak a word of Chinese. . . . As far as the Chinese is concerned, I simply behave like a computer; I perform computational operations on formally specified elements. For the purposes of the Chinese, I am simply an instantiation of the computer program. (Searle, p. 3)

Going beyond Cortana's natural language capabilities, as gamers, do we really care whether the Covenant forces mobilize as a result of making decisions through a human thought process or that they simply behave in a challenging manner? Through the lens of Searle's Chinese room, if I'm only looking for the experience of having a conversation in Chinese, then I disregard the constitution of the interaction. Believability is a matter of behavior and function, as opposed to constitution.

The Seagull Test

But how do we even know we are accurately measuring intelligence through comparison? After all, an instance does not define an entirety. French's seagull test shows another shortcoming of the Turing Test:

> Consider the following parable: It so happens that the only flying animals known to the inhabitants of a large Nordic island are seagulls. Everyone on the island acknowledges, of course, that seagulls can fly. One day the two resident philosophers on the island are overheard trying to pin down what "flying" is really all about. . . . They decide to settle the question by, in effect, avoiding it. They do this by first agreeing that the only examples of objects that they are absolutely certain can fly are the seagulls that populate their island. . . . On the basis of these assumptions and their knowledge of Alan Turing's famous article about a test for intelligence, they hit upon the Seagull Test for flight. The Seagull Test works much like the Turing Test. Our philosophers have two three-dimensional radar screens, one of which tracks a real seagull; the other will track the putative flying machine. They may run any imaginable experiment on the two objects in an attempt to determine which is the seagull and which is the machine, but they may watch them only on their radar screens. The machine will be said to have passed the Seagull Test for flight if both philosophers are indefinitely unable to distinguish the seagull from the machine.

> In fact, under close scrutiny, probably only seagulls would pass the Seagull Test, and maybe only seagulls from the philosophers' Nordic island, at that. What we have is thus not a test for flight at all, but rather a test for flight as practiced by a Nordic seagull. For the Turing Test, the implications of this metaphor are clear: an entity could conceivably be extremely intelligent but, if it did not respond to the interrogator's questions in a thoroughly human way, it would not pass the Test. The *only* way, I believe, that it would have been able to respond to the questions in a perfectly human-like manner is to have experienced the world as humans have. What we have is thus not a test for intelligence at all, but rather a test for intelligence as practiced by a human being. (French, p. 2)

The Seagull-test tells us that believability can only be assessed among behaviors of the natural instances being compared. In regards to *Halo*, whether artificially recreating the experience of gun fights, emotional reactions, or the craft of storytelling, intelligence, when given purpose, is a straightforward endeavor. Believability, in practice, aims to recreate some authored and designed experience, such as human conversation, as the Turing Test demonstrates.

Machines Don't Have Our Background

French continues to say that, "Humans, over the course of their lives, develop certain associations of varying strength among concepts" (French, p. 2), presenting a test that, he claims, a computer would have much difficulty passing. This, he calls "Associative Priming," and illustrates with a hypothetical situation:

> The Turing Test interrogator makes use of this phenomenon as follows: The day before the Test, she selects a set of words (and non-words), runs the lexical decision task on the interviewees and records average recognition times. She then comes to the Test armed with the results of this initial test, asks both candidates to perform the same task she ran the day before, and records the results. Once this has been done, she identifies as the human being the candidate whose results more closely resemble the average results produced by her sample population of interviewees.
>
> The machine would invariably fail this type of test because there is no *a priori* way of determining associative strengths (i.e., a measure of

> how easy it is for one concept to activate another) between *all* possible concepts. Virtually the only way a machine could determine, even on average, all of the associative strengths between human concepts is to have experienced the world as the human candidate and the interviewees had. (French, p. 4)

Halo, as a virtual experience, does not 1. need to be accurately constituted like its natural counterparts as the Chinese room might suggest, nor does it 2. need to perform beyond the natural instance that it recreates as the Seagull-Test might suggest. Nor does *Halo* need to recreate unspecified experiences with high accuracy of precision as Associative Priming may suggest. The success of the series is proof enough of these three challenges do not stifle the overall *Halo* experience. The points made by these three examples may define insurmountable technological roadblocks, but this, by no means, suggests that videogames cannot or should not perform beyond what they are currently doing. The implications of these three challenges give potential examples for richer, higher-agency interactive experiences, but are not sole gate-keepers of greater believability. As the Wright Brothers demonstrated, we are not limited by natural conventions. Believability, as discussed in the Russell and Norvig AI textbook, is still underexplored as a science. Today, game researchers aim to build the bridge that brings the Artificial Intelligence of science towards the Artificial Intelligence of science fiction for its expressive potential as an art form:

Within AI, there has not been a big effort to try to pass the Turing test. The issue of acting like a human comes up primarily when AI programs have to interact with people, as when an expert system explains how it came to its diagnosis, or a natural language processing system has a dialogue with a user. These programs must behave according to certain normal conventions of human interaction in order to make themselves understood. The underlying representation and reasoning in such a system may or may not be based on a human model (Russell and Norvig, p. 12).

Researchers of game technologies have the privilege to develop and understand the science behind the sound and scene of modern interactive experiences. We can see that there've been great advances in graphics, animation, audio, and game mechanics from *Pong* to *Halo: Reach*. The technology which drives the dramatically compelling experiences, however, has made comparably less progress as digital storytellers. The Chinese room makes a good point in regards to the technology that is under-the-hood of virtual experiences: that old technology can be made to do new things, despite not being inherently novel in itself.

Throughout the decades of gaming, conventions were formed around the limits and convenience of development. Game players, perhaps unknowingly, hold many of these conventions to be universal, such as: the blind introduction to a gameworld, death and respawning, and lack of agency. Those examples are three very typical occurrences, but there are many other examples more specific to particular games. Once the narrative (or presentation) of games can be separated from the mechanics and technology that drive the game, we are able to easily identify these limitations.

Advances in Artificial Intelligence not only provide more tools to build with, but more authorial leverage and potential to build immersive experiences. Comparatively, while AI is being researched at a much slower rate, developers, designers, and writers have made their own advancements in the narrative, discourse, and presentation of videogames.

Innovations in Storytelling

So, what breaks your sense of presence in a story? The culture of videogame playing has developed a tolerance for the common practices and limitations in designing and producing games. We've stopped asking "Why?" and have come to expect the typical input arrangements, the impermanence of death, and restrictions of our own free will. I've found, in my personal "research" of popular games, that despite the predictability, certain innovations in narrative are notably novel.

We can break down a game into three layers: paidia, ludus, and narrative, an area that is quite nontrivial is the connection between paidia and narrative. Traditionally in game studies, paidia and ludus are known to be types of games or styles of play. Paidia would be simulation-like through open world exploration, and ludus would be goal and achievement driving through winning conditions. Games however, have all aspects of play to some degree.

Gonzalo Frasca describes ideological rule sets in games as including paidia, ludus, and representation (or narrative).[6] For

[6] Gonzalo Frasca, "Simulation vs. Narrative: Introduction to Ludology," in *Video Game Theory*, edited by Wolf and Perron (Routledge, 2003).

instance, in *Halo*, the paidia is the open world simulation, the movements and actions made available and the experiences that come of their consequences. The paidia or open world of *Halo* is apparent through the rules that drive its simulation of gun fights. The ludus or winning conditions of *Halo* varies in context. In the campaigns, the winning condition is to drive the story forward to completion. As a multiplayer game, the winning condition is typically to have the most kills. Finally, the representation or the narrative of *Halo* is within the context of intergalactic religion and politics. Often, your paidia is constrained such that you don't ruin the narrative layer in the game. For example, it is common that your agency is restricted in order to maintain the story elements—if everyone died at the beginning, there'd be no story left to tell.

In story driven games, the paidia and narrative layers find themselves compromising. Ultimately, the paidia-narrative relationship determines the user's agency in a game and the overall flow and presence in a story. The question I want to pose here is: What breaks your sense of presence in a story? Three typical examples are:

1. Entering a story with no prior domain knowledge
2. The occurrence of dying and respawning
3. Having a terrible sense of agency[7]

In my experiences, I've felt that creative innovations in game writing and game design (or conforming the narrative layer to overcome the limitations of paidia) were apparent in the following approaches:

Introducing a New World

In *Halo*, the opening cut scene briefs the characters in the story, along with the player watching, about what the current situation is. The player is then introduced to Master Chief, or "the new guy in town." Not only is the player unaware of the state of the gameworld, but so is the protagonist. As a soldier being suited up, this also gives the player the ability to learn the button controls as a feature of the story. In later games, there is an apparent expectation that the player understands some of what has transpired, and that

[7] See: <http://eis-blog.ucsc.edu/2009/07/what-do-amnesia-immortality-and-mind-control-have-to-do-with-game-design-immersion-and-suspension-of-disbelief/>.

she has some knowledge acquired from previous games.

Almost every game has some way of introducing a new user to the experience. Usually, this includes teaching a user how to play in addition to priming the user to the introductory narrative context. Early forms of this include opening cut scenes and easy challenges in the early gameplay. *StarCraft* campaigns, for instance, introduce you to the complex build system by composing a story around a mission-based tutorial. With very little contextual priming, the 1995 game *ChronoTrigger* starts with the player character as a red spikey haired young man being woken up by his mother. My initial thoughts as I start this game are: where am I? Who am I? What is going on? What am I supposed to do next? It follows that the protagonist, Chrono, doesn't have much of a personality represented throughout the game. In contrast, player characters such as Cloud from *Final Fantasy* 7 and Pheonix from *Phoenix Wright: Justice for All*, with more complexly defined personalities and lives, are introduced to the player with temporary memory loss. Suitably, the world must be explained to the player character and coincidentally presents information that the user needs to know. As you are discovering the world around you, you are also discovering yourself as a character that is recovering from amnesia.

Death in Games

Death is a common occurrence in many games. There are pretty typical approaches to handling life and death in videogames. It is expected that if you do poorly enough, you lose your life and will be set back in some way. *Super Mario* games employ extra lives. *Final Fantasy* uses save spots. *Halo* uses check points.

In the midst of a big dungeon, there's always that awkward explanation of "here and only at shiny spots like these can you save your progress." When you die, the game ends, but when you start again, you resume from previously saved state. We just accept this as how things are, but *Planescape* takes it a step further. In *Planescape*, the main character is "cursed" with immortality, and when he "dies," he wakes up in a mortuary . . . the closest mortuary to the location of death (and no, time has not stopped nor rewound). In fact, he's lived and died so many times, that his lives, recorded in a tomb, have taken many possible paths (in addition to the path you are currently on). Your living, dying, and resurrection, within play, is just an intentional feature of the story experience.

Mind Control

It goes without saying that stories in games are fairly linear. When it comes to choices, there really aren't many that make a difference. Eventually, you will go from point A to point B to point C with nominal embellishments along the way. If I don't accept the current quest, then the story stops until I decide otherwise. In FPS campaigns, I accomplish the mission objective and await my next orders. *Bioshock*, like *Halo*, is an FPS that progresses quite linearly. You take in the presented circumstances, the interesting setting, music, and dialogue, and you go along with it. For the sake of progressing through the story, you do what you are instructed (I mean, what else would you do?). What's different in *Bioshock* is that you're not meant to have a choice, because you, the player character, were genetically engineered to be mind-controlled by the trigger phrase, "Would you kindly." For the first half of the game, you just go along with your lack of autonomy, and for the second half it is cleverly worked into the story.

And voila, here are three instances where we have gone from typical constraint to novel feature. Until we begin to formalize and create new ways in designing games, our paidia remains a bit limited. Fortunately, we still have the expansiveness of our imaginations at the narrative layer's disposal (in the meantime).

Would Cortana Pass the Turing Test?

Currently, technology enables us to create games in certain ways. The look, feel, and sound of games have changed drastically in the past two decades when compared to other aspects, such as character believability and narrative intelligence. Game players have accepted many of these limitations as game conventions. Designers continuously build different sorts of experiences with the tools that technology makes available. Researchers, middle-ware developers, and (the more adventurous) game developers aim to create new experiences by creating a new toolsets to build with. Increasingly there are university research labs that specialize in this area of study and contribution: University of Alberta, IT University of Copenhagen, University of California at Santa Cruz, Georgia Institute of Technology, North Carolina State University, and University of Southern California, just to name a few.

However far the area of Artificial Intelligence advances, new criticism comes with it—just as it did with the Turing Test, with counterpoints about Chinese rooms, and seagulls. So would Cortana pass the Turing Test? Well, it's relative to the context in which she exists because without the new discoveries about AI that allow for the existence of Cortana, there's the lack of new criticism to evaluate. For example, Cortana exists in a space-age where such AI has been discovered; it's not as though she just appeared at a research lab in the year 2011 at the University of California at Santa Cruz. Likely, Cortana would pass the Turing Test if she were accessible to people in our present time and day. In her time, however, there would be perhaps new discoveries of the limitations or irreconcilable discrepancies between man and machine. Without the knowledge of these limitations, we take one step closer to the dangerous scenarios described in the sundry post-apocalyptic movies. The fear that machines will outdo us and take us over, however, may be a bit far fetched, but there is evidence that our relationships with technology have gone sour in the past.

On one hand, the humanities may take issue with falling short of what constitutes believability and science may find the pursuit of believability a fool's errand; however, in understanding the science behind the stimuli, this gives developers the inspiration to aim for the sky, and *Halo* players, among others, the opportunity to know what is possible will soon be made practical.

But, why would this matter to the everyday gamer? Well, I suppose it's a matter of whether you'd prefer to be a spectator or an influential participant of your own life, whether you'd rather be dictated by technology or be the one to dictate technology. I wrote this chapter to let you know that this choice is available and entirely up to you.

UNSC Debriefing
Don't Look Now, the Boogeyman's Behind You—Or Is It the Flood?

ROGER NGIM

The movie *Halloween* changed the way I look at the world. No, it wasn't *Citizen Kane*, *2001: A Space Odyssey* or *The Four Hundred Blows*. It was a screaming Jamie Lee Curtis running around suburban Illinois while an escaped lunatic butchered her friends with a kitchen knife. Go ahead and laugh, but John Carpenter's film did something interesting and irreversible to the way I experienced filmic space.

Fifteen years later, the pioneering computer game *Doom* had a similar effect on me, transforming my understanding of game space as a vertical plane. Like games in the *Halo* series, *Doom* is a First Person Shooter (FPS), meaning a player can move freely through three-dimensional space and experiences most of the game staring down the barrel of a gun. FPS games are such a staple of the videogame industry that we rarely give a thought to how radically the earliest entries changed the concept of gamespace. Technologically speaking, film has made similar leaps, again largely taken for granted—the invention of devices that allowed smooth tracking shots, for example.

When I was a teenager, I was obsessed with horror movies. I read a magazine for horror fans called *Fangoria* that was so explicit I hid it under my bed right next to—well, whatever teenage boys keep under their beds. I would study the grim photos of gaping wounds and decapitations with the intensity of a forensic scientist, searching for I-don't-know-what—perhaps a reassuring flaw in a bloody special effect or clues as to why slasher movies held me so rapt. No doubt the scares satisfied an adrenaline craving brought on by raging hormones coursing through my adolescing body, but certain horror movies of the 1970s and 1980s, as many videogames would do later, functioned in a particular way: they frequently employed POV shots that forced the viewer to inhabit the body of the killer, an uncomfortable but sometimes exhilarating place to be. In doing so, they brought us into the movie and surrounded us with a virtual world.

Halloween wasn't the first film to do this, but it was the first I remember seeing. The movie opens with a brutal stabbing committed by an unseen person. The perpetrator is unseen because the entire seamless sequence is shown through the eyes of a killer, mostly through the eye holes of a mask, which reduces our vision to two spots near the center of the screen (human sight really doesn't work this way, but we get the idea). We see a hand, presumably ours, grab a knife from a drawer, and then we head up the stairs to commit the act. Only after we flee downstairs and out the front door does the point of view change. As the camera pulls back to a wide shot of the front of the house, we finally see who we are (or were, as it were): a little boy in a clown outfit holding the bloodied weapon.

At several other points in the film, the POV switches to the killer's and we hear the sound of (our) breathing within a mask. Our potential victims glance nervously over their shoulders or obliviously go about their business as we gaze at them from inside a car or around a hedge. As shocking as the opening of *Halloween* is, these quieter moments had a more profound effect on me. In the theater, those shots placed me within the film as a character, creating a kind of subliminal effect of cinematic space around me—there was a left, a right, a forward, a back, an up and a down. I was the unseen menace lurking in the yard. More disturbing, once outside of the theater I realized that my experience of reality essentially was the same: I could gaze at a person who could be my victim, and I could move through space seeing the world as if operating my own Steadicam.

Fortunately, I did not grow up to become a serial killer. Any such tendencies I worked out by playing videogames.

At the time *Halloween* hit theaters in 1978, I was riding my Stingray to my cousin's house to spend the afternoon playing with his Atari 2600. Those were the days when videogames were less about what they attempted to represent than what they were: simple skill games made up of clusters of pixels, accompanied by blips and beeps. *Pong* may have been modeled after table tennis and

Space Race a trip through an asteroid field, but no one playing actually believed they were playing ping-pong or piloting a spaceship, and there were few real-world skills required that were related to the actual activity. I'm going to sound like Grandpa here, but before there was the pressure to create the fastest rendering game engine or most convoluted storyline, games relied on a different kind of innovation that had its own beauty, a kind of visual reductionism that earns artists' praise. I'm talking about the super-low-res graphics the designers of Atari 2600 games had to work with. Yet, they somehow managed to represent everything from E.T. the Extraterrestrial to a Wild West shootout and we could almost always figure out what we were looking at.

Before the perfection of 3D graphics, videogames were not too far from animated board games that could stretch on and on sideways or up and down. I loved my side-scrolling platform and shooting games, especially the strange ones imported from Japan with little or no cultural translation (like *Cloud Master* for the 8-bit Sega Master System in which the player tried to shoot down flying bowls of ramen and gyoza). Much like in the early days of cinema, the action was confined to a planar world, bounded by the frame of the TV or computer screen. No matter how active the imagination of the player, there existed a gulf between the player and the game-as-object. The FPS genre, combined with technology that allows the creation of a three dimensional world that operates by its own clock, has eliminated that gulf. As a result, games are more demanding on players than ever before. Suddenly, we need to know how to move and shoot in every direction. Mastering the controller became much more difficult. In *Mario 64*, the mustachioed character's 3D platform debut on Nintendo 64, you needed to learn how to look all around you in addition to knowing how to move in all directions.

Once you figured out the controls, navigating three-dimensional space was fairly intuitive. However, there was one aspect of this new gamespace that took some getting used to. I remember playing *Doom* for the first time and suddenly realizing I needed to turn around because something was attacking me from behind. This sense of a "behind me" was palpable and new. I wondered, where exactly *is* the behind I need to be concerned about? Certainly not between the back of my chair and the bedroom wall. According to the game's story, I was on some hellish Martian moon, so "behind me" was whatever would be behind me if I were in a hallway on a military base on a Martian moon. I would have to turn around to see. I'm not a programmer, but I'm pretty sure that monster or storage locker or escape hatch behind me wasn't there until I turned around—at least in a form that I could see. (I suppose that monster/locker/hatch existed in the form of rules or lines of code much like that character sneaking up behind me in a movie exists in the mind of the screenwriter.)

This feeling of being surrounded is the primary component of what is commonly referred to as an "immersive experience." I've had an uneasy relationship with the term, and it's not just because "immersive" isn't really a word in the English language. It is most often used in one of two ways: as a synonym for "compelling" or "engaging," or to describe an experience that puts you somewhere you are not. For sure, immersiveness (which is even less a real word) is a quality of many movies and games, but anybody with critical faculties can tell you, is not in itself indicative of quality. Yet, immersiveness persists as a goal in both movie and videogame industries and the term continues to be tossed about by marketing departments as if it were the Good Housekeeping Seal of Approval.

The ultimate immersive experience has been vividly portrayed in the *Star Trek* world as the "holodeck," a three-dimensional virtual reality machine that produces sight, sound, physical matter, and—I'm not certain about this, but why not?—smell. The trajectories of movies and games meet in this imaginary space, for the goal of many game design teams is to create convincing three-dimensional worlds, usually as an arena to run around and kill things. Nothing wrong with that. Hollywood, not content with their flat rectangle of real estate, has resurrected 3D movies. *Avatar* in 3D Imax was spectacular, but was essentially the world's longest cut scene. When do I get to shoot?

The inevitable merging of movies and videogames begins to make sense when we consider the parallels in their opening up of imaginary space and their shared goal of the ultimate immersive experience. In both cases, the experience is no longer a thing to behold; it's a place to be. And not only a location, but a world that invites interaction.

Just don't forget to turn around—there's something sneaking up on you, and it just might be a Covenant soldier.

UNSC Personnel

Ben Abraham is a PhD candidate at the University of Western Sydney and can occasionally be found teaching the designers of the future at the University of Macquarie. He'd tell you his Xbox Live gamertag but would probably just embarrass himself.

Sherol Chen is a PhD student in Computer Science with interest in telling stories through games. She's part of the Expressive Intelligence Studio at Santa Cruz and specializes in Artificial Intelligence for narratives and believability. She's also interested in Philosophy of Mind and the overall impact that technology has on people, as she's trying to find her own way to change the world. She loves Jazz music, Jesus, and had a crush on Super Mario when she played her first video game at the age of five.

Luke Cuddy is the editor of *The Legend of Zelda and Philosophy* and *World of Warcraft and Philosophy*. He teaches philosophy in Southern California. Sometimes he hears a woman's voice in his head, claiming to be an AI inhabiting his consciousness, but then he realizes that it's just his girlfriend telling him to stop playing so much *Halo*.

Tyler DeHaven is a student at Ithaca College studying philosophy and anthropology as a double major. When not attending college, he can be found at home playing video or computer games in his basement as a way to unwind after work. Despite his love of videogames, Tyler understands that he cannot shoot his professors on sight, as he would a Covenant soldier, after receiving a nasty assignment. Currently, Tyler remains undecided about what career he wishes to pursue, though he intends to go to graduate or professional school. Born and bred in a small Pennsylvania town, Tyler lives with his mother, father, brother, and little sister.

Monica Evans is an Assistant Professor in computer game design at the University of Texas at Dallas. Her current research focuses on the design and development of university-level educational games, narrative for interactive systems, and digital ethics. She's spending most of the 2010–11 academic year creating a series of games focused on bioethics and human enhancement as part of the Values Game Initiative. While she admires his persistence, she feels that Guilty Spark 343 could learn a lot from GLaDOS and SHODAN.

A wholly unrepentant camper, **Shane Fliger** is a full time graduate student in Literature Studies at The University of Akron, and holds a bachelor's degree in English with a minor in Philosophy from the University of Akron as well. His primary focus of study is the evolution of narrative structure through interactive media, and has nightmares of laughter in alien tongues at his pitiable efforts to survive. Wort wort wort!

Galen Foresman teaches philosophy at North Carolina A&T State University and is the author of *Why Batman Is Better than Superman* and *Making the A-List*. When he's not teaching or writing, you can find him online, schooling noobs in the art of virtuous spawn camping. Class is in session.

Joyce C. Havstad is a PhD student in the Philosophy Department as well as the Science Studies Program at the University of California, San Diego. At school, she battles with ideas, arguments, and words. At home, she prefers to be armed with an energy sword and a sniper rifle.

Chris Hendrickson graduated from Ithaca College with his Bachelors in Planned Studies: Games and Society. A self-proclaimed ninja, he enjoys practicing with his carbon-steel sword, exploring nature, and riding his motorcycle. You can find him on Xbox Live, running to the front lines and using the armor lock ability to make himself temporarily invulnerable to bullets, rockets, plasma, and confused n00bs.

Sébastien Hock-Koon is a funded PhD candidate studying learning in videogames. He followed the game design course of SupInfoGame. Usual princess rescuer and kingdom protector, he saved the galaxy for the first time by devastating a gigantic alien space donut with the autumnal explosion of a nuclear pillar.

Michael Jenkins graduated from San Diego State University with his Masters in Philosophy. When's he's not pretending to be a logician, he can be found hiding on a cliff or under a bush, sniper rifle loaded, waiting for an unsuspecting Covenant. Though he isn't afraid to get down and dirty with some old school pistol whipping.

Peter Ludlow is Professor of Philosophy at Northwestern University. He is co-author (with Mark Wallace) of *The Second Life Herald: The Virtual Tabloid that Witnessed the Dawn of the Metaverse* (2008) and is also author of lots and lots of papers on technical philosophy of language. In 2006 mtv.com called Ludlow one of the ten most influential videogame players of all time, but his daughter is unimpressed because (a) that was sooo long ago it was probably before *The Flood* and (b) she has more achievements on Xbox than he does.

Roger Ngim is an artist, educator, and former arts critic who has seen every *Friday the 13th* installment but has never seen any of the *Saw* movies. An obsessive gamer, he has taught courses in games and culture at the University of California at San Diego and has a collection of more than six hundred board games.

Felan Parker is a PhD student in Communication & Culture at York University specializing in cinema studies and digital game studies. He is currently studying the "games as art" debate as a popular discourse. His favorite form of expansive gameplay in *Halo* is Jeep Tag. One player is "it" and gets a Warthog, and scores points for running over other players; everyone else gets rocket launchers and frag grenades. When somebody kills the "it" player, they take over the vehicle. Explosions, high-flying jeeps and hilarity ensue.

Chiara Repetti-Ludlow is in ninth grade at the Earl L. Vandermeulen High School on Long Island. She has mad skilz at gymnastics, trapeze, Latin, and Italian, but those are all part of her plan to be the next Ezio Auditore da Firenze. And yes, at the end of the day she likes *Assassin's Creed* even more than *Halo*.

Jeff Sharpless is a recent graduate with his MA in philosophy from San Diego State University and has a BS in psychology from Southern Oregon University. An avid *Halo* player, he would often talk to his fellow players while playing online multiplayer, "Do you think Master Chief's thinks about whether his life is worth living? I mean, think about it, he was stolen from his family and genetically engineered to be a super-soldier" His fellow players would often respond, "Dude! You think too much."

Patrick Tiernan is Chair of Religious Education at Boston College High School where he teaches courses in religion and science, ethics, social justice, and world religions. He is currently a doctoral candidate in educational administration at Boston College. Sometimes he feels his classes de-evolve into the Flood and has to resist the temptation to pull a Forerunner by annihilating everyone. But in the end, he sees the value of disconnecting once in a while and remembering it's just a game.

ROGER TRAVIS is an associate professor of classics at the University of Connecticut. He's also the director of the Video Games and Human Values Initiative, and he writes the blog Living Epic at <http://livingepic.org>. He's still waiting for his invitation to the Grunt birthday party.

FRED VAN LENTE is the writer of the American Library Association award-winning comic-book series, *Action Philosophers*, used across the world to teach thinkers from the Pre-Socratics to Derrida, as well as the chronicler of Master Chief's colleagues Spartan Black in the Marvel graphic novel *Halo: Blood Line* and in the bestselling prose anthology *Halo: Evolutions*.

RACHEL WAGNER is Assistant Professor of Religious Studies at Ithaca College in upstate New York. She has published a number of book chapters and articles dealing with the relationship between religion and popular culture, and is at work on a single-author book on religion and virtual reality called *Godwired* (2011). She has a particular interest in virtual reality experiences that construct other-worlds with multiple media streams, such as *Halo*, *Avatar*, *Harry Potter*, and *The Matrix*. She is grateful that Ithaca College student Tyler DeHaven (co-author in this book) knows that *Halo* isn't real life and isn't going to shoot her for giving difficult assignments.

Index